# Paul Oakenfold

www.**rbooks**.co.uk

# Paul Oakenfold
## The Authorised Biography

**RICHARD NORRIS**

BANTAM PRESS

LONDON · TORONTO · SYDNEY · AUCKLAND · JOHANNESBURG

TRANSWORLD PUBLISHERS
61–63 Uxbridge Road, London W5 5SA
A Random House Group Company
www.rbooks.co.uk

First published in Great Britain
in 2007 by Bantam Press
an imprint of Transworld Publishers

A CIP catalogue record for this book
is available from the British Library.

ISBNs 9780593058954 (cased)
9780593058961 (tpb)

Addresses for Random House Group Ltd companies outside the UK
can be found at: www.randomhouse.co.uk
The Random House Group Ltd Reg. No. 954009

The Random House Group Limited supports The Forest Stewardship Council (FSC),
the leading international forest certification organization. All our titles that are
printed on Greenpeace-approved, FSC-certified paper carry the FSC logo. Our paper
procurement policy can be found at: www.rbooks.co.uk/environment

Typeset in 11/16pt Sabon by
Falcon Oast Graphic Art Ltd.

Printed and bound in Great Britain by
Clays Limited, Bungay, Suffolk.

2 4 6 8 10 9 7 5 3 1

For Sarah, plus one

# Contents

# Picture and CD Acknowledgements

## Picture Acknowledgements

All images have been supplied courtesy of Paul Oakenfold except for the following:

*First colour section*

Page 1: Courtesy of Sheila Oakenfold.
Page 2: Paul with Ian Paul and Trevor Fung, courtesy of Trevor Fung. All other images courtesy of Sheila Oakenfold.
Page 3: Paul with Ian Paul and Lisa Loud © David Swindells/ PYMCA; Dave Little with 'Jibaro' artwork © David Little.
Page 4: Acid house at Spectrum © David Swindells/PYMCA.
Page 5: All images courtesy of Adrian Batty.
Page 7: All images courtesy of Marc Marot.
Page 8: All insets courtesy of Adrian Batty.

*Second colour section*

Page 1: All images courtesy of Grant Fleming.
Pages 2–3: Courtesy of Richard Norris.
Page 4: Main picture and New York, New York theatre image courtesy of Grant Fleming.
Page 5: All images courtesy of Grant Fleming.
Page 7: Nelson Mandela 46664 concert image courtesy of Marc Marot.
Page 8: Paul with Paris Hilton © Browarnik/Wire-images/Getty Images; Paul in Marrakesh courtesy of Marc Marot; Madonna 'Confessions' memorabilia courtesy of Richard Norris.

Every effort has been made to obtain the necessary permissions with reference to copyright material, both illustrative and quoted. We apologize for any omissions in this respect and will be pleased to make the appropriate acknowledgements in any future edition.

## Paul Oakenfold Authorised Biography CD Acknowledgements

'Amsterdam' (Paul Oakenfold/Ian Green) Published by Perfecto Music/Pollination Music. Produced by Paul Oakenfold. Additional production and programming by Ian Green.

'Just The Way' (Paul Oakenfold/Ian Green/Scott Cutler/Anne Preven/Ryan Tedder) Published by Perfecto Music/ Pollination Music/Scottarock Music (ASCAP)/Shigshag Music (BMI). Administered by Kobalt/Write 2 Live (ASCAP). Produced by Paul Oakenfold. Additional production and programming by Ian Green.

'Praise The Lord' (Paul Oakenfold/Ian Green) Published by Perfecto Music/Pollination Music. Produced by Paul Oakenfold. Additional production and programming by Ian Green. Vocals by Sarai.

'Save The Last Trance For Me' (Paul Oakenfold/Ian Green) Published by Perfecto Music/Pollination Music. Produced by Paul Oakenfold. Additional programming by Ian Green. Vocals by Sarai.

'Vulnerable' (featuring Bad Apples) (Paul Oakenfold/Ian Green) Produced by Paul Oakenfold. Additional production and programming by Ian Green. Vocals by Ashley Bottoroff. Additional vocals by Spitfire.

# Acknowledgements

Thanks to everyone at Transworld: Bill Scott-Kerr, Doug Young, Sophie Holmes, Rebecca Jones, Vivien Garrett, Sheila Lee, Sam Jones and all the team. Thanks to my editor Sarah Emsley for her skill and patience in helping shape this book.

Thanks to Gail Haslam for her help in getting this book off the ground in the first place – without whom, etc.

Thanks to my agent, Antony Harwood, for getting it sorted.

Thanks to Marc Marot, Claire, Tracey and all at Terra Artists for their insight and help beyond the call of duty.

Thanks and much love to Sarah Norris for her inspired ideas, speedy transcription, LA driving and all-round inspiration.

Thanks to Dan Rosenthal, Mickey Jackson, Fozia and Alex Hill, Sheila Oakenfold and Sid Steele, Christianne Lambert, Gerry Gerrard, Richard Bishop, Geoff Barnett, Melanie McBride, Ricardo Vinas, Ben Turner, David Levy, Maria Hutt, Guy Oseary, Carl Cox, Greg Shapiro, Adam Clayton, Trevor Fung, Ken Jordan, TC aka Spitfire, Bez, Daniele Davoli, Shaun Ryder, Pete Tong, Kieran Evans and all at C-C Lab, James Barton and Gail at Cream, Andy Carroll, Lee Coombs, Abel Reynolds, Dave Little, Andy Chatterley, Bela Molnar, Johnny

Walker, Alex Patterson, Kris Needs, Matthew Collins, Chris Salewicz, Chris Butler, Jonathan Richardson, Jill Pearson, Alan Lewis, Gary Crowley, Simon Ghahary, Nathan Thursting, Matthew Benjamin, Alfredo, Mark Lewis, Sandra Collins, John Fairs, Pepe Janz, Ian Paul, Lynn Cosgrave, James Nicholas, Nathan McGough, Nick Dewey, Neil Moffitt, Tony Wilson, Keith Allen, Rich Bloor, Charles Cosh, Nicky Holloway, Noel Watson, Matthew Collin, Josh Cheuse and Caro, Steve Osborne, Paolo Hewitt, Jonathan Peters, Else and Roman, Rustam Urmeev, Cello Kan, Pam Hogg, Phil Dirtbox, Steve Proctor, Erol Alkan, Robin Turner, Dave Ball, Jeff Barrett, Darren Hughes, Melanie McBride, Kenneth Thomas, Vello, Grant Fleming, Rowan Chernin, Chris Butler, Sean Rowley, Raymond Blue, Elliot at Safehouse, Gary Stonadge, Bill Brewster, Mark Moore, Johnny Dropjaw, Lisa Horan, Ros Earls, Helen Mead, Jack Barron, Andy Crysell, Zeo Morse, Rob Davis, Steve Lamacq, Justin Robertson, the Bad Apples, Dino Psaras, Tim Sheridan, Ken Jordan, Steve Levy, Tim Fielding, Hernan Cattaneo, Roger Goodman and Jason Bentley.

Thanks to all the Oakenfold party posse who kindly shared their experiences: Craig J. Docherty, Tom Ribitzky, Martin Matthew Heaps, Michelle Monaghan, Graeme Platt, Evan Dilworth, Anthony Francis, Lesley Hall, Jourdan Bourdes, Lysa Oldhams, Jonathan Mosely, Kathy Wilson, Luis Filipe, Synthia, Kate, Angela aka Detroit Pixie, Maxine Richards, Johnny Chazz, Scott Gibson, Bonnie Star, Thomas Tam, Brenda Powell, Maria Chamberlin, Kevin Boyle, K.C. Ray, Wotyzoid, Odessa Aston, Boris Pfeiffer, Daniel Husney, Smokey Azhar, Brian Grecu, Cher Ingram, Ted S., Jamie Hicks, Will Hetzel, Katya Androchina, Stuart Wallace, Kim Dudek, Cheri Lucas, Travis Lewis, Andrew Warsaw, Melissa Gonzalez,

James Campbell, Wesley Tran, Sergey Mayorov, Brenda Cullen, Denise Fernandez, Sarah Woefel, Rachel Blair, Nicole Ruskit, Abril Batallar, Elle Jackson, Steven Chapa, Kee, Rebekah Boan, Jean-Michel Hall, Myles Jacobs, Ashley Harrison, Mike Trelinski, Patrick J. Brown, Trent Smith, Steven Marquiss, Linda Nuanlaoong, Yee Vang, Carlos Martinez, Dan Ko, Justin Reach, Chelle Foronda, Kenneth Pranzo, Michael Neal, Christy Barnes, Steve Wittman, Cheridyn Flynn, Risk One, Natalie Nunez, Matthew Heiser, Christopher Miller, Estefania Montes, Christopher Scocco, Abe Andon, Don Chulio, Dominick Boldi, Beth Richardson, David Garcia, Jesus Gonzalez, Nadya Delgado, Jamie Binns, Kenneth Jarvis, Savanna Searles, Benjamin Mason and Peter Wallace.

Special thanks to Paul Oakenfold for his time, cooperation, diligence and top-quality after-hours sessions.

# Into the Groove

'The most successful club DJ in the world'
*The Guinness Book of Records*, 1999

It's late summer, 2004. Slane Castle, thirty miles from Dublin, is the venue of Madonna's first-ever Irish performance. DJ Paul Oakenfold, opening act for the day, is running late. He's stuck in a snaking queue along with the rest of the eighty-thousand-strong crowd, on a winding two-lane track that stretches back miles from the site. He's flown in from his summer residency in Ibiza, via a triumphant slot at Liverpool's Creamfields festival, and can't get anywhere near the castle. Since he's on first, this is a bit of a problem. Phone calls are made, word reaches the promoter, and soon the DJ and his crew are following a slowly rolling escort down the wrong side of the road. A whole parade of cars sets off in convoy – Paul's agent, just in from New York, his management, DJ Daniele Davoli, a bunch of friends – all dodging traffic, veering up the bank, speeding ahead.

Backstage, it's set up nice like you'd expect at this level – there's turntables, a small PA, plants, comfortable decor, plus the kind of spread a passing rock and roll group might tuck into if they were a bit peckish. It's the same rider Oakey's had for years; nothing too excessive, just beer, wine, sandwiches, fruit. He didn't half get some stick when he first asked for a rider on a British nightclub tour, though – the dance press was full of it. Who did he think he was, since when did DJs get treated like superstars? That seems like a very long time ago.

A couple of members of U2 mill around. Madonna pops in to say hi, but it's only a brief chat; she's getting her thoughts together pre-show, stealthily trying to focus. The DJ and his crew stroll up to the stage, and get their first glimpse of the crowd. Eighty thousand faces stare back. It's the size of a large Irish town.

The revolving stage is a blessing, allowing Oakey his own space to test the equipment where the crowd can't see. He's got three CD players, three decks, mixer, effects, all on a large raised platform. He's filled the available space with brightly coloured inflatables, a video screen, massive on-stage monitors, but even so, in a few minutes' time, it's just going to be him up there, without even a guitar to hide behind . . . facing a town. How do you handle that?

'You've got to learn to hold the stage,' he says with a shrug. 'You can shrink and disappear if you allow yourself to. So I build up my console, bring on the inflatables, the screens . . . you fill the stage, then your presence fills the stage. I might come out from behind the decks and go towards the crowd; you've just got to have the confidence to do that. That's when you're really naked, when you are out there, right at the front, waving your arms about. That's the only time I can ever imagine what it feels like for Bono or people like that. He's got his glasses to hide behind though . . .'

The stage slowly turns, the music cranks up. It's obvious that the young girls in the cowboy hats are here for the main act, but they seem happy enough with Paul's mix of downtempo classics, Irish acts, Radiohead, Coldplay, all familiar stuff. Paul's got about three hours' worth of tunes to play with for this first one-hour set; he feels his way around, sussing out what works and what doesn't, always aware of the crowd. He's not one for slouching moodily behind the decks. 'I changed my approach to DJing a long time ago,' he says. 'You are an entertainer. I got openly slagged for it – the DJ was meant to keep his head down, didn't look at the crowd, all that. I always thought it was very important to have audience participation, to make a connection. I try to have eye contact, if possible. With the residency at Cream, it was like a football match, the whole crowd were so into it.'

The full-on, hands-in-the-air Cream vibe is one thing, but creating a buzz on a festival stage in the afternoon can be a bitch. The revolving platform is something of a luxury, to say the least. Paul's rig can be finely tuned out of sight while the other acts are on, rolling smoothly round into place when the DJ's needle hits the groove. Such elaborate staging comes naturally when you're working with Madonna, but it hasn't always been this way. 'When you are working with a rock and roll set-up, the men in black, the roadies, sometimes don't understand the concept,' says Paul. 'You'll be DJing and they'll be rolling all the kit in and testing it out, making the records jump. You can scream at them, but they don't know what you're on about.' Rock stages can be a hazard. At one gig in New Zealand, Paul managed to misjudge the spot where the white line marked the end of the stage, and sailed clean over the edge. 'I hoped no one had noticed,' he grins, 'but it got the biggest cheer of the night.' The first date he played with U2, Paul managed to knock all his records off stage. The record he was playing was running out; he had to jump into the pit, pick up the tunes, get back on stage and stick the next one on. All the vinyl and sleeves got soaking wet – he had to take every record out of its cover backstage, get on his knees and take a blow-dryer to them. This was the moment U2's manager Paul McGuinness decided to introduce Paul to the band. They thought it was some kind of bizarre DJ cleansing ritual.

At Slane, County Meath, the rain's coming down, a full moon is rising, and Paul's second set is slowly winding up the crowd, pumping up the energy levels in anticipation of the first lady of pop. A dance mix of U2 causes a cheer to spread out wide; outstretched arms arc and ripple over a sea of expectant faces. One-nil to Oakey.

Cut to a cold Friday night a while later, January 2006. It's Paul's first London gig this year. Since the Madonna shows he's extensively toured America, as well as slotting in dates in Canada, Brazil, Chile, Argentina, Colombia, Peru and El Salvador, criss-crossing the globe on a relentless, seemingly endless tour. It's midnight. There are swarms of people milling about, heading for the thousand-strong queue outside Fabric, and a similar throng up the road at Turnmills, where Oakey and Seb Fontaine are headlining tonight. A dude sidles over, spit of Dizzee Rascal, nonchalantly keeping pace down Cowcross Street. 'You going Turnmills? Want pills, coke?' The sign near Smithfield meat market, once the site of a legendary Goa party or two, reads 'Smithfield – hangings, burnings, martyrdom'. Hopefully not tonight.

Inside Turnmills the sound is spacey, breezy European

trance, bass-heavy waves of rolling rhythm. A guy at the bar asks if I'm Seb Fontane's brother. He's a big Oakey fan; reckons Gatecrasher 1999 was the best of many of Paul's DJ sets he's witnessed. Asks me to ask Paul where he can get Sin City's '3 In 1' from the *Oakenfold: Cream Resident* album. Can't find it anywhere. He was going to see him in Marrakesh next Friday, but has opted for Barcelona on Saturday instead.

I head for the DJ booth; Paul's already on. It's a tight space, filled with a few mates, Paul's driver Tariq, and Raymond Blue, a South African promoter who books Paul, Tiesto and Paul van Dyk when they play Cape Town. Paul is a rock star over there, he says. The DJ winds up the crowd with a top-notch blend of dirty beats and skilful EQing, dropping the bass out, twisting it back in right on time as the drums kick off again. He drops a newly minted track, 'Faster Kill Pussycat', from his forthcoming album, featuring Brittany Murphy's dulcet tones. The crowd roar their appreciation – the 'Oakey! Oakey! Oakey!' chant is in full effect. 'I've gotta go for a piss,' says Paul. 'Here, you take over for ten minutes.' I nervously look at the crowd, hands in the air, waiting for the next seamless DJ choice, then back at him, laughing . . . the only piss he's taking is out of me. It's a set-up I'm to see Paul replay over and over again in night-clubs across the globe in the next year or two. His mum tells me he even tried the same gag on his brother's wife at the Grammy Awards party; she was absolutely petrified. Paul never tires of this joke, and laughs like a hyena.

The dancefloor is going mental, lasers flying about, blank white strobe light careering off the roof. Paul drops a Jan Johnson vocal trancer, then 'SOS', a tough, electronic, bootleg rinse-out of an old Police track. The sound is getting a little distorted, but the crowd are still flailing and screaming at fever pitch. Paul notices though, drops the volume to silence and wipes the dust off the needle. They scream all the more as he fades it back in – silence can be a great DJ tool.

The podium in front of the booth is full to bursting, cameras going off every minute, sweaty clubbers asking for an autograph or just trying to catch the DJ's eye. An Italian girl leans in, arms outstretched, crying 'Paaaaul! Paaaaul!' He ignores her for a bit, then smiles and does a little snake dance. The crowd hits another high and Paul starts waving his arms about as if he's addressing the crowd at Wembley – quite a feat in a small, full DJ booth. It's the first time I've ever witnessed a DJ actually conducting the crowd at Turnmills, making such extravagant stadium shapes. He's tearing the roof off.

From mega-festival dates, to globe-trotting tours, to a rocking, sweaty club like Turnmills, Paul Oakenfold can command and energise a crowd wherever he goes. So just how did this dyslexic ex-trainee chef from South London get to be the biggest DJ in the world?

# 1

# Southern Soul

As far as ten-year-old Paul Oakenfold was concerned, Greenhive, Kent, wasn't exactly a hub of musical activity. 'There was the school disco,' he says, 'But that was crap. The only place to buy records was in the post office.' The girls at school were into Bowie or the poppy stuff, David Cassidy or the Bay City Rollers; he preferred the thumping beat of Slade, Gary Glitter, and the Sweet, the shiny glam racket that beamed out of Radio One. The national radio station was a lifeline, as was his dad's record collection – Peter Oakenfold was a part-time musician in a skiffle band, played guitar, with one mate on the tea chest, another on drums; he was also a bit of a vinyl junkie. 'I was given loads of records,' says Paul. 'My dad was a big Beatles fan so I had "She Loves You", "Ticket To Ride" – I had a bunch of records before I ever bought one.' 45s, LPs, the Beatles and the Stones, Paul gobbled them up. The first record he actually paid for was by T.Rex. Peter worked on a city newspaper, the London *Evening News*, and his mum, Sheila, worked for BT. They'd go out dancing on a Saturday night, doing the jive, her dolled up, him suited and booted. Sheila went to the Morgan School of Dancing, and they'd strut their stuff at the Manor House in North London or the Lyceum in town. 'Everyone was smart,' says Paul. 'That was the look. You couldn't be casual.' There was always music around.

Peter and Sheila lived in Beresford Road, in Highbury, North London, when Paul was born, on 30 August 1963. He was born at the Mile End Hospital in the East End, within the sound of Bow Bells, the traditional boundary marking a true cockney. His mum remembers he was always crying; they didn't know why. Turns out he had a painful hernia that the doctors had to sort out. 'My earliest memory is sitting in the outside toilet,' says Paul. 'It was cold, I didn't like it! I was probably about three.' 'That was at his grandmother's,' says Sheila Oakenfold. Peter's mum and dad had a big house round the corner, on Grosvenor Avenue. When Paul was four, his dad decided it would be better to bring up the family in the country; they moved to Kent. Paul went to Greenhithe Junior School, where Sheila remembers him showing leadership potential from an early age. 'We lived on the estate; all new houses. They used to go down to the pit, they called it, because it was near the cement works; he used to go down with all the kids. It was all young children there, and he was king of it all. He was never shy – sometimes he could be a bit bossy. I think a lot of the children seemed to look up to him, as though he was the leader. He was like the Pied Piper; he had a lot of friends. They had so much freedom. He had a good childhood down there.'

Country life didn't last long though; the family, which now included Paul's younger brother David and sister Linda, moved back to the city, to Thornton Heath, near Croydon, South London, when Paul was twelve, halfway through his first year at secondary school. While Greenhithe Junior had been a laugh, Croydon's Lanfranc High School was an altogether different proposition. It was hard joining late – everyone had their classmates, everyone knew what was going on. Lanfranc High had a big Crystal Palace FC stronghold; as a staunch Chelsea supporter Paul was in the spotlight, particularly as Palace drew Chelsea in the fifth round of the FA Cup soon after Paul arrived. 'We beat them 2–1,' he says. 'At school on the Monday I got a right kicking! There were three of us that were Chelsea and we were run all over the place!'

Paul's passion for Chelsea started when he was given a blue Chelsea shirt at a very young age, well before he could go and see a match. It was a bit of a shock for his dad and brother, who were both Arsenal fans, but Paul was adamant. His first match wasn't to Chelsea, however; family friend Sid Steele took Paul to a night game, Charlton Athletic v Preston. Sid worked in construction, and was doing a job on a block of flats that overlooked the ground. He met ten year-old Paul outside the Galleon pub, then took him seven floors up, high above the pitch. A couple of weeks later Paul's brother David wanted to go, too – by this time Sid was working a couple of floors further up, so the view was even better. Paul went to his first Chelsea match with his father. 'I stood in the Shed End at Stamford Bridge,' he says. 'I loved the whole thing – getting into the ground, getting your programme, putting your scarf on.' These early jaunts kicked off a love of football that is embedded into Paul to this day; his LA studio isn't called Stamford Bridge Studios for nothing. Paul's right-hand man at Perfecto in Los Angeles, Dan Rosenthal, knows this all too well. 'You could yell "fire!" when Paul's watching Chelsea and he wouldn't move,' says Dan. 'He'll let his house burn down before he gets up in the middle of a Chelsea match. I can get a call from the head of any record label in the world when they are playing, and I'll have to say Paul's stepped out. His loyalty towards his team is as great as any sports fan I've ever seen.'

At Lanfranc High, Crystal Palace fans weren't Paul's only worry; reading and writing were giving Paul trouble. He'd later discover it was dyslexia. 'They didn't really know I was dyslexic at school,' says Paul. 'It's something I found out later. My parents certainly realised there was a problem; they got me a private tutor, and I worked as hard as I could, but I just couldn't go any further. I was struggling to read, struggling to take things in.'

'It wasn't picked up on in those days,' says Sheila. 'I don't think anybody knew the meaning of it. He did struggle, but we put it down to him always kicking the ball, that's all he wanted to do. We didn't realise – we paid for a tutor to come in, but even he didn't pick it up.'

At least he had his brother and sister to muck about with. 'Like any kids, me and my brother would fight and argue, and we'd bully our sister a bit and get told off,' says Paul. 'My brother would borrow my clothes and go out; they'd stink of smoke when he got back in and we'd get into a scrap.' One battle was a real championship fight. 'We had a loft conversion, and the boys had two rooms up there,' says Sheila. 'One day I heard an almighty scream, and I said to Peter, "One of them's fallen out of the window!" I went running up there, and Paul's slung in the corner with blood all over his face, and David's saying, "He pushed me too far, Mum, I had to hit him!" From that day on, surprisingly enough, they didn't fight. Paul seemed to respect David a bit more.'

Like many an inquisitive teenager, Paul tried to leave home, once. 'I remember one time we tried to run away, we were going to climb out of the second-storey window at home and leg it,' he says. 'I think every kid does that. We didn't get very far. We used to skip school – "hopping off", we used to call it. We'd go into town and hang out.' Paul also had a crafty way of getting out of his piano lessons. One of the earliest ever Oakenfold recordings happened when Paul made a cassette of himself playing the piano. Instead of practising, he'd stick the cassette on in his bedroom so his mum would think he was practising. His mum didn't find out about it until they did a joint interview for the *Sunday Times* many years later.

In general, however, Paul had a disciplined, structured upbringing, a solid family life with firm, hard-working parents. They always sat down and had a meal together; Paul had to shine his dad's shoes, and if he wanted an apple he had to ask for it, or he'd get a whack from one of Sheila's flip-flops. 'My family taught me respect,' says Paul, 'Opening a door for a lady, listening to people, giving someone a smile – that costs nothing, and that's come from my parents. My mum is a strong woman, and I take after her in that respect – you've got to have balance.'

By the time he was about fifteen, thoughts of the opposite sex were no doubt one of the reasons he wasn't concentrating on piano lessons. 'I was a late bloomer,' he says. 'I remember going to the school disco, that dreaded first time when I had to go and ask a girl for a dance. It was one of the slow ones – we're talking cheese here. Her name was Kim Manners. I was extremely nervous, then so excited. She said yes, we had the dance, and then I kissed her. I remember that feeling; it was only a kiss but I felt over the moon. We went out for quite a long time. I lost my virginity to her. It was fantastic, although it was all over in about two seconds! I felt embarrassed, I thought "fucking hell, is that it?" And of course I didn't want to take the blame that it was my fault!'

School wasn't Paul's favourite part of growing up. 'I was never really into school,' he says. 'Wrongly – I wish I had been into it. There's certain areas now where I wish I was better. I didn't know what I wanted to do when I left school at fifteen. I thought, what the fuck am I gonna do? The penny dropped – I wasn't good at anything really, all I wanted to do was play football. It wasn't a case of just wanting to be a footballer when I grew up – it was the only thing I *could* do. I was shit at maths, shit at English, terrible at woodwork, no good at metalwork. I was all right at photography, and all right at cooking. My grandmother, Alice Nicholson, was a chef at a big industrial place, cooking a lot of food for loads of people at County Hall. I loved hanging out with her, and I loved taking photos. I didn't know how to become a photographer, and the band I was trying to get together wasn't doing anything. I was playing piano but I couldn't find a singer, it was really hard to find a proper one. It's much easier to start a band now – it wasn't a trend then, it wasn't an option.'

Out of necessity, Paul's approach to his career was more hands-on than academic. It was either going to be cooking or football. Paul had trials for Tooting & Mitcham United FC, a pretty good team, in the Conference League, just below the Fourth Division; they would scale the dizzy heights of the fourth round of the FA Cup in the mid-seventies. The trials were a success; Paul started wearing the club's black and white strip at thirteen, alternating between midfield, attack, or sometimes playing out on the left wing. His football career was cut short at fifteen, however, when he enrolled as a trainee chef at

Westminster Technical College, where Jamie Oliver, Ainsley Harriott and Antony Worrall Thompson all took their first tentative culinary steps. Jamie Oliver calls it 'the best catering college in England'. As well as playing Saturday games for Tooting, Paul had to train midweek, which clashed with the split shifts in the kitchen. 'You'd work ten till three, then three till five off, then go back to work from five to eleven,' he says. 'Once I became a chef everything had to stop. There was no way I was going to be able to play football. That was the thing that really got me down; you throw any fifteen-year-old kid into a really hard job with split shifts, with trains and buses from Thornton Heath to the West End and back – it was killing me!'

He studied for four years, passing his City and Guilds 7061 and 7062 in French cuisine. 'It's the hardest,' he says. 'You don't necessarily become a French cuisine chef, but if you know that aspect of food, the sauces, the preparation, you can do anything.' His favourite dish remains the traditional British Sunday roast. Somehow DJing and cooking seem to go hand in hand; Danny Rampling's recently been rumoured to be putting in sixteen-hour shifts at certain Gordon Ramsay establishments, prior to opening his own place.

Paul's training included a stint at the Navy and Military Club, a members' club in Piccadilly, central London (president: the Prince of Wales). Paul's crew cooked for between thirty and a hundred, a mix of retired generals, brigadiers and minor royalty. 'It was real old-school English,' he says. 'I'd work under the sous chef, in the pastry section, in the carvery.' He'd serve up joints of lamb, sides of beef; he spent six months in each area of the kitchen, attending college one day a week. He also did a spot of outside catering: 'I worked at Wimbledon during the tennis championships, doing strawberries and cream for J. Lyons; I worked at Brands Hatch for the Grand Prix. It was great, I really enjoyed it.'

Paul's love life was soon to become a bit more complicated. His first real heartbreak was a girl called Linda Paul, a cousin of Paul's friend Trevor Fung, and sister of the DJ's future promotion partner Ian Paul. Linda needed to move out of her home so Paul decided to help out and put her up in a motel. The affair didn't last for long. 'I was really done in,' says Paul. 'I didn't realise that it wasn't true love until years later. It toughened me up a bit.'

In his limited spare time, Paul's thoughts began to turn to music. He borrowed money from his parents, and got his first set of decks, the old mobile disco, double-deck set-up, way before Technics SL-1200s became standard. 'I used to scream at him to turn it down, he played it so loud in his room,' says Sheila Oakenfold. Away from home, Paul began to explore the local soul and jazz-funk scene. 'I think I got into it because it was on my doorstep in South London, in my neighbourhood,' he says. 'Radio One would be playing pop, but the underground would be listening to Robbie Vincent play soul on a Saturday afternoon, on Radio London. You could then go to Tiffany's in Purley and see him play, alongside Pete Tong and Chris Hill. Me and my mates hooked into that scene.'

While Northern Soul's all-nighters, pills and underground fanaticism were rocking the dancehalls beyond Birmingham, a lesser-known soul uprising, centred on the fringes of London and Essex, had an equally obsessive following. The scene took off in the mid-seventies, when promoters Pete Matthews and John Kennedy began hosting all-day events for Northern Soul fans based in the South. The first all-dayer was held at the Top Rank Suite in Reading on 30 August 1976, on a bank holiday weekend, playing Northern Soul in the main room, while the smaller upstairs space, known as the Night Owl, played a mix of jazz, funk and soul from artists like Lonnie Liston Smith, Roy Ayers, Donald Byrd and Herbie Hancock. It was a major success. Subsequent bank holidays were booked; word-of-mouth buzz swelled the crowd, who began to flaunt local identities on T-shirts and banners, declaring allegiance to the 'Paddington Soul Partners', or 'The Brixton Front Line'. The jazz and funk in the Night Owl steadily grew in popularity, particularly after a DJ named Chris Hill, aka Hilly, played at the fifth all-dayer on 29 August 1977. The DJ's reputation had been built at two Essex venues, the Goldmine on Canvey Island, and the Lacy Lady in Seven Kings, Ilford, where he played soul, disco and jazz to a fanatical following, throwing in the odd rockabilly or Glenn Miller tune to break it up, loon-ing around on the microphone. Oakey was a fan – 'He was the king, the godfather,' says Paul. 'His selection of records was very good, all the big tunes like Billy Paul's "Bring The Family Back". He'd also talk a lot. He'd clown about a bit – he was a right character.'

Hilly's attempt at uniting the two all-dayer rooms at the Top Rank was typically eclectic: he led a conga into the main hall to the strains of Roy Ayers's 'Running Away'. The Northern fans weren't impressed – one managed to climb on stage, take the record off the turntable and smash it to pieces. 'I've paid two quid to come in, I'm not listening to this rubbish!' the irate punter fumed, only to be met by a hail of loose change from the jazz-funk crowd. The Night Owl took over. The next all-dayer, on 2 January 1978, was billed as the 'National Soul Festival';

with the help of the South's two best-known radio DJs, Radio London's Robbie Vincent and Greg Edwards from Capital Radio, it attracted a crowd of over four thousand.

New fire regulations forced a move to the larger Tiffany's, in Purley, Surrey. An immense sound system filled the room, a gigantic bank of speakers owned by Steve Howlett, aka Froggy. Froggy specialised in the new disco art of blending two records together in time, rather than simply playing one after another. A new face in the crowd was sixteen-year-old Paul Oakenfold. 'We were too young to get in really,' he says. 'I'd tried to get into clubs before that and got turned away, but once we got in, I loved it. It was my introduction to the soul family. I remember looking up at Pete Tong, and at Froggy DJing – he'd gone to New York and had learned to mix. It was all about the mix. He was the first known mixer on the scene. Everyone else would just play a record, then talk – Froggy took it to the next level. He was the man.'

Paul started checking out local soul nights in Wallington, Crystal Palace, and at Scamps in Croydon. 'This was our area,' he says. 'It was very territorial. There was fighting going on, a lot of local rivalry, maybe down to football.' After a while Paul's gang started to gain the confidence to move a bit further afield. They'd get on a bus and a Tube, and go to the Royalty in Southgate, way up in North London, the other side of town. Wherever the main DJs played, they'd go. Chris Hill, Pete Tong, Jeff Young, Greg Edwards, big Tom Holland, Froggy, Sean French and Chris Brown were the key players, a loose collection of soul DJs who had become known as the 'Soul Mafia'. 'We went to the Goldmine in Canvey Island, Frenchies in Camberley, Flicks in Dartford,' says Paul. They'd get the train down to Flicks, aware that the last train back was at eleven. The DJ, Robbie Vincent, wouldn't go on till midnight. 'We'd have to try to pull a girl and sleep at her place, or crash out on the floor of the train station,' he says. 'No one had a car.'

Paul's compadre and future assistant Mickey Jackson was along for the ride. 'I met Paul in 1978,' he says. 'He was from Norbury and I associated him with the Croydon lot, the soul lot. They used to come to Wimbledon Tiffany's to check out the music, the styles, how people danced, and vice versa. The first time I met Oakey he had this typical mod top on, with the RAF red, white and blue target on it. We got talking; he had a few moves on the dancefloor – he was a bit of a shuffler back in the day. We started going all over to see the jocks. We'd go and see Chris Hill, or if you wanted to go a bit more underground we'd go to see Chris Brown at Frenchies, or Sean French at Dimloes, all these different branches of the family. We'd check out Pete Tong – Tongy was off the hook. He played Dexter Wansel's "Life On Mars" before anyone else – he was phenomenal, he really cut it. He was roughly our age, a bit older; we really looked up to him, he was getting the gigs.'

A loose gang was emerging, drawn together by their love of soul and funk. 'I was going where the music was, meeting different people,' says Paul. 'It was a case of finding people who were as passionately into it as yourself. There were so few people into it, those with a real love of soul music naturally sought each other out.' Paul, Mickey Jackson, Ian Paul, Trevor Fung and Paul's school friend Woody were occasionally joined on these nightclub excursions by Carl Cox, another South London music lover. 'I lived in the Rosehill area,' says Carl, 'around Carshalton, Mitcham, Sutton. There were all these different groups that became as one when we went to the soul and funk parties. We were all the South London crew, we'd all go.'

The anthems that were gradually etching themselves into Paul's brain began to fuel a lifelong vinyl addiction. Favourite hangouts included Groove Records in Greek Street, Soho, City Sounds in Holborn and the Solo record shack at the entrance of Brixton Tube. In 1979 most of the tunes were on albums; the twelve-inch single, initially a promo-only item, cut with wider grooves for maximum playback volume, had yet to make any real inroads. 'I'd buy George Duke, Lonnie Liston Smith or Bobbi Humphrey albums, and there would be one or two tracks to play out,' says Paul. 'Robbie Vincent or Greg Edwards would play them on the radio, so you'd hear it and buy it. I was a fan, buying it all.'

He fed his vinyl addiction by supplementing his wages with various jobs. He started out selling clothes on a market stall in Petticoat Lane with Trevor Fung, then moved to a part-time job at Ice on South Molton St, before a Saturday job at Woodhouse, a menswear shop on Oxford Street, opposite Selfridges in London's West End. Woodhouse sold the latest London soul-boy style – baggy Ball Jeans, thin coloured belts with a clip, deck shoes, loafers, expensive stripy knitwear. Although Paul's taste included soul and jazz-funk, it was the fresh new sound of hip hop that he'd blast over the shop's Tannoy. Much to the annoyance of the other Saturday boy, a sixteen-year-old soul fan with a burgundy wedge named Nicky Holloway. 'I'm standing on one side, getting into the New York hip hop thing,' says Paul, 'Holloway's on the other side, folding jumpers and T-shirts, and we're battling for the stereo. I want Grandmaster Flash, he wants Herbie Hancock. Soul music was an older sound – I'd got into it, but all the musicians and all the albums I bought were older than the DJs! The soul lot lived in the country, they'd be wearing clothes we'd had for ages because we worked in the shop. They were a bit naff. I was into a younger, cutting-edge, New York vibe. Me and Nicky would barter for the stereo.'

The soul fan wasn't too impressed with the competition. 'I was a jazz-funker, into soul,' says Nicky. 'When his tapes were on I would be thinking "what's this shit?" He'd probably think the same when mine were on.' They'd already spotted the music fanatic in each other, though. Both Saturday boys had a passion for vinyl and an overdose of youthful front that would soon serve them well in clubland.

The local DJs Paul most admired were Trevor Fung and his mate Gordon Hughes, known by his DJ name of Gaz Anderson. Trevor and Gordon played local clubs like Tiffany's and Scamps. Gaz would work as the warm-up DJ for Greg Edwards, while Trevor would open for Steve Walsh, who in turn had served his apprenticeship under Tony Blackburn. Paul had met Trevor on a coach heading to a soul night at the Slough Centre. Trevor, from Mitcham, was playing with Steve Walsh; Paul, from Thornton Heath, was along for the ride alongside a bunch of mates who called themselves the 'Norwood Soul Patrol'. 'We were Thornton Heath, Trevor was with the Mitcham lot, and Norwood is near Crystal Palace,' says Paul. 'Because we were the only people in our areas who were into the music, we all met one another.' Paul and Trevor hit it off straight away.

It was through his new friend that Paul got his first proper DJ residency. Trevor was running nights at Rumours wine bar in Covent Garden, a venue well known throughout suburbia as the hip bar to be seen in. Pop royalty and club faces like Steve Strange and Rusty Egan would hang out, listening to Trevor's mix of jazz-funk and soul, before heading off after midnight to the Embassy, up the road. 'I would go to Rumours to hear Trevor or Ray Stevens play,' says Paul. 'I was a bedroom DJ; I had turntables, but I'd never played out. Watching Trevor play got me into it – watching from that side, behind the decks rather than out front, I thought "I'd like to do this." By that time I'd bought one of those shitty DJ double-deck things, a mobile DJ set-up. It didn't have varispeed, pitch control, anything like that; it was a great big heavy thing, but it was handy because it was all built in. I had the speakers, didn't have the lights, but I'd practise on it and try to hire it out as a mobile disco to make a bit of money.'

Trevor was sick one day, so Rumours asked Paul to step in. It wasn't exactly your full-on dancefloor experience – it was a wine bar, after all. 'It was one big lounge area with a little space for chairs and tables, all on one floor, with the DJ booth on the left as you walked in, so you'd always see who was coming through,' he says. 'It was more of a bar than a club. It was very fashion-led – it wasn't "let's finish work and go for a beer" – you'd travel from all over, dress up and go to Covent Garden for a drink. The cool thing was for people to sit down and hang out, with music in the background. Rumours was the place to be. I was really nervous when I first played there.' Soon Paul's love of music would take him on a journey much further than the Tube ride into Covent Garden.

# 2

# New York, New York

'The disco scene is a classic case of spilled religion, of seeking to obtain the spiritual exaltation of the sacred world by intensifying the pleasures of the secular.'

Albert Goldman, *Disco*

The dyslexia Paul battled at school forced him to look beyond South London for education. 'I was struggling to read, struggling to take things in,' he says. 'My learning came through travelling. Instead of learning from a book, I learnt first-hand.' With his mate Ian Paul, Paul began his first world tour. Ian was Trevor Fung's cousin, a tall, gregarious Indian two years his junior. Paul didn't take to Ian at first. 'I thought the same as a lot of people did when they met Ian for the first time. He came over as rude, arrogant and cocky, like he thought he knew it all. But once you got to know him, you realised he was a nice guy. Ian was my partner in crime. He could have taken on the world and won.' Once a year they'd pick some far-flung place, save up their wages and go off on an adventure. The two of them welcomed in the eighties by spending New Year's Eve in Rio de Janeiro. They were both seventeen. 'We had a pure sense of adventure,' says Paul. They flew to Hong Kong, New York, Brazil; they spent five days drifting down the Amazon River, sleeping in hammocks deep in the jungle. 'At that age you don't have any fear,' he says. 'You don't realise you could catch a disease and die.'

Out of all of these teenage trips, New York City was Paul's favourite by far. 'Everyone remembers that first drive across the bridge,' he says. 'I was absolutely blown away. We went there on holiday, came back home and that was it. As soon as I had the money, I had to go back. I was so inspired by what I saw, what I heard, what I could feel – you'd walk down the street and feel it. The old clichés were true. The B-boy with his hat on the side, holding the big transistor radio, kids breakdancing, the music pumping out . . . Then you'd see the dark side – gay cruising, black leather caps and waistcoats. I'd never seen anything like it. It was just brilliant. I thought I've got to be here.'

In 1981 Ian and Paul saved up for a more extended trip. They managed to blag some floor space at Ian's cousin's flat at 118th Street on Harlem's west side; three floors up a brownstone block, heavy metal bars on the door and a cockroach problem. The neighbourhood was mainly Puerto Rican and Dominican. Very little English was spoken. Mornings were heralded by the sound of the police.

New York life was pretty cheap and cheerful for the young South Londoners. 'We were staying at Ian's cousin's, so we had the majority of things paid for, in terms of food and rent,' says Paul, 'but we didn't have much spare money. We lived on the bare basics. It was quite hard to meet people out there. It wasn't like you'd go to a bar and hang out and meet girls; we were saving up enough money to get into Paradise Garage on the weekend.'

Ian and Paul enrolled on a bartending course at Columbia University. 'There would be sixteen, twenty people in the class,' says Paul. 'We'd write the measures down and make cocktails. You were only meant to drink a mouthful, but we'd be at the back of the class like two schoolboys, thinking this was all great. We'd be absolutely hammered.' They'd glide back to Harlem, gaze at the TV – *The Love Boat* followed by *Midnight Interlude*, a bizarre cable chat show with a nude host. 'We'd be off-our-heads drunk, thinking "what the fuck is this?" '

The trainee bartenders arrived in New York as the city was experiencing an extended musical high. Uptown, Afrika Bambaataa and Grandmaster Flash were delivering hip hop to the Bronx at Disco Fever and the Bronx River Center every weekend; downtown the last days of disco were colliding with the emerging bite of new wave. The duo's first port of call was 84 King Street, home of Larry Levan's Paradise Garage. They got there about two o'clock, queued in front of the garage doors in the forecourt, which were bolted shut but had a smaller door-within-a-door for the crowd to walk through, then passed through the metal detector, edging towards the music. Moving to the left, a big driveway was lit up with chasing lights, rising towards the first floor. Roof-high PA stacks filled the hot, dark space. The black and Hispanic crowd, strictly male, were going insane. Up front, in a booth high above the crowd, Levan was in session. 'It was the most exciting club I'd ever been to,' says Paul. He watched, listened and learned. 'Larry's strength was his arrangement,' he says. 'He knew what record to play and when.' Taking two copies of the same track, Levan mixed the bridge out, stretched the breakdown. His mixing was good, but sometimes he didn't blend the tracks – in the era before the rigid beats-per-minute regime of house music, it could be very hard to mix particular records together. Levan would let the record end, leave a gap. It was pitch black. Emerging out of the darkness and silence, you'd hear the sound of a train somewhere in the distance. The train would get louder and louder, in this hot black room. A bright white spotlight would cut through the gloom; seems like the train's coming towards you. Larry would drop a brand new tune, say the Peech Boys' 'Don't Make Me Wait'. The place would explode.

Ian and Paul went every Saturday, falling asleep on the number-one train home, ending up at South Bronx at ten in the morning, way past their stop. Ian's cousin Trevor Fung paid a visit from London; 'I remember thinking why isn't anyone here, it's two o'clock in the morning, I've got to go to bed soon,' he says. 'An hour later everyone starts rolling up, and they didn't walk out until twelve the next day.' The UK contingent wondered how everybody else seemed able to stay awake all night. 'They weren't doing coke or pills in the open,' says Paul. 'It wasn't up front. Maybe we were naive. We didn't see it.'

Paul, Ian and Trevor's road to Paradise Garage stretches back to New Year's Eve 1960, to the opening night of Le Club, New York's first discothèque. French expat Oliver Coquelin ran the venture, hand-picking an exclusive uptown clientele. It was strictly members only. It cost $150 to join, with an annual $35 fee on top. The walls were wood-panelled, hung with tapestries; there were open fires, floral displays, starched linen.

Paradise Garage it wasn't. There was a formal board of directors; financial backers included Henry Ford and the Duke of Bedford. Slim Hyatt, an Afro-American former butler with no DJ experience, operated three turntables some years before Carl Cox, in a room just off the main dancefloor, viewing the proceedings through a pillbox slit in the wall. It was an instant success, and was followed by a string of upmarket New York nightspots – L'Interdit, Sheapards, Ginza, Discoteque-au-Go-Go, the Peppermint Lounge, the Hob Nob. Richard Burton's ex-wife Sybil opened Arthur's on 5 May 1964, a more informal space catering to the newly moneyed *demi-monde*, the emerging fashion and media set. The in-house band, the Wild Ones, were the initial draw, but gradually DJ Terry Noel became the main event, playing Dylan and Sinatra, the Mamas and Papas and the Rolling Stones. The discothèque wave continued into the late sixties, but by the dawn of the new decade the excitement was fading. One new venture was to change all that. The discothèque was morphing into the disco, and the evolution that Paul and Ian witnessed at Paradise Garage began at a space called the Loft.

From February 1970, David Mancuso ran 'rent parties' for friends at his loft at 647 Lower Broadway. He didn't require a licence – it was legal to throw these parties provided the money raised actually paid the rent. Mancuso had enjoyed New York psychedelia at its height, a movement centred on the Electric Circus, Cafe Au Go Go, the Scene and the Fillmore East, the New York outpost of Bill Graham's legendary San Francisco venue. He witnessed counterculture icon Timothy Leary perform at the Fillmore as part of an ongoing series of multimedia events that were part lecture, part theatre, an audiovisual extravaganza. Leary and his cohorts, the League of Spiritual

Discovery, acted out literary, religious, scientific and philo-
sophical scenes, accompanied by sound collages and freak-out
visuals. Leary and Ralph Metzner's book *The Psychedelic
Experience*, based on the Tibetan Book of the Dead, became a
bible for Mancuso. The book's message is enlightenment via
LSD. Mancuso saw this in action when he befriended Leary at
the League of Spiritual Discovery's HQ in the West Village, and
attended the League's private acid parties. The first Loft party,
on Valentine's Day 1970, was called 'Love Saves the Day' – like
Leary's spiritual league, the initials give it away. Years before
1988's smiley culture, or Goa's trance dance, the Loft would
link acid to house.

The Loft was mainly, but not exclusively, gay, black and
Puerto Rican. It was a mixed, intimate affair in a room around
twenty by a hundred feet. You had to be personally invited by
the host; the invite would say how many guests you were
allowed. This made for a close-knit, comfortable atmosphere
where the dancers could freely express themselves. A shrine to
Buddha took pride of place between the speakers. The music
would gradually build and develop as the evening progressed.
The beat intensified, the crowd blew whistles, shook
tambourines, threw shapes; Mancuso served up a finely tuned
selection of African, Latin, rock and soul. The ceiling was filled
with helium balloons, streamers and a lone mirror ball; a
buffet, fruit, and juice were laid on. The bearded, kaftan-clad
host manned the decks, tweaking a phenomenal sound system.
The DJ didn't mix – his skill lay in throwing a party, creating
an atmosphere, weaving an evolving story through his intuitive
music selection.

The Loft wasn't a club, with membership fees, rules and
regulations, Mancuso stressed. There were no VIP rooms, no

velvet rope, and the crowd was a diverse ethnic and sexual mix. The party wasn't focused solely on the DJ – Mancuso was a reluctant spinner, worried that if he stood behind the decks all night he'd be unable to talk to his guests. There was no neon above the door, no bouncer in a penguin suit; many a bemused party-goer would walk up and down Broadway, unable to locate the Loft's entrance. The party didn't even have a name – it gradually became known as the Loft. The name was given to the party by the people, and as a given name, Mancuso thought it blessed. It was more than just a night out; the Loft was truly a special place, and set the template for many fine clubs that followed, including Chicago's Warehouse, the Gallery and the Paradise Garage. David Mancuso continues to spin to this day, spreading the Loft ethos worldwide.

One Loft regular was the DJ Paul Oakenfold would soon be checking out every week – Larry Levan, born Lawrence Philpot on 20 July 1954. A gay, black teenager from the Bronx, Levan bagged his first job at Nicky Siano and Robin Lord's club the Gallery, a large space on 22nd Street that opened in February 1973. Levan, alongside his friend Frankie Knuckles, decorated the space Loft-style, handed out flyers, prepared the buffet and made punch. Levan's first regular gig was at the Continental Baths, a gay hangout under the Ansonia Hotel at 74th and Broadway. The Continental Baths included a pool, gym, restaurants, steamy back rooms, a dancefloor and a small stage that launched the careers of both Bette Midler and her piano player, Barry Manilow.

Levan started dating the PA sound designer Richard Long, who had a showroom at 252 Broadway, near Canal Street. The couple opened the space as a Loft-style party at weekends, which became known as Soho Place. Levan, now nineteen and becoming a formidable DJ, ensured a full house, so full they had to move. Psychiatrist and regular clubber Michael Brody found an odd new space, an old meat locker in his loft at 143 Reade Street, and asked Levan to play. The fridge/loft had some useful attractions, including a killer sound system and a powerful temperature control to cool down perspiring clubbers. The venue shut after a year and a half – it was a fire risk – so Brody moved operations to 84 King Street, a disused garage lot funded with the help of his boyfriend Mel Cheren, head of the up-and-coming dance label West End Records. Paradise Garage opened in a freezing snowstorm in January 1978, with Richard Long's masterful sound system in full effect. The main room needed major structural work, so the party moved to the smaller back room for monthly 'construction parties', before four thousand people showed up for the 'Tut Tut Tut' night in September, a party themed round the Tutankhamun exhibition that had just hit New York. There were mummies and Egyptians everywhere. The sound was clear but threateningly loud; First Choice played live to an energetic, intense crowd. A New York clubbing legend had arrived.

Paradise Garage was the first of countless memorable nights out for Ian and Paul. They went to Danceteria, Bonds, the Roxy, the Funhouse, Save the Robots, Studio 54, even out to Zanzibar, at 430 Broad Street, Newark, New Jersey, where Hippie Torales and Gerald T were residents, where Larry Patterson, Tee Scott and Tony Humphries would also spin. 'Zanzibar was all-black,' says Paul. 'I was literally the only white face in there. It was weird – I didn't expect that. Danceteria and Bonds were more mixed places; even Paradise Garage was more mixed. They were an older crowd, too. They had a great sound system, a fantastic set-up. I was amazed how good the sound was.'

Clubland door policies are difficult to comprehend, let alone conquer; these private parties felt like secret societies, strictly for the initiated. Some places followed Mancuso's lead, employing positive discrimination to keep the club strictly for friends and guests, retaining a non-threatening family atmosphere. This kind of closed community had developed in clubland since the wartime discothèques in Paris, where left-leaning musicians and artists listened to jazz in secret, hiding from the Nazis. The nightclub was a safe space, away from outside pressure. Those hoping for Paradise Garage membership would queue up outside the venue during the week, where they were quizzed by Michael Brody about their sexual orientation before they passed, or more likely failed, the psychiatrist's test. The Garage was fairly mixed on Friday nights, but hard to get into on a Saturday if you were straight. Other venues employed more marked forms of elitism, striving to attract a crowd with a particular social, racial or class background. At 254 West 54th Street, Studio 54's Steve Rubell allowed only the most famous, fabulous or connected through the door. For two straight, under-age South Londoners, this was a challenge. A large dose of South London attitude helped them pass by the door police. 'We never had a problem getting in anywhere, because we had these fake passes,' says Paul. 'It was a false ID with your picture on it, very common in America. We pretended to be English journalists, from the *Melody Maker* and *NME*.'

Not only did this get them into New York's best clubs, they got into the best gigs, too. They'd find out who was playing, ring up the venue, and get put on the list for Maze or Bobby Womack. Sometimes the scam worked too well; not only did they get to see Bob Marley perform, the management thought that the young English journalists might like to interview him, too. 'It was ridiculous,' says Paul. 'What were we going to say? Ian's younger than me, and he didn't know anything about music. But he's totally blasé; Ian thinks he knows everything about everything. Factually he's wrong, but he could make you believe him.' Paul loved this confidence, but Ian could get it so wrong – he asked Bob Marley how long it took to write 'Walking On Sunshine', Eddy Grant's latest hit. 'I'm sitting there, cringing,' says Paul, 'but he's got this confidence and swagger, not even realising what he's done. We got in everywhere because of the good old *Melody Maker* and *NME* – they slagged dance music off for so long, but I used their name to get into all the dance clubs in New York.'

Unlike the Loft or Paradise Garage, Studio 54's focus wasn't solely on the music. The mirror-balled epicentre of VIP culture opened its doors on 26 April 1977, with Brooke Shields, Cher, Donald Trump and Bianca Jagger in attendance. Mick's wife celebrated her birthday at the club on 2 May, nervously parading round the dancefloor on the back of a white stallion, her grin decidedly fixed. The press went overboard; the stunt guaranteed a massive turnout six nights a week. Warhol, Dalí and Yves Saint Laurent all passed through; many less heralded hopefuls were dismissed. Rubell's door policy was brutal. The host attempted to justify his random elitism by arguing that he was 'painting a picture' with his choices of guests. It was that pretentious. By the time Paul and Ian arrived with their dodgy passes, Studio 54's star was waning, but there was still more than a hint of sparkle about. Mainly from Paul and Ian's tailoring.

'I went to see the glamour,' says Paul. 'I had an electric

mauve silk suit on; Ian had an electric yellow one. We were very aware of fashion – I'd worked in Woodhouse, Ian was into early Jean-Paul Gaultier. We bowled up looking like right characters. There was a huge queue but I was with this six-foot black, Indian-looking guy in a bright yellow suit . . . you've got to let him in.' The pair managed to swan past the notorious Studio 54 door, but the club didn't make the same impression as Paradise Garage. 'It was great,' says Paul, 'but it wasn't as musically driven as the other clubs, and we were solely into music. We weren't hanging out in the back rooms of Studio 54, we just touched on the fringes of it.' They left in fairly non-VIP fashion. 'We looked the part, but before we went in I'd got really drunk and we ended up getting chucked out,' says Paul. 'We're sitting on the number-one train, which goes through Harlem and into the Bronx, in these raw silk suits going through the worst parts of New York, drunk, falling asleep on the train. We woke up in the Bronx with all these real hip hop dudes looking at us, going "What the fuck?" I think they thought we were freaks.'

Other clubs fared better. Paul and Ian were spoiled for choice – the quality and scope of New York nightlife in the early to mid-eighties was vast. They took in the Roxy on West 18th Street, where Friday nights were run by the Rock Steady Crew's manager Ruza 'Kool Lady' Blue, a 21-year-old Brit who cut her teeth booking Afrika Bambaataa at Negril. The Roxy's 'Wheels of Steel' night was where the Bronx met downtown, a collision of hip hop, new wave and fashion for a mixed, black and white crowd. The cream of Bronx hip hop – Afrika Islam, Afrika Bambaataa, Jazzy Jay – were regularly featured. Fab Five Freddy mingled with Keith Haring and Debbie Harry. 'The Roxy worked because you'd get the trendy element coming in,' says Paul. 'The fashion crowd would turn up – you'd get models next to B-boys – for me it was the only club that merged it all together.'

The Funhouse, at 526 West 26th Street, had a more Puerto Rican, breakdance vibe, popular with Hispanic and Italian kids from Queens and Brooklyn. John 'Jellybean' Benitez was behind the decks, a young Bronx hustler whose career started with a residency at Experiment 4, further uptown. Benitez, an early Madonna collaborator, spun at a succession of clubs including Sanctuary, Xenon, the Grand Ballroom and the Electric Circus, before settling in at the Funhouse, DJing from a booth decorated with a twelve-foot mural of a clown's head. Benitez displayed a wide-ranging music policy that made a strong impression on the South London teenagers. 'Jellybean ruled the Funhouse,' says Paul. 'He played electro mixed with old hip hop breaks, like "Apache", the breakbeats that have been sampled a thousand times since. There was breakdancing going on, like in the Roxy, but the vibe was pure Latino, not black. You really noticed the separation. All these different scenes were going on, but they didn't really cross over. The Puerto Rican kids didn't mix with the gays, the gays didn't mix with the hip hop kids. I remember going to see Frankie Beverley with Maze and the Pointer Sisters at the Palladium, and being the only white person in the auditorium! We'd go and see Herbie Hancock, Lonnie Liston Smith, Bobbi Humphrey, Teddy Pendergrass . . . if you'd put them on at the Hammersmith Odeon in London, it would have been a ninety per cent white audience – over there it was ninety-nine per cent black. It was a really creative period, and we got to see it all.'

\*

Now that Paul was hearing all this new music, pretty soon he wanted to own it. Larry Levan had a particular technique of getting a record into your head during a night at Paradise Garage. 'One of Larry's strengths, when he was playing for ten, twelve hours, was to play a record two or three times,' says Paul. 'He could break a record that way. You'd hear something like "Don't Make Me Wait", it would sound amazing, then you'd go to this record shop in the Village to try to get it.' Vinyl Mania had Paradise Garage T-shirts and records, but not necessarily the latest tracks. Paul would regularly ask Manny in Vinyl Mania for Garage tunes, like Levan's spacious, metallic mix of Taana Gardner's 'Heartbeat', only to be told that Levan had the exclusive on the record; it wouldn't be out for months. However, there were some gems to be had. 'You could buy promos,' says Paul. 'They had a big sign on them saying "Promotional only – not for resale", but you could buy them. I thought this was unbelievable.' Paul started hoarding vinyl, and residency techniques, from Larry Levan, moves that would stand him in good stead many years later, at Cream.

Taking on temporary work as a courier, Paul delivered packages throughout the five boroughs. His desire for promos meant that his journey around New York was hardly A to B. 'On route I'd make an appointment with a record company, find out who was the head of club promotion and go to see them,' he says. 'I was blagging it.' If the boss tried to find out why he was late, he'd say he'd got lost. 'I hadn't really got lost, I knew my way around New York really well. I'd be delivering stuff on trains, jumping over the barrier.' He'd tell the record companies he was a DJ from London, in town for a few weeks' holiday, with some hot new English music to play them. 'I'd be taking in Haircut 100 and the Human League,' he says, 'I wasn't doing it for any other reason than to get my foot in the door. I'd ask for promos and say you should be aware of this, this is what's going on in the underground. I didn't know that the Human League had already signed to Virgin for a world-wide deal.' The record companies seemed to like the young DJ. 'I think being English and a bit bullish helped,' he says. 'I'd say I'd be back in a few weeks – they didn't realise I'd stay in New York the whole time!' If he couldn't get one of the Paradise Garage tunes on promo at Vinyl Mania, he'd find out what label it was on, and track them down. 'It might be on West End or Prelude Records,' he says. 'I went there and sat in a meeting with François Kevorkian, this little English kid sitting with the guy who's just done the new mix of D-Train's "You're The One For Me", the hot new Paradise Garage record. And I've got it on promo! And he made it! Fucking great!'

One of the people Paul met on his ride around town was Chuck Chillout, part of DJ Red Alert's crew. Red Alert broadcast the most respected hip hop show in New York, on Kiss 98.7 FM. 'I'd got really into the whole breakdancing, B-boy style,' says Paul. 'Chuck Chillout got me into the whole hip hop DJ thing, cutting and scratching. I was checking out hip hop, listening to Larry Levan, listening to Tony Humphries, trying to find my style and identity. Do I want to do the Larry Levan chops, or do I want to do Tony Humphries-style swish mixing? Do I want to scratch? I was finding myself, learning and listening.' Chuck Chillout even took him to the Bronx, which could have been a little taxing for the young white kid. 'I was a bit naive,' says Paul. 'I didn't realise how dangerous it was, but because I was with him and his boys I was all right – I was in their world. I went to his house, we were mucking about on the turntables.' His love of hip hop also led him to meet Cory Robbins and Steve Plotnicki at Profile Records, home of hip hop world leaders Run DMC. Paul took them a record by Boys Don't Cry, who Cory and Steve duly signed. Paul now had his first official music industry job – European scout for Profile Records. The blagging had paid off.

# 3

# From Rock the Bells to Jack Your Body

'I was fortunate enough to spend time in New York when the dance culture was very exciting. We didn't have a dance culture in England, it all came from America. We've just taken it and given it a little twist.'

Paul Oakenfold

With a new job on the table, Paul headed back to England, initially moving back into the family home in Thornton Heath. He couldn't stay in New York much longer, as he was on a limited visa, but armed with his new-found music business contacts and NY hip hop knowledge, he took the sound and the look of the city back to London. 'The first time Paul came back from America, he was completely different,' says Mickey Jackson. 'He'd got into the whole hip hop style – he went out there with a wedge, and came back with a baseball cap! He was fired up.'

On his return, Paul landed a second record industry post, as A&R scout of Mel Medalie's London-based label Champion

Records. 'Champion was a small record label based in Harlesden,' says Paul. 'It was really a one-man show; I'd do everything as Mel's assistant, from press, to marketing, to sending out promos, or going to clubs, plugging the tunes. I used to work in this little bedroom, with a desk and a sofa bed in the corner. Sometimes I didn't leave the office, I just slept on that. I learnt a lot from him; it was like a crash course in the music business. He also learnt a bit from me – he'd come from the seventies pop era and needed advice about dance music.' Mel took a cut of Paul's outside work, and the two parallel jobs didn't seem to worry the label boss. 'Mel was cool about it, I had his blessing,' says Paul.

Paul was soon to take on yet another job, at Rush Release, a UK promo company that was working with the new US label Def Jam. They needed someone with insider knowledge to promote their releases. Def Jam was started by Russell Simmons and Rick Rubin: a black American from Hollis, Queens, and a white Jewish student from Long Island. The label was born in nineteen year-old Rubin's NYU college dorm room in 1984; LL Cool J's 'I Need A Beat' was the first release. Over the next two decades, Def Jam would release many of the most influential hip hop albums of all time, including classic sets from Public Enemy, DMX, the Beastie Boys and Jay-Z. Way before branding became a buzzword, the countless caps and T-shirts sporting the Def Jam logo were synonymous with what was happening on the street.

Through his hook-up with Profile, Paul was getting access to upfront New York hip hop way before anyone else, occasionally passing tunes to other UK DJs like Tim Westwood. This was noted by CBS/Sony, who distributed Def Jam in the UK. Paul was called into a meeting with CBS, Rick Rubin and

Russell Simmons. Russell had been aware of Paul through Profile and Run DMC, whose number included Russell's brother, Joseph 'Run' Simmons. They mapped a plan for label promotion, and promptly got to work. 'All the corporate people didn't know what was going on,' says Paul. 'Def Jam terrorised CBS a bit, saying we won't do this, we won't do that – that's why CBS got me in, to make sure it would happen. My involvement made Russell and Rick comfortable. They played the game really well when they came over, they knew how to motivate, how to terrorise; the record company delivered.' Their acts were delivering, too.

The first Beastie Boys UK tour was a shambolic, riotous success, spawning both hit singles and the kind of mass press outrage not spouted since the Sex Pistols hit the headlines a decade earlier. The Beastie Boys press launch, at the Diorama in central London, was a riot, evolving very swiftly into a food fight that saw a vol-au-vent arc above the B-boy crowd and attach itself to Run from Run DMC's hat. Chaos ensued. The Beasties' habit of wearing Volkswagen car badges round their necks resulted in many UK VWs enjoying a logo-free summer. The tabloids went into bullshit overdrive, falsely accusing the band of assaulting a boy in a wheelchair outside Brixton Academy, and of earlier mocking a group of terminally ill leukaemia victims at the Montrose festival in Switzerland. Tory MP Peter Bruinvels, who'd never seen the band play live, forwarded a motion in the House demanding their deportation. 'Our first impressions of Britain were not great,' said Beastie Boy Adam Yauch. The tour closed with a hail of beer cans hitting the stage at Liverpool's Royal Court – Adam Yauch was charged with GBH over allegedly throwing one at a female fan. 'It was a complete load of bullshit,' says Paul. 'The things that were happening on stage were no worse than at any rock and roll show. CBS put a great spin on it, which wasn't hard to do.' At Brixton Academy, the band performed alongside go-go dancers in two cages gyrating next to an eight-foot inflatable penis. The album shifted three-quarters of a million copies in six weeks.

Paul now had three jobs, and moved to his first flat away from home, in Carshalton, where he started to go out with a new girlfriend, Emma Portius. Twice a month he'd send a package of new music to Profile in New York. Every time there was a Def Jam release he'd work out the promotional plan, fly the acts in for press and club appearances, 'the token white kid hanging out with all these hip hop bands'. Day to day, he'd work with Mel at Champion, sourcing club hits for release. He also began writing a brief column for *Blues and Soul* magazine under the pseudonym Wotupski, named after a track by Funhouse DJ Jellybean Benitez. His dyslexia made this quite a challenging task. 'It was difficult writing it,' says Paul, 'but it was only a page, and half of it was a photo. I put in bits of news, like "Run DMC are going into the studio", or "check out this track, this is happening", things like that, which I'd find out through my access to Tommy Boy and the other labels.'

The column became one of the few regular bulletin boards for the emerging hip hop culture, but was not without its problems. 'I had the biggest fights with *Blues and Soul*,' says Paul. Hip hop had started as a primarily black and Puerto Rican culture, but its move towards the mainstream was bringing in a white, rock and roll influence, through the Beastie Boys, LL Cool J's 'Rock The Bells' and the massive Run DMC/Aerosmith collaboration 'Walk This Way'. Although the staff at specialist UK magazines *Blues and Soul* and *Black Echoes* were predominantly white, the writers, like many an earnest soul music trainspotter before and since, had strong opinions about the racial divide in music. 'Here was this soul magazine with white people writing about black music, telling me I can't write about white music in their magazine,' says Paul. 'Bearing in mind that my school was sixty per cent black . . . I'm like "what's going on here?" I was only reflecting what was going on – I'm just the voice reporting on the music. There were loads of battles. The weirdest thing was, I'd go to the record companies in New York, you'd go into the black division and all the staff were black, in the rock division it was all white. I said fuck that. It pissed me off – the Americans would think I was the token white boy into rap. Even with the rappers I had to prove myself. I just thought "get over it".'

The UK hip hop audience, black and white, was lapping up the emerging culture. In Harlesden, West London, a crew called Mastermind were learning the elements of hip hop, hungrily devouring the New York flavour. The crew's leader, Herbie, was an excellent turntablist. Mastermind and other local crews would emulate the US DJ battles at local parties, rhyming, scratching and breaking. 'They were disorganised,' says Paul, 'but I'd seen the Rock Steady Crew in New York and I thought I could put a whole movement together. We formed the London All-Star Breakers, and we entered the Swatch world breakdancing competition. We all flew to New York! We found ourselves at the Roxy, England's entry to the world competition, battling the Rock Steady Crew. We didn't win, but we did well.' When the crew got back to the UK they made the press; they even appeared on that well-known champion of B-boy culture, *Blue Peter*. 'We went on, they danced, and all got a *Blue Peter* badge! It was great.'

There was soon yet another string to Paul's bow. He'd come across a hip hop record from Philadelphia called 'Girls Ain't Nothing But Trouble', by Jazzy Jeff and the Fresh Prince. The record had a breezy, commercial rap, and was based around a sample of the theme tune from the sixties TV series *I Dream of Jeanie*. The catchy riff had obvious chart potential, but it didn't feature often enough in the song to really hit home. 'I said we need to remix it,' says Paul. 'I was thinking we'd get a remixer into the studio, and I'd tell them where the hook should go and they'd remix it. Mel said "you do it". I'm like "are you sure?" Next thing I know, I'm in the studio. We brought in Herbie from Mastermind, who was more technical. I'm starting to learn, starting to pick it up.' Paul's first remix, featuring the first public outing of Will Smith – soon to become TV's Fresh Prince of Bel-Air – became a UK top-ten hit.

Paul was soon on a plane to Philadelphia to meet the duo and their record company, before they flew back to the UK for their debut *Top of the Pops* performance. 'I took them out and got on with them really well,' says Paul. 'They had such big pop potential. What they were rapping about and the samples they were using were much more friendly than the typical hip hop records at the time. Hip hop was then just a rap with a scratch or a sample thrown in, just anywhere. "Girls Ain't Nothing But Trouble" sampled an old TV programme, rather than just a James Brown break. They were talking about girls, about summertime – normal everyday stuff. You knew straight away that Will Smith could be a star – he had that charisma. That's why I signed him.'

Unfortunately for Paul and Champion, they weren't the only label to take notice. 'We had an option for one record,' says Paul, 'but Jive came along and signed them up. Once they were involved, we were taken out of the loop. That's when Will Smith started his TV programme; he steadily became bigger and bigger. I was really pissed off – we put in so much work and energy into setting the whole thing up, just for Jive to come along in the UK and take it off us. But that's how the business is.'

His next signings were Cheryl James and Sandi Denton, a duo from Queens, New York, also known as Salt-N-Pepa. Their career kicked off with 'The Showstopper (Is Stupid Fresh)', a reply record to Doug E. Fresh's hit 'The Show', recorded as part of producer Herbie 'Love Bug' Azor's college course at the New York Center of Media Arts. The duo went global with 'Push It', originally a B-side that got picked up and given heavy rotation by radio DJs, and led to the breakout album *Hot Cool & Vicious*. Alongside these early successes, Paul masterminded a string of DJ 'battle' compilation albums from Jazzy Jeff, DJ Cheese and Streets Ahead.

As well as plugging, writing, managing, remixing and A&Ring, Paul also managed to fit a bit of DJing into his ever-expanding schedule. He was in the very first DJ roster for London's Kiss FM, which was launched as a pirate station from a house in Peckham by Gordon Mac in October 1985, and built upon the foundations laid down by other pioneering dance pirates such as Invicta and JFM. 'I brought back a sticker from the original Kiss FM in New York, and they just ripped off the logo!' says Paul. 'I had a show playing hip hop, but I didn't like talking on the mic. I realised pretty early on that it wasn't for me – one time I left the mic on when the records were playing, and I was chatting away, without realizing it was going out on air. I was with Kiss for eight months or so. It was raided a couple of times during the time I was a DJ there; if they find you, the DJ gets his stuff impounded. That made me a bit wary! I had conversations with people pretty early on about having my own show at Radio One, but I made it clear that I had no intentions of doing a weekly voice show. I did later become a resident DJ on Pete Tong's *Essential Mix*, however.'

In 1985 Paul started a night called the Funhouse with his DJ friend Trevor Fung, in tribute to Jellybean's New York club of the same name. The Funhouse moved around various South London venues, in Croydon or at the Mecca in Purley, up the road from where Paul experienced his first all-dayer. They'd dress each venue in garish hand-painted banners adorned with hip hop art and slogans like 'Freaks Come Out at Night'. 'They were total fire hazards,' says Paul. The tunes rocking the London Funhouse echoed both the mishmash of styles Paul had heard in the States, as well as the sound Trevor had heard on trips to the Balearic island of Ibiza. 'It was Paul's New York thing mixed with my Spanish influence,' says Trevor. 'We played Thomas Dolby, Japan, all kinds of stuff. We were trying to do something similar to what Eddie Richards and Colin Faver were doing at Camden Palace, but a bit differently, adding our own thing.' The difference took the form of a wide-open music policy. 'If there was something that was out of the genre, that was perceived as a different kind of music, like The Clash's "Magnificent Seven", we'd play it,' says Paul. 'Whatever worked on the dancefloor. It didn't matter if it was Queen, the Beatles, whatever. I got that from Jellybean, from New York.' The music brief may have been open, but when it came to dress code, the Funhouse was strict. 'The attitude was dress up, make a point of it,' says Paul. 'I'd come back from New York, seen the glamour of Studio 54 – I took that back and tried to put it into the Funhouse. It didn't work. Maybe because we were doing it in the suburbs, maybe the timing was wrong. Boy George and Marilyn were doing it in the West End, we were doing the suburban version. The West End was about the whole Rusty Egan, Steve Strange thing – that worked.'

Steve Strange and Rusty Egan started running clubs in the late seventies, in the aftermath of punk. Their first big club hit was Billy's, at Gossips in Meard Street, Soho. Rusty, former drummer with ex-Pistol Glen Matlock's band the Rich Kids, was the DJ; Steve Strange, soon to grace *Top of the Pops* as the face of Visage, ran the door. DJ and future acid-era hit-maker Mark Moore remembers Billy's as 'a really cool club full of rent boys, weirdos and Bowie clones'. Rusty would play a broad mix, from film scores to Roxy Music and Bowie, alongside modern European electronic music – Gina X, the Normal, the Human League and Kraftwerk. After punk, Billy's dancefloor was a revelation. 'Going there opened my mind to a lot of new music,' says Mark Moore. 'Being a punk meant you had to follow a lot of rules and restrictions. You weren't allowed to like pop music or disco music, just punk. By going to this club, I realised the rules don't matter. I stopped hiding my Blondie records when my punk mates came round.' The night was titled 'A Club for Heroes', and the peacocks who flocked to Soho dressed accordingly; the scene was initially referred to as 'the cult with no name'. After Strange and Egan relocated to the Blitz club at 4 Great Queen Street, Covent Garden, up the road from Trevor and Paul's hangout Rumours, the cult gradually became known as the New Romantic movement.

At Blitz, Steve Strange's door antics were becoming more extreme – he famously refused entry to Mick Jagger for wearing a baseball jacket and trainers. An occasional Tuesday-night guest DJ was a young kid from Streatham – Trevor Fung – who played 'white-boy funk, James Brown and a bit of George Duke'. His mate Paul also managed to get a DJ spot at the Blitz. 'It wasn't planned,' says Paul. 'I was playing at Rumours and Steve and Rusty asked me to play. The Blitz was right round the corner; they'd come down and heard me. It wasn't a case of knowing that scene – I was playing stuff that they were into, without even knowing it. Alternative stuff.' Paul and Trevor would check out the Blitz, and later Rusty Egan's Thursday-night sessions at Barracudas on Baker Street, one of the big New Romantic nights. Even later than that, they'd hang out at Playground at the Lyceum, a Steve and Rusty night that featured a thirty-foot-high television wall that dominated the stage, an early clubland version of U2's Zoo TV. 'We were the suburban kids coming to have a look, checking out what the West End boys were up to,' says Paul. 'We started to build a name, and they started to recognise what we were doing. We became friends with people like Rusty Egan and Chris Sullivan at the Wag Club.'

Paul's look at the time included an early sighting of his legendary spiky mullet, eyeliner, and an oversized nylon suit that looked like a pair of pyjamas. It was the coiffure that truly raised eyebrows though – Paul sported the biggest mullet this side of Pat Sharp well into the acid house era. 'The reason I've had so many haircuts is because I'm always trying to reinvent myself,' Paul says with a smirk, not very convincingly. 'I've had the Kevin Keegan perm, the number-one skinhead, the number-three crop dyed blue. I've had the blond bit bleached at the front. In my opinion the mullet was different . . . no one had long hair in that scene at the time. As soon as everyone did have long hair, I went back to a skinhead. I was in Café del Mar in Ibiza, and there was a police raid and they arrested everyone who had long hair because it was a cliché in the acid house scene to have long hair. Thank God I didn't fucking have long hair because I had a couple of pills on me and would probably have got arrested. I look back and think, yep, I had a mullet. But I think my perm was the worst one! Who convinced me to do that?!'

If Steve Strange's door manners were a little severe, the queen of the mid-eighties West End front of house was Philip Sallon, who ran the Mud Club. Initially at Planets in Piccadilly, where Boy George and Jeremy Healy would DJ, the club had moved to Fouberts in Fouberts Place, just off Carnaby Street, back in 1983. Philip would dress in a variety of bizarre costumes – Napoleon one week, a suit made of newspaper or plastic bags the next. He'd take great, dramatic pleasure in loudly turning away outsiders at the door. Those who managed to cross his hallowed portal would mingle with pop royalty (George Michael, Sade, a Bananarama or two) and unconvincing trans-vestites in dresses bought in Kensington Market. The 'Buffalo' look and Vivienne Westwood's pirate collection were the big fashion statements, but most opted for MA-1 flying jackets, Doc Martens, a rockabilly crew-cut and a pair of Levi's. Pink rather than orange stitching in the jeans' turn-ups was an essential detail, for some reason. Malcolm McLaren provided 'Double Dutch' dance lessons on the opening night. Downstairs DJ Jay Strongman blended rockabilly, funk, rap and electro, while upstairs Tasty Tim and Mark Moore provided a more wayward selection. 'We'd play what we called schoolboy disco,' says Mark Moore. Donna Summer, George McRae, Divine, Sparks and Gary Glitter all got an airing, as did the emerging Euro electronics of Cabaret Voltaire and Yello. The upstairs DJs got away with murder, playing the *Rupert Bear* theme, or Julie Andrews's 'The Lonely Goatherd' at the hippest club in town. 'We used to play records to annoy people,' says Mark. 'We grew up with punk, with Throbbing Gristle, so it wasn't just about entertainment. We'd put on Demis Roussos and everybody would stamp the floor in unison; the needle would fly across the record. That was a real success, if the needle jumped across the whole way.'

The pinnacle of West End elitism had arrived on 31 January 1985, with the opening Thursday night of Leigh Bowery and Tony Gordon's Taboo, at Maximus, Leicester Square. Doorman Mark Vaultier somehow managed to be even more uptight than Philip Sallon; he'd hold a mirror up to hapless queue victims and ask 'Would you let you in?' DJ Jeffrey Hinton played the tackiest Hi-NRG possible, while Leigh Bowery and Gary Barnes, aka Trojan, fell over each other, living up to Leigh's maxim – 'Dress as though your life depends on it, or don't bother.' The fashion elite would hang out at the club – John Galliano and Patrick Cox were regulars. The decor was chrome, seventies, tacky. The dancefloor had a backdrop with old cine-8 movies projected on to it, intercut with pop art. You might bump into Bryan Ferry or Janet Street-Porter in the toilets. Although these antics were only a few miles away from Paul and Trevor's nights in Streatham, they seemed worlds apart.

Over in South London, by 1986 Trevor and Paul had replaced the one-off Funhouse parties with a regular Friday night called the Project Club, at a former gay venue called

Chaplins, later known as Ziggy's, at 225 Streatham High Street. It's still there – it's now known as Illusion (ladies free before midnight, no trainers or hoodies). They hired their soul-crew mate Carl Cox to oversee the sound, since he owned a PA; he was later promoted to warm-up DJ. Carl had been obsessed with sound systems ever since he saw the Green Dragon mobile DJ set-up at his school disco, and had built up the best PA spec in the area. 'Even though I wasn't moving closely in Paul's circle at the time, I was someone he could call upon,' says Carl. 'He'd book a hall, I'd bring the sound system. He had Scritti Politti on one time; we were doing parties for sixteen-year-old kids, putting acts in front of them.' Carl brought a bit of Southern Soul history with him to the venue. He brought part of Froggy's sound system from the Sheffield Arms and installed it in the club, including Froggy's mixer. He also doubled up as Paul's mechanic, fixing Paul's bright yellow Mark III Ford Cortina XL at twenty-five quid a go. Paul returned the favour handsomely. 'None of us were earning a lot of money,' says Carl, 'but I wanted to buy my first turntables. Paul said "Look, I'll buy the turntables, you just pay it off on a weekly basis." I was like "Brilliant, I'll have some of that!" I paid it off bit by bit, and I'd got these spanking brand-new SL-1200 decks!'

Paul also managed to set up a record pool around this time, an operation called Opec, based on Frankie Knuckles's Def Mix record pool in New York. Opec provided a service to its DJ members, sending them upfront tunes by mail. 'We had a lot of good DJs,' says Paul. 'Larry Levan, Gordon Mac, all the early Kiss DJs, all the club players like Maurice and Noel Watson.' While Paul was busy promoting hip hop and early house cuts, he would bring whoever was in town to play in front of 250 people, maximum, at the Project. LL Cool J would be playing at the Lyceum in the West End at midnight; by one o'clock he'd be mingling with the punters in South London. 'Run DMC, the Beastie Boys and Marshall Jefferson all played at the Project,' says Trevor. 'No one could believe it.' Carl Cox was similarly impressed. 'Run DMC playing for two hundred and fifty people at Ziggy's? How Paul ever did that, I don't know,' says Carl. 'The old soul lot, Hilly and the rest, were kind of an old boys' network, but there was always room for something new to come through, which no one was ready for, really. Paul had foresight, based on what he wanted to do for people, which initially was putting on hip hop, Run DMC, Oran "Juice" Jones, the Beastie Boys, the list goes on. It was amazing – Run DMC sitting in the corner of Ziggy's! The floor's sodden with last year's beer, there's no air conditioning, it's boiling hot, and there's Run DMC performing! Paul said, "I can put you in front of an audience – it doesn't matter what type of place it is." That's what he did. He put his neck on the line.'

'Run DMC would be playing the Lyceum on the Saturday night, so I'd say "On Friday, let's do this real underground, hot club,"' says Paul. 'They didn't know – I just put it into the schedule. And whether it was my club or not, it was a proper underground club. What was good was that we got them cheap.'

Paul also secured a spot for Darryl Pandy and Farley Jackmaster Funk at the club, promoting Farley's soon-to-be-stellar house hit 'Love Can't Turn Around', a track based on Isaac Hayes' thumping 'I Can't Turn Around' that became a UK top-ten hit in September 1986, despite Darryl Pandy performing the song lying on his back on *Top of the Pops*. Paul had been taking the Chicago duo around the UK's clubs and media. 'I'd be driving them around, doing loads of regional radio stations,' he says. 'I had Darryl, this sixteen-stone black guy, in the back, screaming and kicking off his slippers! He reminded me of Divine. He'd be after all the little white boys in the crowd, that didn't even know he was gay. It was hilarious when he came to the Project Club – he leant back and fell into the audience! Suddenly you could see this look of terror on people's faces as they realised he was going to fall on them . . .' As well as gay Chicago icons, the Project also started to feature a series of guest DJs – soul mafia dons like Jeff Young and Pete Tong, Graeme Park from the Garage in Nottingham, and, on one occasion, an up-and-coming soul promoter called Nicky Holloway.

Since battling Paul over the sound system as a Saturday boy in Woodhouse, Nicky Holloway was becoming a well-known South London promoter and DJ. As all DJs who started in the late seventies will tell you, DJing hadn't been a career move for Nicky. He began playing records in his bedroom, bunking off school when his mum went to work, sticking two primitive hi-fi systems together and taping the results on cassette. Following a stint at Mean Man menswear in Edmonton and the City Sounds record shop in Holborn, he auditioned for the Rainbow mobile DJ agency, who put an ad in the *Record Mirror* classified section – 'DJs required, no experience necessary.' 'It was 1979, I was reading about Paradise Garage, Larry Levan, Froggy,' says Nicky. 'I was counting my BPMs, getting into mixing.' This didn't impress Rainbow – they were more interested in the jovial microphone patter well loved by mobile jocks worldwide. It took Nicky two or three auditions to make the grade, but finally he got a break.

A string of run-down boozers on the Old Kent Road were tarting themselves up in the wake of *Saturday Night Fever*, reinventing themselves as disco drinking dens. 'All these gangster pubs were spending a fortune, trying to outdo each other,' he says. A network sprang up – Sampsons, Jillys, the Duncow, the Green Man. He'd DJ the whole night, from eight until eleven or twelve, for fifteen quid. It didn't seem that bad; most people worked all day for that. By 1980 he was working five nights a week, in pubs he still wasn't old enough to drink in. He was a regular at the soul mafia events, and in 1983 started a night on a Monday at the Swan and Sugarloaf in Tooley Street, Bermondsey, close to London Bridge. He quickly had a couple of hundred coming each week, sometimes more. The suburban soul crew came from as far afield as Southend, Berkshire, Norwich, to hear Sean French, Jeff Young and Chris Brown play, with occasional appearances from Chris Hill when Holloway could afford him. At the same time a pub called the Royal Oak, further up Tooley Street, became available on Fridays, with the added attraction of a two o'clock licence. Special Branch was born.

Like the Funhouse, Special Branch at the Royal Oak was decked with ultra-bright banners, somehow managing to give a dull, run-down Bermondsey pub its own flavour. Nicky and Pete Tong played soul, funk and boogie downstairs, while an up-and-coming jazz DJ, Gilles Peterson, had his first residency upstairs, playing Latin and bossa nova. Pete Tong got a hundred quid; Gilles got seventy. 'The scene was a cross between casual soul boy and London trendy,' says Gilles. 'It was a very important club – out of that scene came nearly everything we have today in the UK.' 'It was a weird little network of people, mostly from the suburbs,' says Nicky. 'They'd meet up at parties all over the place. There was no media to cover it – a page in *The Face* or *i-D* maybe, a bit in *Blues and Soul* or *Echoes*. It was either go to the West End, go to the high street, naff clubs, or come to our scene.' Special Branch, alongside 'friendly rival' the Project five miles up the road, was the new suburban underground.

Following success at Tooley Street, Nicky Holloway began to search for bigger venues to spotlight the younger DJs on the soul scene. The soul mafia's all-dayers at Reading, Purley and Alexandra Palace had been successfully followed by an all-weekend event, at a Ladbrokes holiday camp at Caister Sands, near Yarmouth, in April 1979. It attracted over three thousand, with a line-up including Robbie Vincent, Chris Hill, Tom Holland, Froggy and Sean French, playing jazz-funk, Salsoul, soul, and disco. The 'National Soul Weekender' became a Southern Soul institution. Nicky Holloway decided to throw his own events just after the summer season at Rockley Sands caravan park in Dorset. 'I was a punter on the soul-boy scene but I wasn't getting booked,' he says. 'I became a thorn in their side, the one who nicked their best customers.' Eight hundred turned up to the first of these mini-Caisters; three more followed including one during a massive hurricane. About twenty caravans got blown away, forcing the promoter to rehouse people who'd never met. 'I tried to put two lots of two people in a four-berth caravan,' he says. 'Nobody really minded – we gave them half their money back. A lot of friendships were formed that weekend.'

The holiday camp was followed by a series of Special Branch nights at a string of bizarre venues. Caveman Boogie was at Chislehurst Caves in Kent in 1985; the first Do at the Zoo, at the function room in London Zoo, took place the same summer. 'In those days it was a lot easier to hoodwink people into letting you put parties on,' says Nicky. 'We'd pretend it was going to be some yuppie get-together.' The opening Zoo party was on a Sunday, starting at six o'clock, with free entry to look at the animals beforehand. Two thousand people attended; the bar took so much money that the zoo welcomed the promoter back for sixteen more parties during the next four years. Further 'Do's took place at Lord's cricket ground, in the GLC building on the South Bank, and at the Natural History Museum. The jazz-funkers boogied beneath the dinosaurs.

While Nicky was ushering in a new soul mafia at the Special Branch, Paul began to look further afield for inspiration. He felt a need to broaden his hip hop horizon. 'There was a lot of violence in hip hop – it had lost its edge,' he says. 'We'd toured with the Beasties and Run DMC – we were on to the third generation of hip hop. I was still into it, but I was moving away.' The new sound emerging from Chicago, on small independent labels like Trax and DJ International, began to attract his attention. Paul began tracking down this fresh, emerging sound.

House music took its name from the Warehouse, a club set up in an old loft at 206 S Jefferson, Chicago, which specifically aimed to bring the atmosphere of David Mancuso's Loft to the windy city. The main Warehouse DJ was Larry Levan's old sparring partner Frankie Knuckles, who took the job after Levan had turned it down, refusing to leave New York. Frankie played a bass-heavy mix of old disco classics and current Euro sounds, like Kraftwerk, Telex and New Order, from eleven on Saturday to midday Sunday, mixing them up with the new breed of local recordings emerging from Trax and DJ International. By mid-1985, the sound was beginning to slowly filter through to a handful of UK DJs.

Paul's hunt for house tunes led him to 'Jack The Groove' by Raze, a duo featuring Vaughan Mason and Keith Thompson, which he persuaded Mel Medalie to release on Champion. The track snatches a sliver of the bass line from Cymande's funky, percussive early-seventies hit 'Bra', shifting it into a more European, machine-like groove, a spaced-out robot mantra. It's hard to describe just how alien this naggingly repetitive record sounded at the beginning of 1987. It seemed like it hadn't just been made in another country, but on another planet. 'It sounded raw,' says Paul. 'I'm always on the lookout for new sounds, and the early house tunes had it – the raw sound, that minimalist vibe. It wasn't very fast, only about 118, 120 beats per minute. We were slowly moving towards that tempo. MARRS' "Pump Up The Volume" had been a big hit, and that was at around 112, 114 BPM – that tune brought a lot of energy to the dancefloor. Before that it was the lyrical content and the anger of rap, the mishmash of samples – it was slow, but it gave you energy. The tempo played a very important part in making "Pump Up The Volume" such a big record. It was the only record I played at the time that was that fast, and you still had the blackness, the hip hop element in the vocal sample. So when "Jack Your Body" and "Jack The Groove" came along, this 118, 120-beats-per-minute dirty groove, it had the rawness and energy from rap, but it was different. It was fresh.'

'Jack The Groove' quickly followed 'Love Can't Turn Around' into the charts, reaching number 21 in February. These early tracks made a phenomenal impact – obscure, underground dance records gaining mainstream chart success, with only minimal airplay and little media support. House was truly a dancefloor-led sensation. 'You could see these records were going to be big club hits,' says Paul, 'and with vocal hooks on them, they quickly became pop hits as well. I got immersed in it really quickly, working at Champion. We were putting out twelve-inches, compilations.' Paul's involvement with the early Chicago house scene brought him to the attention of former soul family DJ Pete Tong, who had recently started working for London Records. 'I'd met these guys from the Chicago house labels – Rocky at DJ International and Larry at Trax,' says Paul. 'They'd come in the Champion office with a suitcase almost the size of the desk, open it up and it would be full of cassettes of new Chicago tracks. Some of them they didn't even own! They'd try to sell them to you anyway . . . all of a sudden, without realising it, we were becoming the label that was putting out more house records than anyone else. Because of this, Pete Tong then hired me to promote Steve "Silk" Hurley's "Jack Your Body" for London. I ended up doing club promotion on it, and because of that simple lyrical "jack your body" hook, it suddenly crossed over to the pop charts.' The record was an even bigger success than 'Love Can't Turn Around', reaching the UK number one spot in January 1987.

London has always been seen as painfully slow to pick up on house music, while the rest of the country embraced the new sound. DJs like Winston and Parrot in Sheffield, Steve Proctor in Liverpool, Mike Pickering in Manchester and Graeme Park at Nottingham's Garage are all noted for playing house music early on, while London was supposedly still wholly immersed in the retro cul-de-sac known as rare groove. To a certain extent this is true, but it's not the entire picture. Rare groove, which took its name from Norman Jay's Saturday-afternoon *Original Rare Groove Show* on Kiss FM, was a natural step on from the jazz, funk and soul scene catered to by the soul mafia and Special Branch. The sound had a dedicated following at the Wag Club in Wardour Street, at Gilles Peterson's Talkin' Loud Sunday sessions at Dingwalls, at Norman Jay's Shake 'N' Fingerpop, and at Judge Jules's Family Funktion events. It was given saturation coverage in the style press during 1987, and with triumphant gigs by the J.B.'s and a string of re-releases, it did dominate the capital's musical brew for a short period.

Yet small outbreaks of house music started to filter through; you can only listen to Maceo and the Macks' 'Cross The Tracks' so many times. Some of the soulheads saw that something was afoot. 'All the early Trax and DJ International records were played at Special Branch,' says Nicky Holloway. 'They were big records.' Mark Moore was another early convert; the first house record he heard was JM Silk's 'Music Is The Key', played by DJ Colin Faver at Jungle, a Monday-night session at Busby's on Charing Cross Road, which was generally known for more soulful tunes. Mark was DJing at Asylum at Heaven, a gay night run by Lawrence Malice and Kevin Millins, which later became known as Pyramid. He'd spin alongside Colin Faver and 'Evil' Eddie Richards, DJs who'd made their mark as residents at Steve Strange and Rusty Egan's Camden Palace from 1983 onwards. Mark, Colin and Eddie played a more left-field selection than the usual Hi-NRG associated with gay clubs. Hi-NRG producer Ian Levine dismissed Asylum as 'the place that all the freaks went' – naturally Mark Moore took that as a compliment. 'We were playing a lot of Euro stuff – Front 242, Yello, Cabaret Voltaire,' he says. 'Around 1985 there were all these tracks coming out from Chicago and Detroit. We didn't know if it was house or disco – it didn't have a name at the time, it just fitted in with what we were playing.' Early house tracks such as Farley Jackmaster

Funk's 'Funking With The Drums Again', JM Silk and Jesse Saunders, were mixed with the Italio disco sound of Gino Soccio's 'Dancer' and 'I Remember', or 'Droid' by Hypnosis. 'We didn't know the difference between them,' says Mark Moore. 'The Chicago and Detroit records were just more primitive versions of what we were already playing.' The DJ found Farley Jackmaster Funk's 'Love Can't Turn Around' at Record Shack, a London Hi-NRG store. Nobody wanted it – it was in the 50p bargain bin. He started playing it at Heaven and the Mud Club. Everyone went ape.

Noel and Maurice Watson's Delirium night also championed house music, at the Astoria, and later at Heaven, although their mainly hip hop and soul crowd were none too keen. A massive cage was installed at the Astoria to keep bottles and other flying objects off the decks. Mike Pickering and Graeme Park were openly taunted and threatened when they played house music in the capital. Despite this, practically all of the movement's key figures came out to play in London; Larry Heard's pioneering act Fingers, Inc. graced the stage at Delirium, as did Marshall Jefferson and Derrick May. Frankie Knuckles had a two-month residency when the club switched to Heaven. And in the corner, a tiny cluster of South London dancers with strangely baggy clothes and floppy haircuts, including Ian Paul, Trevor Fung and Paul Oakenfold, were leaping about to the new noise. The Watsons initially thought they were a bunch of French students who'd wandered into the wrong night. 'We were the only people who really supported it,' says Paul. 'Noel and Maurice were well before their time. They were the only other people we knew who were playing house, so a crew of about fifteen of us would go down, get on the dancefloor and go mad. At the time people wouldn't look at the DJ; they'd be dancing, doing their own thing. Cut to us lot, all looking at the DJ, all going crazy . . . the DJ was getting a response, so he was loving it. It was one of the only places you could hear the music. I think if Delirium hadn't stopped when it did, at the end of '87, it would have been a much bigger club. There were more and more of us coming down, getting on the floor, getting the place going. You could feel it.'

Central London's night scene was pretty flat in 1987. There were occasional hints at a brighter future: Delirium, Phil Dirtbox's parties in Earls Court, the early Mutoid Waste Company events, Jeremy Healy's Circus warehouse nights. The Jamaican-blues-party-inspired sound systems like Soul II Soul and Shock hinted at what was round the corner. These were the exception rather than the rule; the fuck-you, door-bitch attitude, that stretched from the Blitz to the Mud Club and Taboo, still hung around the club entrance like an unwanted guest. It was tough to get in, and once you got inside, posing, standing at the bar and checking out each other's shoes was the norm. Only half the crowd seemed to want to dance. Nobody talked to each other. The first wave of rap had peaked; hip hop crowds were increasingly moody and introverted. The main media focus was on rare groove, on throwing funky shapes to old – admittedly fine – James Brown records. Everyone was dressed to the nines in a formal, restrictive monochrome, or perhaps, by winter 1987, in floppy seventies blaxploitation chic, acting out *Shaft* fantasies in Soho. The gay scene – traditionally the barometer of where straight dance culture is heading – was in crisis, hit by the double whammy of AIDS and a spiralling hard drug problem. 'People started disappearing and you didn't know why,' says Mark Moore. 'Were they dying, were they dead? You'd hear reports. Nobody wanted to be a freak any more, they wanted to look healthy, be a bit more normal. 1986, '87 was really quite boring. Something had to fill the void.' Paul, Trevor, Ian, Nicky, Carl and their mates were about to find out exactly what that was.

# 4

# Balearia

'When we came up on the E we didn't know what the hell was going on – only that we felt fantastic, everything looked sparkly and colourful, and we were up for a great night out.'

Johnny Walker

Did you hear the one about how Paul Oakenfold and his mates went on holiday to Ibiza and brought back dance music? I thought so. We all have; it's a nightlife fable that's been told and retold many times, developing its own particular mythology along the way. The official story goes like this.

Four friends from South London take a two-week trip to a sun-kissed island off the coast of Spain, hear a DJ called Alfredo play a genre-spanning selection of good-time tunes at Amnesia while out of their gourds on ecstasy, become fervent disciples of the Ibiza sound, triumphantly return to London armed with the new sound . . . *et voilà*, modern dance music as we know it is miraculously born. It's an easy, media-friendly shorthand that now seems cast in stone, with hindsight ignoring some elements, highlighting others. But it certainly isn't the whole story. The general outline of the tale may be true, but for Paul Oakenfold and friends, the story's a little broader, a little deeper, and started long before that fateful summer of 1987.

Although Paul had only been going to Ibiza for a couple of seasons before that fateful 1987 trip, the mates who introduced him to the White Island had been going for a few years. Nicky Holloway and Trevor Fung, Paul's teenage friends, stalwarts of the Southern Soul scene, were old hands when it came to Ibiza. 'The first time I went was on a lads' holiday when I was really young,' says Nicky Holloway. 'We were drunk before we got there, on the flight out from Gatwick, and just stayed in San Antonio, hanging out in all the bars. We didn't really see any of the other nightlife.'

Paul's DJ sparring partner Trevor Fung had reached the Balearic island even earlier. 'At the end of the seventies, as well as DJing, I was working for a travel agency in West Kensington, for a friend of mine's old man,' he says. 'I did it as a summer job. Because of working there I got a free holiday to Ibiza, with Club 18–30 to San Antonio. I was just a kid, sixteen years old. I loved it. Every year after that I went two or three times. Every season I'd meet loads of people. It was about ten per cent English tourists at the time, if that; it was mainly Swedish, Norwegian, Germans, a lot of Americans and Italians. I started DJing for these two brothers, Billy and Felix, who owned a club called Fred and Ginger's in San Antonio, which was opposite Legends. They asked me to go to Ibiza for the whole summer, in 1983. They'd just bought this club called Amnesia. I was doing a lot of gigs at the time, the

Caister soul weekenders and all that, but I'd got pretty fed up with it, bored with the music. I wanted to find something new.'

Trevor took Billy and Felix up on their offer. His cousin (and Oakenfold's future co-promoter) Ian Paul was supposed to come along for the ride, but he backed out at the last minute. Trevor went anyway. 'I played at Amnesia every night for about a month, maybe six weeks, and then it gradually shut down. The most you'd get was about five, six hundred, but not on many nights. It hardly opened – it was only open at the weekends. It was dead. Absolutely dead.'

Amnesia was so quiet that Billy and Felix had to let Trevor go. 'They couldn't keep me on so I started looking for other work,' he says. 'I ended up at the Star Club. I'd met another DJ called Carlos; he was the main DJ on the island, before Alfredo was around. He was playing at Exstasis and Café del Mar. He was the man; he got me into all this other music. He was brilliant, a really good DJ. That was where the whole early Balearic thing came from. Most of the stuff he was playing would be indie records from Leeds, plus the Fini Tribe, Front 242, that kind of feel. I thought these tracks were all American when I first heard them. It wasn't until a bit later on that I found out a lot of the records were from the North of England. It was quite a shock. A lot of the tunes were raw, quite industrial, but a lot of it was good. I loved it. You'd hear it at Glory's in San Antonio, which had the equivalent of the harder, techno-based feel of more recent Ibiza clubs, like the main room inside Space. It was the late-night spot, where all the DJs would finish.'

Ibiza's charm was beginning to cast a spell on the young DJ, a welcome antidote to the grey skies of South London. 'The island's spirit and openness appealed to me,' he says.

'Everything you were told you couldn't do by your family and employers, you could do. There was a feeling of freedom there.'

Returning again in 1984 and 1985, Trevor occasionally stepped out of the tourist enclave of San Antonio to taste the more refined pleasures of the larger clubs, like the eight-thousand-capacity Ku club, later to be renamed Privilege, now home to Manumission, where he saw the likes of James Brown and Roxy Music perform. 'People used to go there from the London club scene, people like Steve Strange and Rusty Egan, but there weren't a lot of English people there,' he says.

Ibiza's burgeoning nightlife scene received its first in-depth UK press attention in September 1985, when style bible *The Face* ran a lengthy feature with the front-cover headline 'Ibiza: Holiday Babylon'. The article centred on a gig at Ku by a fairly nondescript Latin funk act called Animal Nightlife, but the story around the party held much more promise. The article hinted at the fun to be had on the island where a certain British pop duo had shot a video, at Pike's Hotel, two years previously. 'At £157 a fortnight, anyone can purchase a chance to visit Wham's mythical Club Tropicana,' noted writer Don MacPhearson. The drinks on Ibiza aren't exactly free, mind. 'The aptly named Club Amnesia does not even open until five thirty in the morning,' noted MacPhearson, 'and it would be impolite to depart before 8 a.m. . . . For the serious Ibiza hedonist, life is not complete without a major readjustment to the body clock.' Reading that in the UK at a time when pubs closed in the afternoon, and everyone was supposed to go to sleep at eleven, felt like a passport to paradise indeed. Quite a few *Face* readers, along with Paul Oakenfold, made the trip the next season.

In the same year as *The Face* hit Ibiza, Nicky Holloway

organised his first Special Branch overseas jaunt to the island. It was a rather shambolic affair. 'The first flyer we did was unbelievably bad,' he says. 'It's a bit of wobbly Letraset and a picture nicked out of an old copy of *The Face*. I can't believe I actually got two hundred and fifty people to send me two hundred quid in the post off the back of this photocopied bit of black-and-white paper. But they did, and off we went. This was May 1985 – it was before the season started so it was really quiet. It was all in San Antonio then, centred around the Star Club and places like that. We also did a thing at Café del Mar. It was a little quiet place on the seafront, away from the West End, that people in the know used to go to. There was nothing else around that area at the time. They'd shut the doors and we'd set up inside. There was no one DJing, we just had tapes on; they had decks but they were all closed up.'

In 1986 Special Branch went to Corfu instead; many japes were had the last night when Nicky deemed it 'topsy-turvy' night. 'There were three hundred of us, all the girls dressed as blokes and vice versa. Danny Rampling, Gilles Peterson, Trevor Fung, Bob Jones all went out dressed as girls.' Trevor made it to Ibiza in 1986 however, and there was a new ingredient to add to the mix at the end of the season – a previously little-known drug called ecstasy. 'A friend of mine used to give me this stuff that year. I was working for him and he said, "I can't pay you – I can pay for all your expenses, but I'll pay you the rest in drugs." I said, "All right then . . ." We went backstage at his club, he opened his bag and said, "Help yourself." I picked up some Es and about five grams of charlie, all in little bottles. The thing was, I was flying out the next morning at eleven o'clock. I did some of the E. It was amazing, but I had to give the rest away . . . by the next year everyone would be on it.'

Returning to the Balearics in 1987, Nicky Holloway's trip got off to a flying start. 'We went over there a week before, to make sure everything was OK,' he says. 'I'd block-booked this hotel for three weeks. On the first day there we got pissed up and climbed into the swimming pool area. We were out of it, and thought it would be a great idea to go skinny-dipping. There's all these houses and flats overlooking the pool, with mums and dads and kids in them. It's seven in the morning and we're running round bollock naked. The owner of the hotel came out, took one look at us and chased us out of the hotel, whacked us about the head as we left with an umbrella. I was banned from the hotel that I'd filled up before anyone else had even got there.'

Trevor Fung had rather better luck. 'I'd already lined up a spot from the year before, with a friend of mine called Manola who ran the Project Club in San Antonio,' he says. 'He'd had the place for years. He was operating downstairs, but the upstairs never used to be open, so me and Ian Paul rented it off him. By then I knew everybody. I was sorting out all the island's DJs with records. Most of the records I'd sell direct to the DJs, then give what I had left to the shops. I'd get them from distributors cheap in England; they'd go for a fortune out there, because they were imports. I was getting them for one pound eighty and selling them for a fiver a time. I used to go backwards and forwards to England, bringing in records every two weeks, selling them to DJs and record shops in Ibiza. I'd fly in from Bristol, Manchester – any way I could get in. There was big money in it.'

The Project Club was a small venue away from San

Antonio's main West End strip, just an everyday side-street bar that could hold maybe fifty people, with an overspill of more than twice that hanging out in the street. The only unusual feature was the fountain in the basement. 'We didn't want to be in the West End,' says Trevor. 'The Project Club was on the road down to Café del Mar. There was nothing else around there; all the other big bars down there like Mambo didn't exist. We were doing something different. We even had people from Ibiza Town, on the other side of the island, coming down to listen to the music. I was getting involved in Amnesia, the bigger clubs like Ku . . . I used to have all their T-shirts up and sell their tickets in the bar, this tiny little place in San An. We also used to go to Pike's, where they shot the "Club Tropicana" video; I went to a brilliant Freddie Mercury party there in 1987. There were all sorts of people there, pop stars like Nina Hagen. It was amazing. There was loads of cocaine laid out in bowls.'

Gradually the island's laissez-faire attitude was creeping into the music selection. 'We were playing early house, a bit of hip hop,' he says, 'blended in with Prince tracks from the *Sign Of The Times* album, like "Starfish & Coffee" and "If I Was Your Girlfriend". All the English people that came to the Project were workers on the island. Lisa Loud and Nancy Noise used to hang around our bar. There were people from Sheffield and Manchester there, working for me.'

One new face hanging out at the Project bar was Paul Oakenfold. 'I first went to Ibiza in 1986,' says Paul. 'Trevor and Ian had been doing summers, working the season; I went there on holiday, and the next year I went back again. The Project was great, this little underground bar tucked away in the back streets of San Antonio. They were really mixing the music up there, a good Ibithenco style of music.'

Paul headed back to Ibiza at the beginning of the season in June 1987. For his birthday, later in the season, Paul asked Trevor to look out for a place he could stay with a few mates. Paul, Nicky Holloway, Danny Rampling and Johnny Walker all headed to Ibiza in August 1987. The four, plus Trevor and Ian, all knew each other to varying degrees. Johnny Walker was a soul music fan working for ffrr records with Pete Tong. Nicky had brought his mate Danny Rampling along, another South Londoner who he'd first met outside the Tropicana in San Antonio's West End. Danny had just returned to the UK from a long trip to America, where he'd worked on building sites and in restaurants, and had a life-changing narrow escape from a car crash. Danny was a regular at Special Branch parties, and had even decorated Nicky's flat. Trevor got them all a nice villa at Port Estrol, round the other side of San Antonio bay. It was quite a flash thing to do, quite unusual at the time, but allowed the group a freedom that they wouldn't have enjoyed at a downtown San Antonio hotel.

Paul was twenty-four on 30 August, two days after Johnny Walker had turned thirty. Paul, Johnny . . . Nick and Danny arrived on the island to find Trevor and Ian noticeably looser, more laid back than they had been in June. 'Paul was a bit shocked when he saw us,' says Trevor. 'We were being a lot more open than you would be in England. Everyone's guard had come down a bit; we were having a great, free time in the sunshine. We were coming out of our shells. The E helped!'

Although the birthday evening was soon to turn into a very happy one indeed, it didn't get off to a very good start. The night began at Nightlife in San Antonio, a typical beery Brit hangout in the West End. 'It was crap,' says Paul. 'I wasn't into the San Antonio scene much.' It was here, however, that Paul and Danny took one of the little white ecstasy capsules they'd heard so much about from Trevor and Ian. Johnny Walker and Nicky Holloway were more cautious. 'I was very apprehensive about doing it,' says Nicky. 'It wasn't until I saw the others having such a good time that I thought I'd try one. When I finally got that first rush, it was fucking great, and that was it.'

At Ian and Trevor's suggestion, the whole crew floated down to hear the DJ spin at Amnesia. The DJ was Alfredo Fiorito, known to one and all as Alfredo, an Argentinian former film and music critic who had first started DJing on the island in 1982. He'd fled Argentina's repressive rule after being jailed following the right-wing military coup of 1976, settling in Spain, and finally Ibiza. It took a couple of depressing, empty seasons at Amnesia before the DJ's alchemy began to work, but eventually it did. There's something about the sunshine and the warm breeze that made particular records perfect for Amnesia. Alfredo would mix up Bob Marley with Tears For Fears, Donna Summer's 'Love To Love You Baby' with Depeche Mode, hip hop and early house tunes; these records would come alive. By the time Paul and his friends headed for Amnesia, Alfredo had guaranteed the venue was *the* after-hours party spot on the island. 'We all paid to get in,' says Paul, 'we weren't on any guest list. Then the fun began.'

Amnesia was formerly a *finca*, a set of farmhouses that had gradually been converted into a nightclub. It had the distinct advantage of having an open-air dancefloor and an inter-national clientele. 'It was a very mixed crowd,' says Paul. 'It was very European, aged from about eighteen to fifty. That's why it was good, because it was so open.'

Alfredo started weaving his magic on the decks, the pills began to kick in and another world began to slowly take shape. 'It was a completely new experience,' says Johnny Walker. 'Everything felt much warmer and larger than life. We were lucky that we did it in such a perfect environment. We were dancing all night in the open air, under the stars. That warm, Mediterranean air was so much part of it.'

'The penny just dropped,' says Nicky Holloway. 'We now knew why we were living. I remember that euphoric feeling, thinking "this is great". We thought it was something special, that we'd keep for special occasions. Of course we did it every night after that . . .'

'There were roped-off sections, loads of different bars,' says Trevor Fung. 'You had a real mix of different people. The only workers in there were a few Spanish people and some Italian boys, and us lot. There used to be a swing in there; there used to be a little pool there – everyone used to jump in that. It was quite brilliant. Just nuts. Imagine us skipping round the club to the Nightwriters' "Let The Music Use You", or Frankie Knuckles' "Your Love" . . . Johnny Walker was inside a speaker, hanging out of it. We were like kids in a candy store.'

'I don't remember skipping round the dancefloor,' says Nicky Holloway, 'but it could have happened. There were pyramids, everything was white . . . We did sit inside the speakers. There were people dancing in the fountains.'

'I can remember being absolutely nutted,' says Johnny Walker. 'I was holding hands with Lisa Loud and Nancy Noise at seven a.m. in the morning. Alfredo the DJ was playing U2's "With Or Without You". It was just a really fabulous, loved-up experience.'

'For me, up until that point it had been all about the music,' says Paul. 'But then I took this pill and it was, like, "Oh my God!" I've always been a sharing person; when I find something I love I just want to share it with other people – a record, a film, an experience, whatever it is. Straight away, when we found this thing, we wanted to share what we'd discovered.'

The party continued the next day at the villa. Danny and Nicky were so excited they wrote a letter to their mate Gary in America, urging him to come and experience a night like they'd just had. 'We had "Moments In Love" on the tape player, and we were all holding hands in the pool,' says Nicky. 'We didn't know what this feeling was, but we'd never felt like that before.'

The wide-open music policy was certainly as revelatory as the little white capsules. 'One track really captured the spirit of that holiday,' says Paul. ' "Why Why Why" by the Woodentops. It was the last record on, one night at Amnesia, this 150 bpm live version, with all the crowd cheering along to it. It sounded so unique and different; I just had to stand there with my mouth open. I couldn't believe they were playing this mad record by an English indie band as their last record of the night. The whole place went off.'

The only club comparison the English contingent could think of was New York's Paradise Garage. 'I went to Paradise Garage with Oakey in 1986,' says Nicky Holloway. 'It was Gwen Guthrie's birthday; Timmy Regisford was on. They were blacking the room out and playing Master C & J's "When You Hold Me", with its big weird long intro; they were playing the early house records, and people were going mad to it. I couldn't understand it at all – there was no drink there, I just didn't get it. I didn't know they were all off their head on Es . . . I didn't know what an E was! You couldn't really tell – it was all black gay guys in shorts. I didn't get it at all. It wasn't until I did a pill at Amnesia that I realised what had been going on the year before at that club I went to with Paul.' Paul spotted the similarities too, but was more blown away by the differences. 'The atmosphere and buzz of Paradise Garage was a lot more intense,' he says. 'It was the same in that it was certainly about the music, but I felt this was a lot more free. In Paradise Garage you're in a dark, very gay club, whereas at Amnesia you are in an open-air resort, with a mixture of good-looking people. It was a different vibe, a different feeling.'

The gang soon took in the other delights Ibiza night culture had on offer. 'We'd go to Es Paradis,' says Paul. 'We'd hang out at Café del Mar, and go to clubs like Manhattan's, Glory's, Amnesia and Ku. We'd go to Amnesia at two, leave at seven and then go to Manhattan's, which was the underground club, the late one. Glory's, which was on the road to Ibiza Town, was more *NME*-style music more indie, things like the Cure, Simple Minds, U2. Not so much Pacha, that wasn't as good then.'

'Ibiza could be whatever you wanted it to be,' says Trevor. 'It could be dead quiet, really relaxing, or it could be manic. Sometimes you'd go up to people's houses in the hills, and it would seem quiet, and you'd see fifty or sixty people running round off their heads.' Navigation was particularly challenging. 'You couldn't get anywhere – no one knew how to get there, no one knew how to get back. You'd be up there for days – you'd stay there till someone came to get you.'

This broad musical melting pot had a marked effect on the young English crew. 'We were total black-music snobs in those days,' says Nicky Holloway. 'We were hearing white dance music for the first time.' 'Nicky and Johnny came from the soul scene,' says Paul. 'Hearing Alfredo play Kool Moe Dee, the Beastie Boys or the Woodentops . . . it changed them. It affected Danny Rampling differently; he hadn't been a DJ before. It didn't change me – I was into hip hop and rock, a lot of different styles. What really influenced me was how Alfredo got away with playing all these different kinds of music in one room. We'd tried it at the Funhouse, and it didn't work – in London you'd go to a club and just hear one sound. I thought "This is fucking amazing, you can put all these kinds of records together." It broadened a lot of people's minds.'

The next step on from hearing the music Alfredo was spinning at Amnesia was actually tracking down the vinyl. This was no mean feat, as Alfredo's selections were a glorious mish-mash of styles, sourced from a number of vinyl specialists in more than one country. Trevor may have been importing UK tunes to the island, but out of the four DJs, Paul was particularly keen to hunt down the new Alfredo-endorsed tunes. He had quite a head start on the others: not only was he already working in the music industry, he had a long history of blagging upfront vinyl, of sourcing a wide selection of tunes from record shops. 'I was working for Rush Release, so I had access to promos,' says Paul. 'I started giving Alfredo records, which meant we'd get into Amnesia on the guest list. I started talking to him, finding out what the tunes were. I went back for the closing party in September that year, and brought him back a load of records. We got tapes off him. Danny Rampling was desperate to get those tapes! Later on he taped my set at Shoom, without me knowing, and went out and got the records! I'm not saying that in a bad way – if Alfredo played a record, I'd go up to him and find out what it was – Danny could have done the same. That's the funny side of it – we were all after the same records. I was lucky in that I'd been into alternative music before I went to Ibiza; I'd find the records, either in Rough Trade or HMV, or I'd ring up the record company and track them down. There was also a record shop in Ibiza where you could get a lot of the records Alfredo was playing. You could have access to Belgian, Italian, European records that you couldn't get in England. If you go to those shops now, the records are all English.'

The return trip wasn't as euphoric as the birthday sessions, however. 'We were so hyped up about it, me and Paul went back for the closing parties,' says Nicky Holloway. 'We went back for the closing night of Amnesia. There was a big thunderstorm; we got to the club, did a pill, and about three-quarters of an hour later all the electricity on the island went out and never went on again! We ended up sitting outside the Star café, Eing off our tits, after we'd flown all the way out there. We'd bought the T-shirt, bought the poster, were coming up on our first pill, and the whole fucking thing went down!'

Despite this, nothing could dampen the group's enthusiasm for Ibiza. Paul and his friends were convinced they could import their new discovery back to the UK. 'We became like salesmen for the place,' says Nicky Holloway. From the distance of London, in autumn, the need to bring a bit of Balearic sunshine to clubland grew more vital. 'I don't think it crossed Paul's mind to get Alfredo to come over to England and DJ straight away,' says Trevor. 'It was when everyone went home, sat down and thought about it. You've got to realise music in London was pretty depressing at that time – it needed something that could shake it up. Rare groove was boring, it wasn't happening. It needed something new.'

'I just knew we'd found something special,' says Paul. 'The spirit, the energy of the island was amazing. There was no real plan, no let's start a club, let's do this or that, but there was something we'd found there we wanted to take home with us. We were totally on a mission.'

# 5

# Aciieed!

'In November 1987 we came back to London. It was awful; we couldn't give up what we'd started in Ibiza. Three weeks went by and everyone's dying for a party. I didn't know what to do, so I called Paul Oakenfold – meanwhile he's buying up every record that was played at Amnesia. He's already got more than Alfredo. Paul's found his niche and he's ready.'

Ian 'St' Paul

'The key, the secret to the whole thing, is fun. People never had so much fun.'

Paul Oakenfold

Bringing sunshine to a wet autumn in South London was quite a challenge. Recession was beginning to creep in, highlighted by the 'Black Monday' stock market crash, which signalled the end of the eighties economic boom. The yuppie dream was fading. The Conservative Party had been re-elected for the third time in the summer of 1987. You couldn't have got much further away from the carefree, open-minded Balearics, but it didn't matter – the newly minted Ibiza-inspired fervour wasn't to be dimmed.

Nicky Holloway held a Special Branch party at Bentley's in Kingston, a couple of days after returning home. 'We had some of Trevor's crowd there,' he says, 'probably about twenty people who'd been to Ibiza in the last few months, and a hundred and fifty people who hadn't. Me and Johnny Walker found ourselves playing to the twenty people, totally getting off on it, while everyone else was standing around, not knowing what to think. We were wearing our Amnesia T-shirts, playing Cyndi Lauper's "What's Going On", "Jibaro" and all that, and the soul boys were like "What's this shit?" Within a few months they all knew.'

Paul Oakenfold and Trevor Fung had a much better result. The pair were running the Project Club at Ziggy's in Streatham, and decided to host an after-hours Ibiza reunion party. After the main club closed, they let the regular Friday crowd out, and snuck the new crew in via the side door. Unlike Paul and Trevor's earlier Funhouse night, where attempts at a broad church of musical styles fell on deaf ears, this time round the tunes, the crowd, the energy was right.

'A few of our mates had been out all season in Ibiza with us,' says Trevor. 'It wasn't just me and Ian. By the time we came back to South London everyone knew about it. The Project Club was rammed solid. It was brilliant. Everyone knew it was going to be busy – it was packed during the normal night, earlier on; everyone had heard something was going on, and were all trying to get in. We were changing the music then, switching it over. Everyone was totally up for it.'

The desire to put on a great party overtook any regard for

the usual confines of the law – a situation that was to be played out again and again in the coming years. 'We didn't have a licence,' says Paul. 'The Ibiza reunion was completely illegal.' Unlike many a future gathering, however, this didn't stop the party. 'At half past two we opened the side door, and all these people poured in,' says Paul. 'Everyone had stayed in touch from Ibiza, they knew that we were having the after-party, so they all came down. People came from Sheffield, from Manchester, a couple of lads from Birmingham; all the workers we'd got to know from Ibiza. A whole load turned up.'

The party carried on until seven in the morning with no hassle, a new box of records with tunes from Nitzer Ebb, the Woodentops, Thrashing Doves and Elkin and Nelson; some of the little white pills had found their way back to South London, via Manchester, via Amsterdam. The spirit of Ibiza had now officially gone international.

The look was beginning to take shape, fast; within a few months the Gaultier suits and shiny shoes of mid-eighties style culture would be merely an upright memory. The change was almost instant. It probably took about three months for the whole of London clubland to change its clubbing style and loosen up. Previously London clubbing had centred on posing at the Wag or Mud Club, chatting people up, beer in hand; now it was all about the dancefloor.

'It was all Converse trainers and baggy trousers, because all you did was dance,' says Paul. 'You were dancing for hours, so everything had to be baggy. The look was a South London thing; it was the way we all were. It wasn't about what label you wore that got you into a club, like it had been before, it was your attitude. In Ibiza nobody dressed like that; they were still dressing up when they went out for the night. This was more about the workers from Ibiza. The change really was quick. We had the after-party on the Friday – by the following Friday everyone was wearing baggy clothes; you noticed the change straight away. We were straight away dropping the tunes, and you had the likes of Carl Cox saying "what's this?" and seeing us lot going absolutely mad. It changed very fast.'

One group of club faces Paul invited down to the Project were a bunch of characters soon to be known under the name of Boy's Own, a collective who would spawn a small-scale but highly influential club fanzine, a record label and the careers of a handful of DJs, remixers and producers, including Andrew Weatherall, Terry Farley and Pete Heller. 'I was DJing for Boy's Own parties at the Wag, and I played at the Raid a lot,' says Paul. 'I knew Gary Haisman, Terry Farley and Paul Dennis, so I invited them down to the Project. They all turned up in floppy cloth hats, that rare groove look; they'd come from the rare groove scene. They were not expecting to see what was going on. When they saw it, once they'd seen what was going on, it all changed for them, too.'

The Project Club sessions went on for a further few weeks, but an incident in the sixth week, with Alfredo, newly arrived from Ibiza, guesting on the decks, saw the club come to a close. A Project Club punter had parked their car blocking the delivery entrance of the supermarket across the road from Ziggy's, which resulted in the police sniffing around and finding a bunch of baggy-trousered revellers having a rare old time in a venue without a late licence. Amnesia might have kicked off in the middle of the night, but Streatham had to answer to Her Majesty's finest. Goodbye Ibiza reunion.

Alfredo's central London debut, at the Raid night at the

Limelight the following evening, was a bit subdued. 'There was a little bit of a "what's this all about?" thing going on,' says Paul. 'It was the same lot who'd been at the Project, and a few more who'd heard about it. There were maybe ninety people there that knew what was going on, and the club holds a lot more . . .' Unfortunately Alfredo wasn't going to be the triumphant hero of the West End – he ended up being asked to vacate the DJ booth.

These early setbacks didn't deter Paul. In November he hooked up with Ian Paul to launch a night at a venue called the Sound Shaft, which was an intimate space behind the much larger Heaven nightclub, under the arches at Villiers Street, down by Trafalgar Square. Heaven was the home of Delirium on a Thursday night, one of the only places in the capital Paul and his crew could go to hear house music, so it was decided Thursday was the perfect night of the week to hold a smaller gathering round the back. 'I was running into problems with the Project Club because of the music policy,' says Paul. 'We couldn't change the Friday night that drastically, otherwise we would have ended up with a club with only about sixty people in it. Ian wanted to do a night in the West End, so we decided to do the Thursday night.' The club, with a nod to the possibilities that lay ahead, was called Future. One slight problem, however. Ian and Paul didn't have enough money to cover the £300 hire fee. Caught a bit short, the promoters had to wait outside the main entrance to Heaven, until enough of their mates had turned up and paid their fiver entrance fee, before everyone trooped into Heaven towards the Future.

The club was the perfect breeding ground for the new culture. Unlike the Limelight, ninety people at Future was quite enough to make the place catch fire; any more lifted the roof.

It had a unique ambience; a special place that felt particularly dark, clandestine, underground. After the finance fiasco of the first week, the crowd didn't have to stomp through the main club to get to Future. The Sound Shaft had its own entrance round the back of Heaven, down an industrial-looking alleyway that added to the night's mystique. 'What was great was that you'd come in the back door,' says Paul. 'It was still like a little secret.'

Musically, Paul at last had found the perfect space. 'Future quickly found its own legs, its own sound and themes,' he says. 'I'd gone in there thinking musically I'm going to play indie with rap, rock with dance – I'd gone in there with the true Balearic sensibility. My interpretation of the Balearic beat is that you can play all kinds of music together; it doesn't mean only tracks you'd heard on the island. I was playing a small amount of Ibiza tunes, and the rest of the night it gave me a chance to play all the other alternative stuff I was into.'

Playing alongside Paul was a female DJ called Nancy Noise. 'Nancy would have all her records mapped out,' says Paul. 'She knew exactly which one she was going to play, in a certain order. When she got to her last record, that was it. I really believed she was a great DJ and I wanted to encourage her to play longer, so I would sometimes deliberately disappear downstairs when I was meant to go on. She'd go mad! We had a couple of guests occasionally. I think I had Johnny Walker as a guest, but me and Nancy were the residents.'

Working the lights was Paul's mate Mickey Jackson. 'Future was the one,' he says. 'That was the proper, serious club on the early scene. There were people from all walks of life there, loving it because it was a completely different environment. We had the Cure there once, Michael Clarke the ballet dancer, who'd worked with the Fall, Leigh Bowery, Arthur Baker, fashionistas mixing with the underground people you respected.'

Another DJ who first got noticed at Future was Paul's new girlfriend, Lisa Loud. Romance had blossomed during those intense few months, after the pair had met in Ibiza. 'It was a whirlwind,' says Paul. 'We were out twenty-four/seven, everyone was. I fell for the best-looking girl on the scene, as far as I was concerned. I had no intention of wanting a girlfriend; I was having a great time, we were all wrapped up in the scene, but I fell for her – like everyone else. She was a good-looking girl, and out of all the guys she chose me. So I ended up going out with her. She started DJing a bit later. We also opened a small side club for Lisa and Nancy, called Loud Noise, on a Tuesday. We'd all go down and support them and hang out. Ian ran it.' Ian, by this time, had decided to canonise himself, adding 'St' as his middle name. 'After '87 Ian decided he was going to be a saint,' says Trevor Fung. 'He was doing a lot of drugs by then . . .'

Paul and Lisa's romance wasn't to last very long. They went out for around a year before splitting up. 'It took me a while to realise that the relationship was great for what it was, but it shouldn't have happened. We'd come home, we'd be lying in bed talking about music, going "anyway, what do you think of this record?" It was all too much – we needed personal space. She's a great girl and I won't have a bad word said about her, but it's difficult talking about record releases in bed!'

Meanwhile in South London, Danny Rampling had also come back to the UK with a similar idea. Hiring out a basement fitness centre in Southwark Bridge Road, just south of the river, he opened Klub Schoom on 5 December, with Danny and

Carl Cox on the decks. As with Ziggy's, Carl supplied the sound system for the new club in its early weeks, but was now also DJing, immersing himself in the emerging sounds of Chicago and Detroit. 'As soon as I heard the new jacking sound, this trippy kind of jack, I was on it,' says Carl. Trevor Fung and Colin Faver were early guests. The name came from something Trevor Fung had said to Danny in Ibiza – 'Are you feeling schoomy?' It was a made-up word that expressed positivity and good times, very much the spirit of the club. 'Sensation seekers, let the music take you to the top' beamed the flyer. About a hundred and fifty people came the first night, enjoying free Lucozade from the bar. The night wasn't as successful as hoped – the music mix wasn't quite right yet, and some people weren't quite used to the new sound, more comfortable with the rare groove and funk they heard elsewhere. 'There was a transition going on,' says Carl Cox. 'Everyone was putting on afros, putting flares on, platform shoes, but also hearing this tweaky acid music. Everyone was like "what's this?" Some people hated it; with others it was like "sod this" – the wigs and the flares came off – "aciieed!" It was a great time, because we all ventured into the unknown. You had to let go of the past, and enter the future.'

By January, with the name shortened to simply Shoom, the club was rocking. Arriving in Southwark Bridge Road, the first thing you'd see from the road outside were the basement windows, all steamed up with sweat. If you managed to negotiate your way past Jenni Rampling's über-strict door policy, you'd walk down the stairs to be confronted by some random stranger with a large grin and a small hat trying to shake your hand, with a 'Hello, my name's Polo, who are you?' Ten minutes' conversation later, your new best mate would introduce you to all his mates, then lead you to the bar on the left, for a soft drink. Alcohol was pretty much frowned upon in the early acid house days – 'ruins your buzz' was the general consensus. After a swift Lucozade it was off to the steaming, dry-ice-filled dancefloor on the right. Sweat would drip down the gym's mirrors, off the ceiling, everywhere. For most of the night the dry ice was so thick you couldn't see two feet in front of you. When the strobes kicked in and Mac Thornhill's 'Who's Gonna Ease The Pressure' worked its stuttering magic, the sensation was one of total immersion. 'Release it!' would be the cry, and the pressure of grimy, grainy London life would rise out of your sky-high hands, your backbone would unwind and the music would, indeed, take you to the top. Sweets, ice lollies and fruit were handed out now and then. New anthems were being discovered on a weekly basis. '"Acid Trax" by Phuture was just sick,' says Carl Cox. 'It didn't do anything apart from eleven minutes of that acid sound. In amongst all that smoke and haze and fog it would just do your head in; that track was amazing. Bear in mind Shoom was a fitness centre, that was all. All the machines were put away, it was just a room with mirrors in it. Banners, big sound system, loads of smoke, a couple of oil wheels, two strobes and "let's go". I'd probably go there today and think "was this it?"'

'The first time I went to Shoom it was all smoke and strobes, people wandering around like *Night of the Living Dead*, waiting for their Es to come up,' says DJ and S'Express main man Mark Moore. 'I was confused – Colin Faver had told me this place was really rocking, but everyone was just shuffling round like zombies. I didn't get it. Then, slowly, people started getting madder and madder. I looked into their eyes and thought "Hang on a minute, I know what's going on here!"

For some reason Shoom was more debauched than Future.'

As with Future, the dress code was rapidly changing. Graphic designer Dave Little remembers his first trip to Shoom. 'We were all still bedecked in Gaultier, the long coats, suits with little clips in the back,' he says. 'We walked in and it was full of trainers, the South London lot in pods and dungarees. I think that look was already there – it was the street look amongst your barrow boys, anyway.'

By now the club also had a slogan, 'Happy Happy Happy!', and a logo – the smiley face. The smiley, initially an early-seventies icon, was currently in vogue. Club runner Nick Truelocke used the image on flyers for his seventies-influenced Discothèque night; it was the key image in Alan Moore's seminal graphic novel *Watchmen*, which was widely read. *i-D* magazine's December 1987 edition was titled 'The Happy Issue', where 'Everybody's Gonna Be Happy!' The magazine featured a winking smiley on the cover and a fashion spread dedicated to 'smiley chic'. The magazine illustrates the changing nature of 1987 London clubland – stylist and model for the issue Barnsley may be wearing a smiley T-shirt, but he's surrounded by people who look like they've walked straight out of a blaxploitation movie. In their chart of 'the best things to happen this year', rare groove is in at number ten, just behind singer Terence Trent D'Arby, whilst house music scrapes into the top fifty at number forty-eight. The smiley would soon be reanimated for a new generation. Danny Rampling spotted stylist Barnsley in his coat made of dozens of smiley faces, and thought the emblem perfect for his new club: a happy, smiley gang that were, in soon-to-be derided slang, getting right on one, matey.

Not everybody saw Shoom as one happy family, however.

Jenni Rampling's strict door policy seemed a harsh throwback to mid-eighties style culture, to Philip Sallon, Taboo or White Trash. People would turn up week after week, and never get in. The crowd that did get in was an eclectic mix – Ibiza veterans, media types, suburban kids and minor music celebrities – the Fitness Centre would be as full of pop glitterati as the Mud Club. On any given week you'd spot someone out of boy band Brother Beyond, Kevin Rowland looking dapper, Paul Rutherford from Frankie Goes to Hollywood, dancer Michael Clarke, shoe designer Patrick Cox . . . all these West End profiles crammed into a tiny, fog-filled South London sweatbox. Martin the Poet, Shoom's resident wordsmith, might have been spouting flowery verse, but on the door it certainly wasn't all peace and love. 'Whatever you say about Future or Boy's Own,' says Dave Little, 'I found more than a hint of elitism at Shoom. Maybe that was because it was South London and the other nights were in the West End. Jenni Rampling was an absolute sod on the door.'

There were reasons for this however; the Ramplings were working hard to retain the magic that went alongside clubbing with a small, known group, aiming to preserve 'that wonderful feeling, feeling that you are in on a big secret', as one fanzine put it. 'When it started off in London it was cliquey,' says Mark Moore. 'You had to know someone to get into Shoom. I loved Jenni, no matter how bonkers she got on that door. I thought it was great – you need this. They weren't letting journalists in, which was a good move. The media missed the boat on it – the music journalists decided '87, '88 in London wasn't going to be year zero, it was going to be 1990, in Manchester. They said dance history started then; they had the bands, they could hang it on something. When they let the ITN crew into the

Apocalypse Now rave it was a big thing; everyone said "oh my god! they are letting cameras in!" It was such a big deal. Everyone who was in that early Shoom scene was very much like they were in the sixties, on the bus with Ken Kesey, but the opposite – Ken Kesey was trying to advertise it, whereas we weren't. I admire Jenni for doing what she thought was right. There were loads of people trying to get in, and some of them you wouldn't want in your club.'

Back in the West End, things were speedily expanding for Paul. 'It was escalating out of control really fast,' he says. 'We went from doing a little club in South London, a club that we could manage, to doing a club in the West End that we didn't even have enough money to pay for. The whole scene was spreading like wildfire, and I was just trying to get all the music, trying to get it together. It was going crazy.' And it was going to get a lot crazier. Not for nothing was Paul and Ian's next venture dubbed the 'Theatre of Madness'.

On Monday 11 April 1988, Paul Oakenfold and Ian Paul embarked upon a massive gamble: their new night, Spectrum, opened in the main arena at Heaven. While Paul and Ian had comfortably been able to cover the costs at Future for some time, the move from a couple of hundred clubbers in the Sound Shaft to eighteen hundred in Heaven seemed like a wildly optimistic leap. Monday nights were traditionally slow; there were mutterings throughout clubland about the size of such an undertaking. 'Do you know how many people told me I was absolutely crazy to do a club on a Monday?' says Paul. 'All the London club promoters told me we were fools. They thought it would never work. Me and Ian knew it was going to go off, though. We knew that if people came down they'd enjoy themselves so much they'd tell their friends. We believed in it a hundred per cent. We were determined to make it happen.'

The early nights were a lot of fun, despite being worryingly populated by a mere fraction of the club's capacity. The Future posse showed up, along with Ibiza contacts from around the country. 'It was so exciting,' says Paul. 'There were no boundaries. I had this Japanese electric guitar player, Kenji, set up in the middle of the dancefloor, or Zeo, one of my studio collaborators, playing live keyboards. I'd have Mike Pickering and Graeme Parke come down from the Hacienda to do a battle of the DJs with me and Colin Hudd, with four DJs playing against each other . . . The club was really happening every week.'

Paul and Ian, alongside Spectrum co-promoter Gary Haisman, went at it full throttle. The sound system was immense, the lights and lasers unbeatable, the flyers and T-shirt design immaculate. Geordie designer Dave Little, whose reputation had been built with early sleeves for Rhythm King records and the massive, thirty-foot-long canvas mural he painted for the Raid parties, was brought in to conjure up something special. 'I first met Paul when he wanted to start a club called Back to the Future and got me to design the logo,' says Dave. 'For Spectrum, Ian said he needed a flyer and Gary Haisman came round, waving his arms about, and said, "I can see it now . . . a big eyeball looking at you, the all-seeing eye!" That was all the brief I needed. I'd been a right old acid head at college, and I'd just acquired this book called *The Art of Rock*, which had all these Haight-Ashbury psychedelic graphics in it by people like Rick Griffin, who did the designs for the Grateful Dead. At college I was into *The Electric Kool-Aid Acid Test*, Ken Kesey and the magic bus; we were doing acid, reading that shit when we were nineteen. I saw the scene, with the strobe lights and the sound of it, as a recurrence of the happenings of the Haight-Ashbury period. I took that on board; that's why the Spectrum design had a psychedelic flavour to it. We got everything gloss-laminated, we did full-colour posters and T-shirts. None of the other club graphics were following a psychedelic flavour before that. They all did after!'

Like David Mancuso's Loft parties in Manhattan almost two decades earlier, the links between psychedelia and house were becoming apparent. 'People saw the link to the sixties, because it was our interpretation of it,' says Paul. 'We also had Maggie and Roger Beard, the travellers, coming down, who had a direct sixties connection. Roger would DJ reggae tunes with Terry Farley upstairs. And we had those great, glossy flyers. They said we were a club that was different. The flyers were the best quality we could afford – we felt to put ourselves across to people that might not know us, they needed to see something different, something with class. The colours!'

Debts were mounting, however. A few weeks into the new venture, Gary Haisman got cold feet and pulled out; it seems he was much better at coming up with catchphrases than pro-moting a giant nightclub. Both 'Aciieed!' and 'It's all gone Pete Tong' were Haisman inventions. This left Ian and Paul to go it alone. 'There was pressure on, because we didn't have any money,' says Paul. 'We had to give them a certain amount, and the debt was building up, building up . . . but every week more and more people would come. You could feel the buzz. David Hinches, the manager at Heaven, was great – if it wasn't for him the club would have closed down. He believed in it; he'd never seen anything like it in his life. He kept putting the debt off, every week we owed more money. We got to the sixth week and we owed twelve grand. And then . . . that week we broke even! Then we started to pay the money off, and then we started to make. It was word of mouth that did it.' In the space of a single week, there were queues snaking right round the block under Heaven's arches.

The curtain had finally risen at the Theatre of Madness. Unlike the cosy enclaves of the Sound Shaft or the Fitness Centre, here was a gigantic, purpose-built space that demanded big-room drama and grandiose statement. It was here that Paul Oakenfold's DJ style was truly cemented. Opening with the set piece of A Split Second's 'Flesh', an expansive Belgian New Beat tune that has all the cinematic sheen and atmosphere of many later trance anthems, Oakenfold would command Spectrum from the DJ booth, set up high over the heads of the crowd at one end of the club, pushing the assembled throng into orbit. This was to be the start of Paul's long-running penchant for signature opening music. '"Flesh" was massive,' he says. 'The intro would start and it would all come up, the lasers were on and you'd know I'd started, I set out my stall with "Flesh"; I needed to find a big record that said "this is it". My closing record was a classical piece, from the movie *Excalibur*. I had Jenni Rampling coming up and saying "Turn it off, that's devil music! Why are you playing that?" It was in *The Omen* . . . I was like "fuck off!" It was just an intense piece of classical music.'

It took countless crate-digging trips to get the sound sharply focused for Monday nights. 'Spectrum was a lot of work,' says Paul. 'I spent a lot of time looking for records and finding the right ones for the place. Future was more about skipping around the room; it was lighter, slower, a bit more rocky. I could slam in an out-and-out rock record at Future; I wouldn't do that at Spectrum. The pace of the records was faster, there was more intensity. It was more housey . . . it was acid house.'

Tracks like 'Jibaro' would be played at Spectrum, but it's no accident that the acid sound and proto-trance anthems like the KLF's 'What Time Is Love?' were the real floor-fillers here – the club was built for them. The sheer size of the place, the great sound, the swooping green lasers and the swathes of dry ice were a potent combination. It was spectacular. 'The first time you'd walk in you'd be like "fucking hell, what is this?"' says Paul. 'It was amazing.'

'The first few times I went to Spectrum there were about two hundred people there,' says Mark Moore. 'On the opening night, the front of the stage was made up to look like a Jeep, with the DJ decks in the middle. It was absolutely fucking brilliant. Around this time S'Express took off, and I went off doing promotional tours. When I came back there was a huge queue round that corner. I thought "this is it . . . the whole thing is going to take off now".'

The club kept getting better. Paul's showmanship was developing apace; one particularly over-the-top trick was to plunge the club into darkness, then silence, then Tchaikovsky's 1812 Overture. Live acts such as Guru Josh and Flowered Up took the stage; KLF did their first live performance at the club. 'I was playing "What Time Is Love?" – it was an anthem,' says Paul. 'They hadn't figured out their image then, it was very early on. Their track was massive.' A number of famous faces started to show up – mainly unbeknown to Paul, who was DJing at the time. 'They wouldn't make a big entrance with an entourage,' he says. 'They'd observe the madness from the balcony upstairs that runs the length of the club. I heard George Michael was there, I heard Bowie was there, Duran

Duran, Simple Minds . . . we were too immersed in our own thing to realise what we had. We didn't give a shit – we didn't really want those kind of people in there, they could spoil it for us. We wanted people who were really into it, not just coming to observe it. We were anti all that.'

The ubiquitous 'Aciieed!' chant, created by Gary Haisman on the Spectrum dancefloor, even turned into a hit. 'That was one of the biggest situations that I totally missed,' says Paul. 'Danny D came to the club, he'd never been before, walked in with fresh ears, heard the chant and thought "I'll make a record out of that." It was number one in something like twenty countries. I was sitting there, scratching my head, thinking "why didn't I do that?" '

If you were up for a boogie, you were in for a good night. Spectrum had noticeably less of an elitist feel than the more intimate Shoom. 'I liked that,' says Mark Moore. 'You felt like anyone could come in. With a club that size, it made sense. But everyone who went there was pretty cool – they were in the know, you had to have heard about it via word of mouth. You had to search for things then – you had to have an interest in it, you couldn't just casually dip into it. The fact that it was all linked by a friend telling another friend made it good, it gave it that family feel. I'm sure the Shoomers looked down on it, thought it was a bit more mainstream – as Jenni Rampling put it, you started to get the "lilac-clad camels" coming down – but it was still pretty underground. It very quickly became like a Fellini movie, with all these bodybuilders doing poses on the podium, a few gangsters here and there . . .'

Throughout spring, Spectrum got hotter. 'The pace was so fast,' says Paul. 'On one Monday night we had Spectrum at Heaven, and an outside Spectrum over the river Thames, on the same night.' Bank holidays were particularly insane – Paul and Ian initiated the Spectrum 'On One All Day' sessions. Carl Cox was asked to DJ at one of these marathons. 'It was the first or second one they did,' says Carl. 'It was great for me – Paul could see what I was doing, but no one had given me the opportunity to do it. This was a place for me to prove myself and shine through. What a great concept – on one all day! You'd be in there at twelve o'clock in the afternoon, and it would be going mental.'

The Spectrum imprint quickly found its feet nationwide. 'We were sending Colin Hudd and Trevor Fung to do a Spectrum night every Monday at Legends in Manchester, and running Spectrum in Birmingham,' says Paul. Trevor Fung has fond memories of the Manchester night. 'It was brilliant,' he says. 'We'd hire a 5 Series BMW every week and bomb down the motorway and back. We had a big following from Manchester who used to come down to the London club every week.' A couple of the Manchester crew would soon be known as lead singer and dancer for a certain band who were certainly up for enjoying happy Mondays. 'Then we started Spectrum tours,' says Paul. 'We became like a superclub – we were doing what Cream, Ministry, or Godskitchen went on to do years later.'

The impact of Spectrum made itself felt on other nights at Heaven, particularly at Rage, a new Thursday-nighter that opened in the main room soon after Spectrum's initial success. The night was run by Kevin Millins, who'd previously organised Heaven's successful Asylum night. 'He took the idea of what we were doing and put Fabio and Grooverider on at Rage,' says Paul. 'Trevor Fung played there too. It was a continuation of what we were doing. Future was about playing indie-dance and Balearic, whereas Rage was about playing acid; more the Eddie Richards end of DJing.' Rage was a darker, moodier, more stripped-down take on the acid and techno scene; cuts like Bam Bam's 'Where's Your Child?', 4 Hero's 'Mr Kirk's Nightmare' or Innerzone Orchestra's 'Bug In The Bassbin' fitted the vibe powerfully. The club was a breeding ground for the sounds that were soon to become hardcore: breakbeat and jungle. Many of the leading lights of drum and bass, such as Goldie and Kemistry, would be turned on by Rage.

Designer Dave Little remembers the difference between Rage in the main room, and Future, round the back. 'Because I'd designed the flyers for both clubs, I was one of the few people who were allowed to go through the double doors, straight into Rage from Future,' says Dave. 'The atmosphere was completely different – in Future you'd have everyone loved up, jumping around, singing along to "All You Need Is Love", then you'd go through the doors and be hit with NWA, Public Enemy, hardcore, this speed thing. You wouldn't see people really dancing at Rage, you'd see people on the dancefloor nodding aggressively. There was nobody talking to each other. Then I'd go back to Future, where everybody would be waving their arms about and hugging each other. The two sides were totally different.'

In April 1988, the newly loved-up acid house crew decided to share their passion for the new sound with the old guard at the Prestatyn Soul Weekender. The blend of old and new didn't exactly gel. 'We were in what they called "the warehouse room",' says Nicky Holloway. The soul mafia even put up 'No Acid House' banners, such was their concern. 'The other area was called the "house-free zone", but we just took it over. Our room was packed; we were just playing what we wanted.' Paul Oakenfold could sense change in the air. 'They didn't like it at all,' he says. 'We were added to the bill, as the new generation that was going to change everything. No one was rude to me, but you knew they felt threatened. I wasn't a soul head, but I knew everyone in that scene. They were watching me. Adrian Webb gave me a little bit of a warning – he told me this is how it works, this is what goes on. It was a soul weekender, and I'm not a soul DJ, so they were concerned. I didn't give a shit and did what I did. I had to fall in line, but in my own way I didn't. I'd already got my little scene going on, so anyone who'd been to the Project or the other nights expected to hear what I'd normally play. And that's what they got.'

Come early summer, the acid house secret was well and truly out. 'I realised things were getting big when I went to Hyde Park on a sunny day,' says Dave Little. 'I must have spotted about forty people in Spectrum T-shirts.' The press was beginning to sniff out a story, too. First off the block were the style press, with both *The Face* and *i-D* running acid house reports. The timing was just right for another veteran of Paul's Ibiza birthday jaunt, Nicky Holloway. He'd decided to shut down Special Branch in February 1988, and on Saturday 4 June opened the Trip at the Astoria on Charing Cross Road, a sizeable gig venue smack-bang in the middle of London's West End, opposite the Centre Point block. The flyer promised 'For five weeks only, acid house, fat funk and Balearic beats. Opening night T-Coy live, Mike Pickering, Paul Oakenfold . . . upstairs Cloud Cukooland with Ravi Shankar.'

'*The Face* and *i-D* did stories about this new big scene in the June issues, which came out mid-May,' says Holloway. 'There'd only been Monday and Thursday nights in town, little bits going on, no one had done a big legal night on a weekend before. The timing was just fucking perfect. Mike Pickering came down, Andrew Weatherall and Terry Farley played upstairs. I thought there would be about six hundred people there. We'd arranged it so that if there weren't enough people, we wouldn't open the balcony; we were going to put drapes up, to make it seem smaller. We didn't have to, though – there were twelve, thirteen hundred people in there. From day one it was full. It closed at three, and everybody left on a high.'

Scenes outside the Astoria following the Trip were soon to become tales of legend. Chaos ensued outside – hundreds of clubbers poured on to a busy West End crossroads still up for a party. House music blared out of cars in the YMCA car park up the road, a few brave ravers dipped into Centre Point's fountains opposite, and when the police turned up to move people on, the crowd cheered when they turned on their siren, echoing, as it does, the hook from Todd Terry's 'Can U Party?' My one abiding memory of the scene after the Trip is of a few moody police officers huffing and puffing, and hundreds of people on the street, giggling, looning about. Acid house was now well and truly overground.

The euphoria of the initial ecstasy experience made anything seem possible. Club promoters like Paul, Ian and Nicky Holloway proved it could be done; their expansion of the close-knit initial scene, although frowned upon by the elite, paved the way, by late summer, for even larger, more outlandish out-door events, like Tony Colston-Hayter's Sunrise and Jarvis Sandy's Biology, among scores of others. Enthusiasm levels were sky-high; there was a tangible sense of possibility. Margaret Thatcher may have maintained 'There is no such thing as society' in a 1987 magazine interview, but the acid house crew were creating their own utopian alternative. If punk's DIY ethos taught us that anyone could do it, acid house went even further. In the new climate, everyone could do it.

Conservative MP Norman Tebbit famously recalled his grandfather, who'd got 'on his bike' to look for work in the thirties, and thought the modern-day unemployed should do the same. The E generation did exactly that, but not into the kind of employment the minister would have necessarily approved of. The new, continually expanding gang that had bonded on the dancefloor began to form a loose, alternative business network. DJ, record company boss, club promoter, graphic designer, T-shirt seller, musician; these were now obtainable positions, even possible career options, rather than pipe dreams or a hobby on the side. And those were just the legitimate jobs. The new network wasn't getting its information out of the mainstream press, but from flyers, fanzines, pirate radio, word of mouth in record shops. People used to turn up outside Spectrum or the Trip for the flyers alone, eager to find out what was happening next.

At which point, the few hairline cracks that had developed between Paul and his club-promoting friends began to widen and multiply. When Shoom moved to the YMCA in town on a Thursday night, in direct competition to Future, there were a few grumbles – was it possible to split your loyalties between these two small clubs, which basically shared the same crowd? A Future trip to the coast deepened the rift. 'On one Saturday we did a party on Brighton beach and took two coachloads of people down there,' says Paul. 'Their club was empty, apart from the new lot who were coming; all the faces weren't there. Jenni Rampling had an argument with Ian, saying you've taken our crowd, and then stopped a lot of them from coming into Shoom the following week. That's where the fallout happened, that's when the scene split.'

It was a shame that the common bond of Ibiza '87, a bond based on positivity and shared experience, was shattered in under a year. 'There was no rivalry to start off with,' says Paul, 'because everyone had their own nights. We didn't do a Saturday night, so the rivalry occurred more between Nicky and Danny. Nicky was doing it to the masses; Danny was doing a small club. The "teds", as we called them, were going to Nicky's, the people in the know were going to Future and Shoom – that's the way it was set up. Until Jenni started all that and people fell out.'

'There was a lot of green-eyed monster in those days,' says Nicky Holloway, who took most of the rap for taking the scene overground. 'I was running a club and making the money. People like Andrew Weathcrall and Terry Farley always thought I was a wanker. It got a little bit like a competition, but mainly we were all still friends. Paul played at the Trip a few times.'

Throughout the year new nights had been springing up at a staggering rate – soon there wasn't a day of the week to be had that didn't feature at least one acid night. Warehouse parties, parties on farms, away trips to Amsterdam were happening every weekend. 'There were loads of warehouse parties,' says Mark Moore. 'The Mutoid Waste parties were fantastic – it was like *Mad Max*. There was a great one in King's Cross where I DJed and Soul II Soul DJed . . . there was one out at the back of Ladbroke Grove, which was just insane – there was a bunch of nutty gangsters trying to smash the door of the DJ booth down. They'd brought their own records! There were tons – every week there would be a different warehouse party.'

'The best house party was up by Kingston Bridge,' says Trevor Fung. 'It was me, Paul and Carl Cox, playing at a derelict house by the Thames. One of my mates who worked in property got the owner to agree to have a party there. We hired generators, it went on right through to about twelve o'clock the next day.' Carl Cox remembers it well. 'I don't know what it was about that party, but it was just great,' he says. 'It was the right people at the right time, and we're playing the right music. It was all about what we were creating; a lot of people saw what we were doing, saw that it made sense.'

Spectrum, Shoom and Boy's Own all began putting on small-scale events. Tony Colston-Hayter and Roger Goodman took over a film studio in Wembley for the first big rave event, Apocalypse Now, at the end of August 1988. London's nightlife was jumping. In the West End? Try Dave Dorrell's jumping, sweaty Friday night, Love at the Wag, a far cry from the self-regarding rare groove nights of a few months before. Fancy more of a hardcore night out? RIP at Clink Street, a phenomenal night out in the grimiest, dingiest warehouse, where E-Mix hollered down the mike, Kid Batchelor, Shock and Mr C manned the decks, and the whole thing resembled a dirtier, more raucous take on the Prodigy's 'No Good' warehouse video, right down to that bit where Liam Howlett smashes through a wall with a big hammer. A mighty fine time was had by one and all, a more experimental, urban thrill, illuminated more often than not by a single, swinging light bulb. As Paul Oakenfold told the *NME*, the secret to the whole thing was fun. Big fun.

# 6

# Over the Rainbow

'After Spectrum, you realised something was happening here, people were spreading the word. It's going to get bigger.'

Mark Moore

Such large-scale fun and reckless abandon wasn't going unnoticed by the tabloid press. On 17 August, the *Sun*'s first target was Paul Oakenfold and Spectrum. 'Scandal Of The £5 Drug Trip To Heaven' screamed the headline. 'It was known that this place was absolutely crazy and people were taking drugs there,' says Paul, 'but the press were mainly interested because Richard Branson owned Heaven, and the media's view was that Richard Branson was allowing this to go on in one of his venues. They felt that there were a lot of drugs being taken in Spectrum, and there probably was, to be honest. But the *Sun* tried to target Branson.'

The article wasn't particularly well informed. The journalist takes the phrase 'acid house' rather too literally, and rather luridly. 'LSD – a favourite with seventies dropouts – is now popular with yuppies,' it shudders. 'Junkies flaunt their craving by wearing T-shirts sold at the club bearing messages like "Can you feel it" and "Drop acid not bombs" . . . the youngsters, mainly in their mid-twenties, try to escape the pressure of work by getting high on acid every weekend.'

For your average suburban teenager, the article, and the many that followed, had a completely opposite effect to the one desired. 'The whole acid house, ecstasy thing became bigger after that,' says Paul. Nicky Holloway agrees. 'The *Sun* newspaper did the biggest PR for us,' he says. 'If you were a young kid and hadn't been to one of these things and you were reading about that, you're gonna go "that's fucking great, we've got to go to that". They spread it round more than anyone. They were the biggest bunch of hypocrites – they did an anti-acid house piece, yet they were selling acid house T-shirts at the same time.' Indeed. 'It's groovy and cool – it's our Acid House T-shirt! Only £5.50 man,' chirped the paper on 12 October, next to an article outlining ten reasons not to take LSD.

Richard Branson was naturally sensitive about his entertainment licence, so the entrepreneur came down to Spectrum the next Monday night. 'I was DJing at the time,' says Paul. 'He came in, looked around, realised he'd seen it all before. He wasn't pissed off about it, but the club had to be seen to be doing something. They didn't want to lose us, as they were making shitloads of money out of it, on a Monday night, until three thirty in the morning. So he said take a month off, close the club and then reopen it under a different name. That's what we did. It was exactly the same!'

Spectrum came to a halt in October, but reopened again as Phantasia, complete with a new Dave Little design. Unfortunately for Paul and Ian, the press had picked up on a rumour that the next generation of ecstasy was called Phantasy, or Phantasia. Phantasia, the club, was on and off in weeks. The name had to be changed again, this time to something still reasonably psychedelic, but with less of an overt drug association. It was time to wander down the yellow brick road, towards the Land of Oz.

Land of Oz took Spectrum's theatre of madness and tweaked it, buffed it up, made it even shinier. 'It was all about following the yellow brick road,' says Paul, 'which was a special road we built that you followed to get into the club. We really started dressing the place up; we'd have a big thing on stage every week. Oz was much more theatrical – we didn't really have the money to do it at Spectrum, but we did now, so we went for it.'

Snowstorms, giant spiders, glittery explosions, castles, ghosts on chicken wire that flew across the stage – Paul and Ian upped the drama. Land of Oz was a land of sensation, of stimulation overload. Different rooms catered for different senses. In the main room, Paul delivered the big, celebratory tunes. The pounding rhythms and heaving mass of people made for a tribal, bodycentric experience. It hit you in the chest, and made your whole being move. Upstairs, a new DJ team was catering more for the head.

Running the show in the VIP room were the DJ duo of Alex Patterson and Jimmy Cauty, with occasional appearances from Alex's flatmate, Youth, who would 'turn up when the photographers were there', according to Alex. Alex and Youth used to attend the same church-run school; Alex had previously been a roadie, for bands including Youth's outfit Killing Joke. He gave up the touring life in 1986 due to back injuries, landing an A&R job at EG Records, best known for its Brian Eno releases. 'Ambient' was Eno's description for a series of EG albums, a theoretical update of Erik Satie's 'furniture music', designed for a specific atmosphere or environment. These releases, now highly cherished, were derided by the rock press on release, yet a few years later, their time had come.

Paul Oakenfold's Land of Oz was the perfect platform for a new school of ambient music. Paul himself dabbled in slower tempos and a more relaxing groove with his studio project Movement 98, which featured acclaimed 'lovers rock' vocalist Carroll Thompson, and even built their first single, 'Joy And Heartbreak', around Satie's melody from his *Gymnopédies*. The track made number 27 on the UK chart. 'People wanted a downtempo vibe, and Movement 98 was a response to that,' says Paul. 'All the tracks were around 98 bpm.' The slow groove was an antidote to the frenetic action of the main room, and was a big sound during the 1990 Ibiza season, but in the VIP room at Land of Oz Alex and Jimmy were developing something far more abstract.

The Orb's Alex Patterson recalls the days of the Land of Oz from his flat in Battersea, London, the very same flat, a couple of decades before, where Paul Oakenfold, Andrew Weatherall, Jimmy Cauty and Youth hatched a plan for the VIP room at Heaven. 'It was a meeting of DJs,' says Alex. 'We all sat round here on the sofa and got on these brain machines that this girl from Manchester had given us.'

The meeting led the way to a regular Monday-night slot upstairs at Land of Oz. Paul gave the DJs free reign to play whatever they liked. 'The only instruction he gave us was "Don't get them to dance,"' says Alex. The advice was purely practical – Paul wanted to create a space away from the main-room frenzy, a place where people could talk and relax, but Alex and his cohorts took it upon themselves to deliver something unique – a new kind of DJ set, specifically tailored to this environment. They'd been experimenting during after-party sessions at Trancentral, Jimmy Cauty's large squatted house on Jeffries Road, Stockwell, using the newly affordable sampling equipment, some basic recording gear, turntables and tape recorders, creating a new, do-it-yourself music. The seeds of these sessions would eventually flower on the *Chill Out* album, by Jimmy and Bill Drummond, released as the KLF. 'We were having these parties, after things like Shoom, that went on from about seven in the morning to about two, three, four, five in the afternoon,' says Alex. 'We'd have people back and let them watch us sample stuff up, watch us develop a track. We very much thought this is for everybody now, it's not just for musos, it's for everyone. Everyone could get involved if they wanted to.'

They brought the same spirit upstairs at Heaven, as well as a bulky stack of equipment. 'We were carrying boxes of records in,' says Alex. 'It wasn't just one box of records, because of the length of time we were playing for, we had to take several boxes. We were using a DAT machine and an Akai multitrack recorder, a twelve-track reel-to-reel. That was always taken every week out of Trancentral. We'd put this sound effect record on for twenty minutes, and see how people liked it. And then we'd put the loop on it, and then build another layer of ambience over the top. It was totally experimental.'

When I ask Alex what was the earliest ambient album he got into he tellingly refers to David Bowie's seminal, Brian Eno-produced album as '*Low* by Eno'. And rightly so – the producer's role in the record is immense. 'That's the one,' he says. 'Youth and I used to share a bedsit in Earls Court, before Killing Joke. We had one of those record players that could replay the record automatically. We'd play the same record all night; we'd listen to side two of *Low*. Fast-forward to 1980 – Killing Joke are on tour in Germany, and we go to an after-party in a mad block of flats in a place near Düsseldorf. I've now spotted EG as a label, because Killing Joke are just about to sign to them, I saw a load of EG records on the floor. Admittedly I was tripping, but I stuck on Eno's *Music For Films* and I fell completely in love with it. Along with Philip Glass's *Koyaanisqatsi*, that really got me into this music. I was a fan for a long time, I never really contemplated doing music of my own.'

The sound coming out of the VIP room was a far cry from the DJ skills on display downstairs; its layered drift many moons from the main floor's precision beats. But in Alex, Jimmy and Youth's blend of film and atmosphere, Paul had stumbled across a DJ team whose influences mirrored his own cinematic leanings.

The upstairs area was called the chill-out lounge, sometimes known as 'the white room'. 'This came about because we had white drapes everywhere,' says Alex. 'A friend of mine, Roger T. Smith, would turn up with these camcorder recordings and play them over this white screen. It would usually be films of the ducks in Battersea Park! It was very lo-fi, loads of funny little films.' There was a bar in the middle, a large window with blinds across it, and an entrance, which cut everything out from the main room . . . almost. 'We were right behind the main booth of the dancefloor in Heaven,' says Alex, 'so every time a DJ came in through those doors, it would be like whooom! We'd be playing Satie or Eno, and all you got was this noise coming in over the top. That added to the general ambience of it all really. Not to mention the drugs.'

A small handful of devotees would sit in the chill-out room all night, oblivious to what was going on downstairs. 'Lots of people sat on the floor like weebles, doing weeble dancing,' says Alex. 'There weren't that many that came into our room – that's what created the mystery about it. Not many people could get in because you needed these bloody VIP badges, you needed a pass.' This kind of cordoned-off behaviour could have been a cliquey disaster, but Alex thinks it helped. 'It could have gone either way,' he says. 'Luckily for us, I think it made it a bit more special. It became a mystical thing. People would come out of there saying "I'm really chilled out," and walk straight into the techno – boom boom BOOM . . .'

Alex and Jimmy's spot, from ten o'clock until four in the morning, earned them the princely sum of £90 – forty-five quid each for six hours' work! But it was worth more than the wage; the Monday-night gig was enabling them to develop their own music and hear it before an audience. 'What we tended to do was take the flavour of the week, our favourite track of the moment, and spend an hour on the Sunday looping the front end. That would be the repetitive theme for the night. We were taking everyday noises, putting them in. The Orb worked like that for maybe a year or so, as a Sunday-afternoon band, and a Monday-evening DJ unit. We'd play things like "Huge Ever Growing Pulsating Brain . . .", which we'd just written. It was a tune that we just tripped over. We'd been to a Shoom party in Brighton, up on the hills. We ended up on the beach, and got home about ten o'clock at night. It was a mash-up. We came down in one of Jimmy's American police cars, then went back to Trancentral and did it. We'd been working on it for quite a while, and both had massive headaches, so I said "Let's get rid of the drums . . ." Weatherall was a great champion of that tune, as were Trevor Fung and Nancy Noise. I realised they all liked chilling out to it. What we'd set out to do, the pair of us, was to chill out the techno nation. We had a slogan for it – "Ambient House for the E Generation".'

Strange new sonic bedfellows emerged out of the woodwork. 'Steve Hillage came along one night,' says Alex. 'He said to me, "You're playing my record"; it was one of about five playing at the same time, so he could have been from the BBC Radiophonic Workshop for all I knew! Bless him.'

The record Alex was playing was Hillage's *Rainbow Dome Musick*, a chiming, loping, arpeggio-laden piece that sounds like a direct precursor to ambient house. The album, recorded with French keyboard player Miquette Giraudy, was a sound-track recorded to accompany a large rainbow dome structure that was built for the Festival of Mind, Body and Spirit at Olympia in London in 1979, a full decade earlier. 'He told me a story about how he'd been raped and pillaged by the press, made a scapegoat in the punk days. I was pretty full of myself in those days, so I said I'd sit in with him in his interviews and get him back on track. If anybody had a go, I'll have a pop back, punk that I am. It gave him a bit of confidence.'

The two, along with Miquette Giraudy, would soon become the first live incarnation of the Orb, at Olympus Studios in Battersea. Just as the VIP room was breaking new DJ boundaries, it helped Alex focus his ideas of bringing the Orb to the live arena in a new and refreshing way, using his new DJ technique alongside a new type of live band. 'Land of Oz gave me the kind of desire to be a DJ on stage,' he says. 'I wanted to break the mould, and have a connection with musicians as opposed to becoming a musician directly. I didn't want to compromise being a DJ by learning an instrument to be on stage with a band, I wanted to develop a style that would suit the DJ as well. We could fit in on stage as an ambience, as a great big watercolour behind all the music. And it worked, for sure.' Paul recalls the upstairs room at Land of Oz fondly. 'It became its own club, a club within a club,' he says. 'It was brilliant. Alex did really well there. He started a whole movement out of that VIP room.'

The large-scale parties that had followed in Spectrum and Land of Oz's wake had royally roused the tabloids, which quickly adopted a stance of righteous moral indignation. A week after the *Sun* had tried to flog their 'cool and trendy' acid house T-shirt, the *Sun* doctor, Vernon Coleman, was frothing at the mouth about the evils of ecstasy. 'You will hallucinate,' said the good doctor, before really laying it on with a trowel. 'For example, if you don't like spiders, you'll start seeing giant ones . . . there's a good chance you'll end up in a mental hospital for the rest of your life.'

In the same month, a more distressing, concrete result of ecstasy usage forced the wider public to take notice. Twenty-one-year-old Janet Mayes died after taking two ecstasy tablets, one more than her usual single pill, at the Jolly Boatman pub in Hampton Court. The media reaction was swift. 'Shoot These Evil Acid House Barons,' bellowed the *Sun* in November. After Gary Haisman and D-Mob's appearance on *Top of the Pops* with 'We Call It Acieeed', all records with 'acid' in the lyrics were banned by the show's producers. National fashion outlets banned smiley T-shirts. The first serious bust occurred on 4 November, when two East London promoters were sentenced to six and ten years apiece after putting on a boat party in Greenwich, found guilty of 'conspiring to manage a premises where drugs were supplied'. When Paul Oakenfold was interviewed by ITN at the time of the furore, his half-hour interview on the club and music scene was cut to a few seconds concerning drug-taking. Throughout the summer of 1989, the tabloids ramped up the moral panic to national security level. In June, the *Sun* reported fifteen thousand people at one event, dubbed 'Ecstasy Airport!' It was, said the paper, the 'worst ever!' There were 'drug pushers galore!' Kids of twelve were said to have gone 'wild', while 'thousands of empty ecstasy wrappers littered the floor'. Visiting the scene, Thames Valley Police's Supt. Anthony Howlett-Bolton took a more balanced view. 'Drugs were not a problem,' he told Channel 4's *Hard News*. 'In reality, I suspect drugs were part of the scene, part of the festival, but I don't think they were the main reason for those attending,' he said. He denied there were children as young as twelve at the event, and 'saw no extensive evidence of drug use at all'. The 'ecstasy wrappers' came from silver balloons that were part of the party's special effects.

In August 1989, one hack embarked on a trip into even wilder realms of fantasy, reporting that at one party 'Beheaded pigeons littered the floor ... youngsters were so high on ecstasy and cannabis they ripped the birds' heads off'. The *Sun* baited the constabulary, asking 'Don't the police care about enforcing the law of the land? Are they not troubled about what is happening to our young people? Just when will they decide to smash the evil drug pushers in our midst? Only when the drug habit has spread to all of Britain? When the party stretches from shore to shore?'

The establishment responded by setting up the Pay Party Unit, a police task force that set up road blocks, searched and arrested ravers, confiscated equipment, even set up fake pirate radio broadcasts to divert party-goers. A Pay Party Unit report of April 1990 detailed the task force's success; they'd monitored over three hundred parties, of which 167 didn't take place, 106 were stopped by the police and 68 went ahead. As the promoters' use of call-centre phone technology was becoming ever more sophisticated – they would leave party details on secret recorded messages, activated at staggered intervals to confound the police – the cat-and-mouse game became increasingly elaborate. The *Guardian* reported 'fear of a spring acid house boom' in February 1990, which was to be counteracted with 'a combined intelligence unit drawn from twelve police forces, the Home Office's most powerful computer system, sophisticated radio scanners, monitoring of underground magazines, light aircraft, helicopters and arbitrary arrests'. All because of a branch of youth culture, a form of dance music.

Graham Bright, Conservative MP for Luton South, parliamentary private secretary to John Major, took it upon himself to introduce a parliamentary bill on the matter, which became one of the small number of private members' bills to actually become law. His Entertainments (Increased Penalties) Bill became law in 1990, raising the maximum fine for putting on an unlicensed party from £2,000 to £20,000. He referred to it as 'the acid house party bill'. The tabloids were beside themselves. 'Ecstasy! The party's over!' trumpeted the *Sun*. Some were not so sure the police effort had been worthwhile. 'I wonder whether the amount of time, resources, money that has been ploughed into this has been all worth it,' said Ken Tappenden, head of the police's Pay Party Unit. Graham Bright's links with lobbyists Ian Greer Associates, whose clients included the drinks brand Whitbread, were disclosed in 1994 during the 'cash for questions' scandal. The drinks industry had a lot to lose from a young population raving in the open air, rather than sitting in their pubs like previous generations.

Later measures drove the party underground more specifically, such as the Criminal Justice Act of 1994, which was brought in to stem the tide of mass parties like 1992's Castlemorton rave, among other widespread measures. Sections 63, 64 and 65 of the act notoriously defined a dance music event as a gathering of a hundred or more people in the open air, playing music 'wholly or predominantly characterised by the emission of repetitive beats', possibly the only time in British law that a style of music has been categorised in an act of Parliament. One side effect of such law enforcement was to steer dance music away from the fields and back into clubs. It was no coincidence that Ministry of Sound was granted its licence around the time when the Bright bill became law; it is also no coincidence that the rise of the superclub such as Cream, Renaissance and Gatecrasher followed the introduction of the Criminal Justice Act.

Whatever the legal outcome, tabloid and law enforcement pressure took the wind out of the acid house scene. On the surface, the dawn of the nineties was the peak time for the E generation, as new friendships formed and top nights were endlessly repeated, but behind the scenes the smiley façade was beginning to shatter. Many large-scale promotions were now being run not by wide-eyed party idealists, but by gangsters smelling profit. Paul acquired a booking agent at around this time, David Levy, who he'd met when David was representing Marshall Jefferson. David's main role was to stop people putting Paul's name on flyers for parties that Paul hadn't agreed to play at. 'These were the dark years,' says David. 'You'd ring people and say "Take Paul's name off the flyer" and they'd say

"Oh sorry mate, I'm going to have to break your fucking legs, get off the phone!" It was a horrible time.'

This heavier undercurrent was beginning to affect Paul's nights at Heaven. There was a noticeable change of clientele and atmosphere as the night continued. Dave Little's imagery for Land of Oz was a little starker than the technicolour art for Spectrum; it was as if he had sensed a sea change. Cocaine was beginning to make its presence felt as a club alternative to ecstasy. 'Nightlife got more coke-y, and I don't think it's ever got out of that since,' says Dave Little. 'The Land of Oz flyer was based on a really vicious face, a chiselled, pale, slitty-eyed robot face that was modelled on something from *2000 AD*, with a really tight, almost sad mouth. I don't know if I was projecting some subconscious thought, but I could see that cocaine was cutting through the club scene like a knife. Maybe it's no accident they called it Land of Oz – oz is also an abbreviation of ounce! People started getting banged up for drugs. By the time of Land of Oz, one of the managers at Heaven got five years for dealing coke. This was the underbelly. It was like the sixties had been compressed into a year and a half – you had the euphoria of the beginning, the explosion, the Summer of Love, then the cocaine and the comedown.'

For Paul and Ian, this was where the bright idealism of the Summer of Love truly turned against them. While Paul was busy DJing, Ian's entrepreneurial activities now included a spot of dealing on the side. One situation, a deal Ian was brokering, became a lot more serious than just knocking out a few pills. Ian's contacts decided to get scarily physical when things didn't go their way. 'Basically, it was a drug deal that went very wrong,' says Paul. 'They sprayed ammonia in his eyes. I went to see him in hospital; he was partially blinded. He said he was going to hire these guys who were going to take out the guys who did it to him, he was gonna kill them. And I said don't – you just can't, you mustn't go along that route. And that's when it all changed for him. He lost that edge. It's good that he lost it, because he was such a bolshie drug dealer. He got scared. He either had to go down that route or not. At that time he felt like he had to, but you can't start killing people.'

Various rumours circled this incident. It was alleged that Ian was so well connected, he put the word out and the money came straight back to him, briefcase and all. This wasn't so. 'Of course he didn't get it back,' says Paul. 'He was trying to save face saying that. Ian got hurt big-time. He nearly lost his sight. I think it really hit me when I was sitting there in hospital with him and we were talking it through. I was like, "You've got to get out of this game. Next time you'll get shot or something." '

Having a known drug dealer on the team was becoming an increasing worry for Paul. His old, valued friend and travel companion was becoming a dangerously loose cannon. 'I went round to Ian's house one night and they were all sitting there doing fucking hard drugs and I thought, "I better get out of here," ' says Paul. 'If this place gets raided I'm in trouble. Ian Paul became a huge liability. He became that cliché drug addict and wouldn't listen. He was my best friend, but he wouldn't listen to anyone. He was bringing all these dodgy people around. He was a bomb waiting to go off.'

'He's a fantastic bloke, but there was a real mad side to him,' says Ian's cousin Trevor Fung. 'When he's down there's a side to him you don't want to see – he'll take you and everybody else down with him. He used to literally live round my house;

I couldn't get rid of him. He's brilliant, a really generous, genuine bloke, but he got a little bit messed up.'

It's a shame that the real driving force of acid house got knocked off course; in an ideal world, Ian St Paul would be lauded as the linchpin of the era. 'Ian was the man behind the scenes,' says Mickey Jackson. 'He was the one who had the ideas, but he wanted to stay out of the picture, for his own reasons. He was in his own world. He organised everything; Paul did all the interviews, booked the artists and was behind the music, but Ian was the architect.'

Ian and Paul's paths grew further apart, but the link was too strong to break completely. Ian headed to LA, and helped kick-start the American acid party scene, before following the hippy trail to Goa, India. In both places Ian's crusading zeal to get the party started reverberated once again, resulting in new dance spaces and musical experiments that would influence and inspire Paul Oakenfold far into the future.

In September 1991 a new nightclub was launched in Gaunt Street, Elephant and Castle, London – the Ministry of Sound. The club was founded by ex-Eton school friends James Palumbo and Humphrey Waterhouse, alongside DJ Justin Berkmann. Like Paul Oakenfold, Justin Berkmann had experienced Larry Levan at the Paradise Garage, and wanted to import the sound of the Garage to London. 'Justin Berkmann brought me in as the first resident at Ministry,' says Paul. 'We'd both been to Paradise Garage; we shared the same vision. I was resident for the first six months – I was playing on Friday nights, back when the DJ booth was a hole in the wall on the side. I'd play for the last three hours, then go straight out to the West End – at ten on Saturday morning, I'd be in Soho, buying records. As a club they had a lot of problems, but as a venue, as a sound system, it was fantastic. There was an air of expectancy that this was going to be the best club in London, but they thought they could cut corners and not pay the DJs a lot of money. The reason I left was because they promised me money down the line, but I never got it. I wanted to be part of the club, so I did it on the basis that I'd get paid later. Of course the money didn't happen, so what do you do? Do I let them walk over me or take a stand?' Paul left the Ministry, but would still return occasionally, mixing an early Ministry compilation and performing at their Millennium Dome New Year gig many years later. The DJ residency idea wasn't totally shelved however; it just lay dormant for a while, to resurface in Liverpool at Cream.

**Right:** *Peter and Sheila Oakenfold, Paul's parents, on their wedding day.*

**Above:** *The Oakenfold family on holiday.*

**Left:** *Peter Oakenfold (pictured right)* with *his skiffle band.*

**Clockwise from top left:**
*Paul (pictured right) with
his brother and sister, David
and Linda; Paul with furry
friend; David, Linda and
Paul with monkeys; Cub-scout
DJ; Ian 'St' Paul, Paul and
Trevor Fung at The Copa,
New York City, 1980; Paul,
aged nine.*

**Right:** *Aciieed! Paul, Lisa Loud and Ian Paul at Shoom, 1988.*

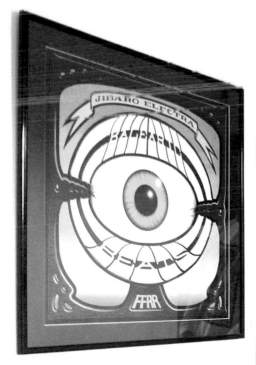

**Below:** *Designer Dave Little with his artwork for 'Jibaro'.*

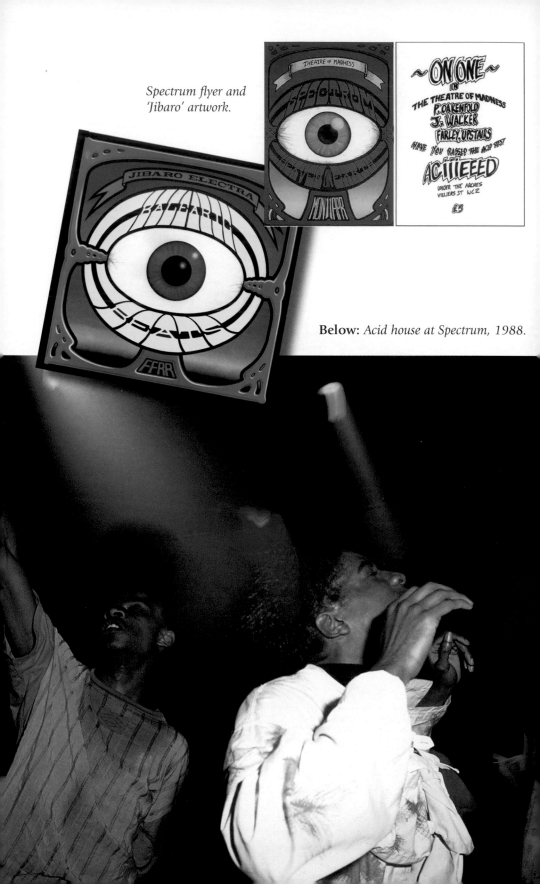

*Spectrum flyer and 'Jibaro' artwork.*

**Below:** *Acid house at Spectrum, 1988.*

**Left:** *Perfecto party at Ku, Ibiza, 1995.*

**Below:** *The fabled free party at Can Punta, Ibiza, 1995.*

**Left**: *Paul (centre) with The Edge and Larry Mullen of U2.*

**Below**: *Paul and Bono, living it up on the Italian Riviera.*

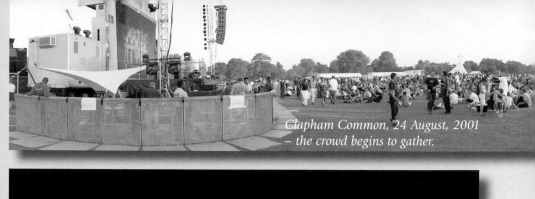

*Clapham Common, 24 August, 2001 – the crowd begins to gather.*

*Paul surveys the ever-expanding crowd at Clapham Common.*

*Blue is the colour: Paul with silverware at Chelsea's Stamford Bridge stadium.* **Insets**: *James Barton, Paul and Darren Hughes celebrate Paul's signing with Cream.*

# 7

# Wrote for Luck

'Happy Mondays are as good as Mozart'
Tony Wilson

'I can't be doing with all that bollocks'
Shaun Ryder

After scoring a debut top-ten remix with Jazzy Jeff and the Fresh Prince's 'Girls Ain't Nothing But Trouble', the track that introduced Will Smith to the world, Paul returned to the recording studio in 1988. His first Balearic-era recording project, Electra, on London/ffrr, opened with the Ibiza club staple 'Jibaro'. The track was originally written and recorded in 1974 by brothers Elkin and Nelson Marin. The duo left their native Colombia and moved to Spain in the early seventies, swiftly becoming major figures in the Latin music world with their fusion of Afro-Cuban beats, Santana swing and James Brown soul. They played on a handful of smash-hit Latin crossovers, such as the Gibson Brothers' 'Cuba' and 'Oh What

A Night', but it was 'Jibaro' that got non-stop rotation in Ibiza when it was re-released in 1986. The original is a percussion-heavy, sun-drenched call to arms, fusing Latin rhythms and Euro production, a formula that the Oakenfold version sticks pretty close to. The main difference between the two tracks was that the original wasn't accompanied with a Balearic-ed up video featuring a South London DJ with a tremendous, *Dallas*-tastic mullet and a gleaming white, shoulder-pad-heavy jacket, pretending to play a Spanish guitar, grinning his face off. Paul, Mickey Jackson, Johnny Rocka and their pal Nick had swiftly formed a makeshift band to promote the record, and shot the blissed-up visual in about fifty takes, waiting for the sun to come up in Ibiza. A string of PA dates, a spot on Pete Waterman's clubtastic TV show *The Hitman and Her* and an interview in the *NME* followed, as the song hit the lower end of the UK chart.

Working alongside Paul in the studio on the Elektra project was Rob Davis, former guitarist with glam rock outfit Mud, who scored a string of naggingly catchy UK hits in the early seventies, three-minute slices of stomp'n'shout bubblegum that seemed to be in the top ten for months on end. Davis obviously learnt a thing or two about recording from Mud's producers, glam rock studio wizards Nicky Chinn and Mike Chapman, as when the Mud finally dried, he set up his own studio in Surrey, planning a Hall and Oates-style duo project with ex-Darts vocalist Stan Alexander. The duo didn't quite pan out, but they managed to score a US hit for disco outfit Liquid Gold, buying Rob the time to concentrate on writing and production. One of his contacts was Oliver Cheatham of Champion Records, who introduced him to Paul Oakenfold in 1988. Rob lived in Epsom, Surrey, while Paul was a short hop down the road in Carshalton. 'Paul said to me, "I know where music is going to go to – the house thing is going to be big," ' says Rob. 'He started playing me all these things. I quite liked it, but it needed a bit more melody. I saw an opening, to write top lines, melody lines, and get more vocals into the club tunes.'

Rob used to frequent Oakey's club nights every month or so, nipping in to Spectrum to hear the reaction to a freshly minted acetate. His new musical partner didn't have an inkling about Rob's glam past, however. 'Oakenfold didn't know about it for a couple of years,' says Rob. 'Then he saw me on the telly one night and phoned me up, laughing his head off, and it was all exposed. It wasn't very credible!' Rob's years in Mud left more than an impression on one fan, however. 'This girl used to fly over from Germany,' says Paul, 'a Mud fan from years and years ago. Rob used to describe her as "big . . . big . . . BIG . . ." She used to camp out on his doorstep – he'd come out for a pint of milk in the morning, hair would be all over the place, and she'd be like, "Rooooob! Rooooob!" And he'd go "arrghhh!" and quickly slam the door! She would just wait for him. She was the only fan he had, who became this psycho. Bear in mind he was married . . .'

From being mainly an ideas man rather than a hands-on technician, Paul gradually started to get a more developed feel for the studio, with Rob's help. 'We were writing the Grace album, and I was learning from Rob in the studio,' Paul says. 'He was kind of doing it all, engineering and programming. I'd learnt piano at school, but I had no fucking clue how to work a studio. So I would watch him, and start to learn through him.'

Rob also brought Paul into contact with his first manager, Brian Reza. 'Brian was in the studio with us one time, and said to me "I'll manage you," ' says Paul. 'I said I didn't really need a manager . . .' He did take Brian on board though, and it proved to be a smart move. One of the first introductions Brian set up for Paul was with a studio engineer called Steve Osborne, who'd trained at the legendary Trident recording studio alongside many of the great UK recording engineers of our time, including Flood, Alan Moulder and Mark Stent. 'Me and Rob needed a good engineer,' says Paul, 'so Brian brought Steve Osborne in. Suddenly me and Steve just clicked, and we now had a great team. With Rob it was more of a songwriting team – we wrote the whole Grace album together – with me and Steve, it was more about mixing. We were getting offered shitloads of work.'

The first Oakenfold/Osborne remix collaboration was one of the very finest, a track that was to help shift the direction of many a late-eighties dancefloor. The remix was 'W.F.L.', a version of the track 'Wrote For Luck', by Manchester band Happy Mondays. And by God did the alternative scene need a band like Happy Mondays. Mid-eighties indie was a painful, serious, introverted affair. Thankfully, years of morose, navel-gazing tedium were about to be shaken off. Here was a multicoloured noise that would make the pallid indie crew shake their scrawny butts and free their lively minds. A match made in Heaven on a Monday night, in the Hacienda the rest of the week.

The Oakenfold/Mondays connection that led to 'W.F.L.' came about via a growing network of London/Manchester Balearic links. Paul and Ian held Spectrum nights at Legends in Manchester, whilst a number of Manchester faces, some of whom had hooked up with Paul and gang in Ibiza, would regularly make the trip south to check out Spectrum at Heaven.

'I knew a few people from Manchester,' says Paul, 'people like Mike Pickering. The Mondays used to come down to Spectrum.'

It wasn't just fate that led Happy Mondays to work with Paul Oakenfold and conjure up their particular brand of baggy-assed dynamite. Unlike many indie bands, who suddenly decided 'there's always been a dance element to our music' some time in 1988, the Mondays' dancefloor connections were firmly in place right from the off. For a start, they were from Manchester. It's no accident that Manchester was one of the first UK cities to champion the embryonic sound of Chicago house and Detroit techno – the city has a long history and affinity with club culture. Pop-picking sensation Jimmy Savile ruled the roost in the late fifties and early sixties, spinning at Manchester's Plaza. Before becoming a *Top of the Pops* legend, Savile allegedly ran the world's first-ever disco, in Otley, West Yorkshire, in 1942, at a time when the idea of dancing to anything other than a live band seemed ridiculous. In the early seventies, Manchester's Whitworth Street was home to the Twisted Wheel, a club which, alongside the Torch in Tunstall, Blackpool's Mecca and the Wigan Casino, was one of the key venues for Northern Soul, a scene whose vinyl obsession, all-nighters and pill-popping mirrored the house scene a decade before acid house. A few years after the Twisted Wheel's peak, a new club hit Whitworth Street. A former yacht showroom was taken over by fêted local record label Factory Records, opening in May 1982. The club was called the Hacienda and was soon to become the Mondays' – and Manchester's – dance headquarters.

The Hacienda took some time to find its audience. Initially set up by New Order and Factory as a home-town version of the clubs they'd frequented in New York, such as the Funhouse and Danceteria, there was yet to be a dance crowd large enough to fill the place, despite a few key early gig nights with performances from New Order, the Smiths, and an early sighting of Madonna, captured for *The Tube* TV series. The Ben Kelly design was beautiful, but pretty stark – if you walked into the Hacienda in the mid-eighties, you'd encounter concrete, metal stairs, the low stage, functional Highway Code graphics and some long sheets of industrial plastic that seemed to have been imported from an abattoir. Not the second Summer of Love, exactly. DJ Justin Robertson, who moved to Manchester to study philosophy in 1986, describes his first visit. 'I went there as an indie kid,' he says. 'I was quite into Factory but I'd lived a vaguely sheltered life, and never really ventured out. Someone took me to the Temperance Club, which was Dave Haslam's indie night on a Thursday. I remember walking into this stark, industrial space. Dave Haslam was playing Shinehead, "The Cap Fits", which has this electronic backbeat that sounded incredible in there. I fell in love with the place. From going on that Thursday, I started basing my entire life around going there. Dave Haslam was DJing bits of hip hop, all quite drum-machine-driven . . . it was very stark but massively cool.'

A couple of years after that, there was a strong sense of change in the air. On a Friday night Mike Pickering and Mike Prendergast were DJing under the name MP2, at the legendary Nude night, dishing out early Chicago house and Detroit techno. 'I remember walking in and hearing Rhythim Is Rhythim,' says Justin Robertson. 'I remember thinking "this is why I need to stop buying Soupdragons records!" ' The look was slowly changing too. 'Nude had a really mixed crowd,' says Justin, a man rightly famed for his sartorial elegance. 'They were dressed in black suits, a few MA-1 jackets, that black-polo-neck jazz look,' he says. 'A pivotal night for me was a Wednesday night called Zumbar, a very theatrical, cabaret night. They had all sorts – comedians, people pulling razor blades out of their stomachs, fashion shows and music. In early '88 they did a party for *i-D* magazine, with Mark Moore DJing. A load of people came up from London for it. I was wearing some kind of suit, and this guy with mop-top hair, wearing Converse and this psychedelic T-shirt, totally out of his mind on ecstasy, came up to me on the dancefloor. He gave me a teddy bear! Over the course of that night people's dress sense seemed to be changing – we were all loosening our suit jackets and untucking our shirts ... We were already aware of acid house, and were listening to the music – Manchester was well ahead for playing house music – but it didn't have the culture that went with it in London, the clothes, the scene. But from then on there was a meeting – of vocabulary, of the look. That's when it changed.'

Nude was followed in July 1988 by Hot, which replaced Zumbar's Wednesday-night cabaret show with a mini-Balearic getaway, complete with a swimming pool next to the dance-floor. Jon Da Silva and Mike Pickering manned the decks for one crazy summer. 'It was a bit more mad at Hot – it felt more illicit because it was a Wednesday night. Nude was a better night generally, but Wednesday was more nuts. You'd see people coming in with their old-style dress, thinking they were going for a few beers, and you'd see them going from some go-go, hip hop dance, looking at people, to doing the full-on trance dance. They were being converted before your eyes. And obviously the drugs were quite important!'

Ah yes. And if you looked under one of the pillars off the dance-floor, in an area that was soon dubbed 'E Corner', chances are you'd spot a particularly wide-eyed gang nodding in time to the music. Ladies and gentlemen, let's hear it for Happy Mondays.

The Mondays were pretty much born in the Hacienda. Their first manager, Phil Saxe, got them their first gig, a 'battle of the bands' contest at the recently opened Hacienda in 1983. Saxe was the former Twisted Wheel Northern Soul DJ who also ran the Some Wear clothes shop in the Arndale Centre, where the Mondays could be found eyeing up job lots of extra-wide jeans that Phil was having trouble shifting. They didn't win the Hacienda competition – opinion varies as to whether they came second or last – but their performance alerted another DJ to them, Hacienda resident Mike Pickering, who persuaded Factory to sign the band in May 1984 and produced their first single, the three-track 'Forty Five'.

The Mondays certainly had a different vibe. Most of their indie contemporaries were shambling introverts, with a range that stretched from dour to grim. Here was a new proposition, one that couldn't quite be pinned down. An early convert was Jeff Barrett, now head of Heavenly Recordings, then running a record shop in Plymouth. 'The lads who used to buy records from me were seriously into Factory,' says Jeff. 'The label had a really interesting period in the early eighties with artists like Quango Quango, ACR and Marcel King. They had groups like 400 Blows and Colourbox, this whole white-boy funk thing going on. I remember when the first Mondays single came out thinking it was really good, but it was also really odd – where does it fit?'

Barrett got a job as the first-ever employee at Alan McGee's Creation Records, whose offices were the floor below Factory's press officer, Dave Harper. 'I picked up a test pressing of "Freaky Dancing", the second Mondays single, from him,' says Jeff. 'It was fucking amazing, absolutely the dog's bollocks. We played it for ages. To me it was the natural progression of everybody's dance influence. We had a band on Creation called the Weather Prophets who needed a band to support them for a London show at the Clarendon Ballroom, Hammersmith, so I said you've got to put the Mondays on. I played the test pressing to Pete Astor of the Weather Prophets; he reckoned it was like the Fire Engines, with a bit of Captain Beefheart . . . like Can, but wrong! This was a good thing.'

From the off, Jeff Barrett knew the band were resolutely individual. 'The first time I met them I was actually trying to throw them out of the venue!' he says. 'The Weather Prophets were doing a soundcheck in the afternoon, and Pete's ego wasn't working too well, because there were people sat in the room and he wanted them out. There was this lot in the corner, with snorkel parkas on, drinking bottles of cider. Hammersmith Broadway was a renowned hangout for alkies at that time – I thought they were alkies and said "Would you mind leaving?" It was the Mondays. I took another look at them, and thought "of course you are!" They looked amazing, unlike any other indie band. They didn't have fringes or Chelsea boots like every other band at the time. They had flares. And they were big flares! It was completely individual. They looked great.'

This debut London gig lived up to the promise displayed on the band's early singles. 'The gig was phenomenal,' says Jeff. 'They blew my mind. You could tell they came from Manchester – they were absolutely Northern, absolutely psychedelic. It was shambolic, but everything that was in there made sense. They were Beefheart, there was a Northern Soul thing going on, it was rhythmic and it stomped. The guitarist immediately got to you, because he had this weird sound; with the singer, you thought "what is that guy on about?" You couldn't really make it out, but there was charisma there. They were just different.'

Barrett supplemented his Creation gig with promoting bands at various pub dives around town, and booked the Mondays, sharpish. 'I put them on five or six times. The first time was at the Black Horse in Camden. Shaun and Paul's dad Derek was doing the sound. There was no stage – they had to play by the fireplace with a big mantelpiece and a stuffed heron over it. It could hold maybe sixty, seventy people. Bez and Cressa were both dancers, before Cressa jumped ship to the Roses. There were tons of them, smoking away. Shaun comes up and says "Where's the stage?" I told him there wasn't one and he wasn't pleased. I told him they'd look great under the stuffed heron. Straight away afterwards, his dad comes up to me and says "He hasn't just asked you for acid has he?" I mean, it's Sunday night at this pub in Camden – nobody's asked me that question for years! I'm hardly walking around with pockets full of it. He said "If he asks you for acid, don't fucking give him any." They covered "She's Crafty" by the Beastie Boys. It was amazing. With a stuffed heron behind them!'

Unfortunately this early live and recorded promise was yet to excite the music press. *NME*, the music paper that was to soon feature the band many times on its cover, gave their John Cale-produced debut album a proper pasting. The album may have had a right mouthful of a title – *Squirrel And G-Man Twenty Four Hour Party People Plastic Face Carnt Smile (White Out)* – but there was no need to describe their 1987 début as 'someone shouting in a Manchester accent over weak and watery foonk like nearly everything else on Factory'. It may be a bit wonky in places, but any album that contains a track like '24 Hour Party People' can't be all bad. The band were, however, a big hit with other Manchester musicians, including New Order's Barney Sumner. 'Like us, they weren't musos,' he says. 'They couldn't have cared less about writing proper songs or showing people how well they could play their instruments. All they really wanted to do was take loads of drugs, shag tons of girls and have a laugh. Hooky and I thought that was an admirable outlook on life.'

Following the release of the album, the Mondays swapped management from Phil Saxe to Nathan McGough in the spring of 1988. Son of famed Liverpool poet Roger McGough, Nathan entered the music business running a night called Plato's Ballroom at a working men's club called Mr Pickwick's in Liverpool in 1981. It was a bit of an art happening – three bands on, a performance artist, a cabaret act and a few Jean Cocteau movies projected on the walls for a couple of quid. It was inspired by Tony Wilson's early Factory club, in Hulme, Manchester – four nights of music and dance that featured Cabaret Voltaire, Big in Japan, the Durutti Column and Joy Division. McGough went on to manage the Pale Fountains, getting them a deal with Virgin Records. 'It was the biggest deal Virgin had done since the Sex Pistols, for silly money,' he says. After falling out with Pale Fountains singer Michael Head, the Factory-inspired manager moved to Manchester. 'I was very tight with Tony Wilson and the Factory lot,' he says. 'I'd been kind of involved with Factory, as a friend of Wilson's, from the very start, sitting in the flat at 86 Palatine Road, which became the Factory office, hand-making the silver and black *Factory Sample* EP, with Barney and Hooky from New Order. So I went to Manchester and worked at the Hacienda as a barman.' At the same time McGough continued his management interests, looking after a couple of bands including the Bodines, who were solid eighties indie fare, not without a certain charm, but hardly likely to set the world on fire. A more exciting proposition was a band that McGough had booked for a handful of Bodines support slots – Happy Mondays.

'Happy Mondays were every band's favourite band in Manchester,' says Nathan. 'In the spring of '88, the Mondays had decided that they wanted a new manager because Phil seemed to be very busy with his stores. Shaun Ryder came up to me in the Hacienda one night and said to me "We've fired Phil." I said, "Are you telling me some information or are you asking me to manage you?" He said, "What the fuck do you think?" I said, "Oh right. I'm in!" They had some new songs written, for the album that would become *Bummed*. We went and did session demos, and then got into making the album.'

McGough got together with Alan Lazarus from Factory and came up with the idea that Martin Hannett, legendary producer of classics for Joy Division and a handful of other Factory acts, should produce the new record. 'I was a massive fan of Joy Division and A Certain Ratio,' says Nathan, 'they were my favourite bands, even when I was still living in Liverpool as a teenage kid. I loved Hannett's production of *Unknown Pleasures* and *Closer*, and the very first Certain Ration twelve-inches like "Flight" and "Do The Du". I just loved them, and still do to this day. I was a huge fan of Hannett. So we came up with the idea of Hannett producing. We wanted that sort of exotic spatial dynamic that Martin brings to music. We thought it would be a good mix. And sure enough, it was. We went off to the Slaughterhouse Studios in Driffield, Yorkshire, with these massive bags of LSD, and the band and Hannett were just taking ecstasy twenty-four hours a day and making this record, for four weeks. As far as I know it was the first ecstasy-fuelled rock record ever made.'

Factory boss Tony Wilson was initially unconvinced that Hannett was right for the project – the pair had clashed over whether the producer could buy a Fairlight synthesizer out of the profits from Joy Division albums. 'Wilson baulked at the whole idea, didn't want to know, but we kind of pushed it through,' says Nathan. The label boss's mood soon changed once he got to the studio, however. 'The central moment in my life with that album was driving to Driffield and going into the studio,' says Tony Wilson. 'Martin was mixing the album on one side of this little courtyard. On the other side was that room where the band goes, where they play pool . . . In this case it was dark, and there was this beating, booming noise. You walked into the room and it's all dark, and you begin falling over black vinyl, which is scattered all over the floor, and the musicians, who are scattered all over the floor. They're just lying there, off their heads, listening to this beating, banging house music, these very first house imports. All the rhythms that are feeding them, coming in from Chicago and Detroit into their brains.'

'The Mondays had always been into their drugs,' says Nathan. 'It seemed unusual in those days for working-class kids like them to be into pot and LSD. Now it's not. In 1987, it was.' Martin Hannett was similarly keen to experiment. 'When I first met Martin, when I was fourteen, he had a thumbnail two inches long on his left hand, which is used as a coke spoon,' says Nathan. 'Martin had actually been a chemist at ICI, and knew the chemical make-up of all sorts of pharmaceutical prescription drugs. He knew what they would do to you, and if you combined them, what would happen.' The major drug dynamic in the studio was ecstasy, which the Mondays' Shaun Ryder insisted was good for the producer. 'It stops him getting too bladdered,' Shaun told Nick Kent in *The Face*. 'We were givin' him two a day and this was when they were twenty-five quid a go, right . . . He kept saying, "I can't feel anything, but I'm in a fucking good frame of mind." '

'When I got involved in the Mondays' world, Shaun and Bez were popping ecstasy on a daily basis,' says Nathan, 'but they were doing it in a way that they would do quarters and halves, like, for breakfast and just getting on their E-vibe for the whole day, going about their daily business. Not getting monged, but just using it as a groove rider. The deal was that Shaun and Bez had an Amsterdam connection with a friend of theirs, a Mancunian who lived there who was sharp and on his toes, and was just doing his business out in Europe. A lot of the boys from Manchester were, because it was easy pickings in Europe. He was basically shipping the drug through to them, and they were knocking it out on the corner of the Hacienda, and at parties.'

The local army contingent, stationed near Driffield, also managed to kick back a little in their down time. 'There was a pub with a club upstairs next to the studio,' says Nathan. 'The squaddies used to come in, and the band would be selling Es to them, getting them all fucking pilled up. Which was nice! Kill with a smile! Love the one you kill! My memory of the studio is being under the desk a lot . . .'

One of the records strewn about the studio floor was 'Jibaro', the early Oakenfold, Osborne and Davis collaboration. 'Shaun had this twelve-inch of "Jibaro",' remembers Nathan. 'It had a pyramid with a great big eye in the middle of it, and a picture of people dancing. Shaun loved it, he was playing it non-stop in the studio for fucking weeks, and he was going, "It's this guy called Paul Oakenfold from Spectrum that's done it." Our relationship with Ian St Paul and Paul Oakenfold developed throughout that summer. When we came to launch the album in November 1988, we did it at Spectrum.'

The *Bummed* album launch was a key moment in the music media romance between dance and indie. The evening started with a playback at Heaven at six, which was followed by a boisterous gig for a couple of hundred invited guests at Camden's Dingwalls. John Peel was positioned down the front on the right, digging it, furiously taking notes. It was also, somewhat bizarrely, filmed for a children's television documentary about how to form a band and succeed in the music business.

It was the first time Paul Oakenfold had seen the Mondays live. 'It was amazing,' he says. The crowd, which included a large Manc contingent, were bouncing, shouting, shimmying. Many of the assembled rock journos got their first taste of E culture that night, albeit a craftily stage-managed one. 'The band made more money selling ecstasy to the journalists at the album playback than we did by getting paid for the gig at Dingwalls!' says Nathan.

Launching the album at Spectrum sealed the growing relationship between Paul Oakenfold and Happy Mondays, and the band's relationship to dance music in the eyes of the assembled media throng. 'It was our way of positioning this music within the cultural framework of acid house,' says

Nathan. 'From the beginning of '88, through to the album launch in November, the whole scene had exploded. It had this fucking vertical take-off from the spring through to the autumn. There was a feeling at the time that was very tangible. We were experiencing a paradigm shift.'

The music press, who had been initially wary of acid house, and hadn't started reporting on it until the scene was nearly a year old, were slowly waking up to the biggest youth-culture shift since punk. The idea of promoting a band like the Mondays as a useful bridge between the emerging dance movement and their mainly 'indie'-based readership became more and more appealing. Around this time Dave Harper left Factory for a press position at BMG, handing over the mantle to Mondays fanatic Jeff Barrett. 'I was over the moon,' says Jeff. 'I was working with a group that I loved, that I thought were completely counterculture, the most exciting thing out there. Dave Harper had done a good job setting the band up with certain journalists, who thought they were an interesting Factory art group, but I knew they were more important than that. I got the test pressings of *Bummed* . . . what a record! It was mind-blowing. I started getting them down for interviews.'

Not that the band were that arsed about their rising press profile. 'I remember Bez coming over to me at the bar about three interviews in,' says Jeff. 'I had long red hair at the time. He said, "Oi foxhead, why do you keep sending students over to talk to us? I'm trying to have a bevvy and you keep sending students over." They'd just been interviewed by the three main music papers! They had no concept of career. They had their own language – calling themselves X, Horse, Horsehead . . . the keyboard player's nickname was Knobhead. I remember the first time an article ran in the *Melody Maker* and

they called him Knobhead. He rang me up and complained –
he rang up and says "No one calls me Knobhead." Everyone
called him Knobhead.'

The tide was even turning at the *NME*. 'I remember the
editor at the time, Alan Lewis, saying "I am never going to put
that band on the cover,"' says Jeff. 'Sure enough, a year later
they had eight covers.' They found a staunch champion in
features editor James Brown, who kicked off a lengthy
campaign with a 9-out-of-10 review for *Bummed*. He wrote
them up a storm: 'If you love the energy of acid and the
awkward aggression of good independent rock, but want your
music to be scarred with the characters of Dennis Hopper,
Charlie Bukowski, Hunter S. Thompson and Johnny Rotten,
then you can stop looking to the past and taking these
pleasures separately by getting *Bummed* for a truly stimulating
contemporary, sensory thrashing.' The band couldn't have been
better positioned for your average *NME* reader if Jeff Barrett
or Dave Harper had written the album themselves.

The first single taken from the album was 'Wrote For Luck', an
inspired groover with a loping, circular guitar riff, topped off
by Shaun's incisive, observational spiel. The single and the
album did reasonably well in the first few months of release,
selling around fifteen thousand by March '89, but not doing
the numbers Nathan McGough and Tony Wilson would have
liked. 'The E scene, the acid house scene, was going from
strength to strength,' says Nathan, 'but the Mondays as a band
hadn't grown in tandem with that scene, in terms of actual
sales. Tony Wilson and I sat down and I said, "We have here
the band that's the musical mouthpiece for this generation. All
these kids are piling into warehouses and raves on the

weekend, ten thousand at a time . . . these kids need to connect with Happy Mondays and this album. How do we do it?" Wilson said, "We need to make a record that's going to cross over into that scene; we need to get someone from the scene to do a remix." The first name that came to mind was Oakenfold, because of our connections with Spectrum and everything else.'

Despite the band being pretty much born in a corner of the Hacienda, the management and the label didn't want it to appear that the Mondays were riding on the coat-tails of the new dance scene. 'By that time, there were quite a few dodgy acid house records and mixes coming out,' says Nathan. 'What we didn't want to do was be seen as having some naff ravey remix. So I called Pete Tong, as the band were published by ffrr music. I explained what I needed to achieve, and he came back and said "Oakenfold's your man". Paul was top of my list, and sure enough, he'd been doing some belting mixes. So we sent him "Wrote For Luck".'

McGough also handed the track to Vince Clarke of Erasure, who'd never previously done a remix. He handed back a throbbing, stripped-down, electroid monster, adding a European, Teutonic spin to the mix. But the mix that really delivered on the dancefloor was the 'Think About The Future' mix by Paul Oakenfold, aided and abetted by Terry Farley and Steve Osborne.

Oakey attacked 'Wrote For Luck' from the beats up. 'The problem with indie band records was that the rhythm was all wrong,' says Paul, 'I couldn't play them out. I wanted to keep the spirit of the original in the mix, the looseness, the way he sings. The rhythm, the arrangement, and the structure were wrong for the clubs, so I came up with an idea of taking an NWA loop and putting that underneath.' He also added a mesmerising, floating top-line hook, some stuttering, gated keyboards, and turned Ryder's 'Ahaaa aah haaa' refrain into a mesmeric E-mantra. As well as NWA's 'Express Yourself' beats, a sample from Prince's *Batman* soundtrack sneaks its way on to vinyl at the end of the mix. 'Think about the future,' says Prince, as well he might. The record, released as a single in September 1989, was a crucial release. 'That's the record, that's the single song that broke the Mondays,' says Tony Wilson.

The band first heard it as they were on their way to their first tour of America. 'We went off to tour with the Pixies, and on the way to the airport I was handed a cassette with Oakey's mix on it,' says Nathan. 'We all listened to it in the van – everybody thought it was just the nuts! It just completely hit all the targets that we wanted. It just absolutely kicked in. I love Vince's mix, it's so electro and robotic, it's just precision, digital bliss, but Paul's mix was special because it's got the throbbing bass and kick drum which became the prominent rhythm pattern of all those baggy records. If you take a pill and listen to that record, it's on the money!' It strode boundaries like no other. As well as being a guaranteed floor-filler, the track also impressed the indie-guitar-fixated press – *NME* crowned it dance record of the year. As the Stone Roses' Ian Brown put it, 'The black kids always had something going, and '89 was the year the white kids woke up.'

Armed with a killer remix, the track, now known as 'W.F.L.', needed a suitably deranged video to accompany it. The Mondays' small-screen auteurs turned up in the form of two likely Geordies, Phil Shotton and Keith Jobling, aka the Bailey Brothers. The duo went on to make every single Mondays video bar one, and the more manic of the pair, Keith Jobling, later coined the term 'Madchester'. Capturing the spirit and feeling of a great club on film is no easy job, but the Bailey Brothers clip nails it, big-time. The city's nocturnal antics were represented remarkably accurately, as a throbbing mass on the dancefloor of Legends nightclub, a mainly indie venue that had gained favour during acid house, including hosting Oakenfold and Ian St Paul's Spectrum offshoot. Paul had tried to get a Spectrum night at the Hacienda, but had been turned down. 'We had a meeting with Paul Cons, the manager of the Hacienda, in early 1988,' says Paul. 'They just wouldn't have it. They said it wasn't happening, so we did it at Legends instead. They came down and saw it was blowing up, and then tried to get us shut down!'

'Spectrum at Legends was good,' says Justin Robertson. 'Mike Pickering and Graeme Park had gone down to play in a DJ soundclash with Oakey at Spectrum in London, so there was a connection,' says Justin. 'Danny Rampling had done a Shoom night at the Hacienda, but Spectrum was the first London club that had their own night in Manchester. Despite what people might think, it was well received – there wasn't any sneering about Southerners coming up to Manchester. This guy called Jeff the Chef would be standing on tables, shouting, yelling "Come on Manchester!" People were pretty open-minded. There were Spectrum tapes floating about – we were all excited about it, we thought it was the real deal. The music was different – it was similar, but had more of a wobbly, Balearic bass-line vibe, a lot more of a European flavour. Things played at Spectrum, like A Split Second's "Flesh", weren't big at the Hacienda. The Hacienda was very much about straight-up Chicago house and Detroit techno. The way it was put together seemed to be different as well. It was quite unusual at the time – the guest DJ thing wasn't really established then. It was quite a bold move.'

It was certainly a move that worked, if the 'W.F.L.' video is anything to go by. The Mondays' new remixer was suitably impressed. 'If you can't explain what went on in the scene, just watch the "Wrote For Luck" video,' says Paul. 'That's what we were doing with Spectrum in Manchester on a Monday night. The band had been to Future; they understood where I was coming from. That video sums the whole fucking thing up.'

'It's a fantastic video,' says Nathan. 'You watch it and you feel like you're off it! It's a snapshot of something totally real. The Bailey Brothers had this very simple idea. Everybody was out seven nights a week, doing pills easily four nights a week, drinking double Rémy Martins and Coke. They said, "We've just got to film what's happening." So we hired Legends and we put the word out; we told all our friends, we said, "Right, everyone get down for six o'clock, they're gonna film for six hours." Someone brought down a fucking massive bag of pills; lots of 'em brought their own supplies. I don't even think we had a free bar to be honest, I think we just had a night! We put Shaun in the middle of that dancefloor, and they just filmed him. He had that little Joe Bloggs coat on, and we just had these chicks stood around him, he's just there in the middle. It's this seething mass of ecstatic oblivion, but in the centre of it is this little shining light – it's him, direct to camera. There's all this chaos around him, but he's this voice from within it, which speaks directly to you, the viewer. It's fabulous.'

For some reason the Bailey Brothers were convinced they also needed to do a slightly more junior version. 'I don't know why this happened – it doesn't make sense to me to this day,' says Nathan. 'Keith the director said, "We're going to do a kiddies' version, because we want the kiddies to get into it!" The kids that did it weren't twelve or thirteen, they were seven and eight-year-old kids! They came down in the afternoon from some stage school. Shaun was doing his do, with little kids doing the rave dance around him, with little white socks and sandals. It was just weird. I don't know why it was done! It was never used. It doesn't make any sense when you're watching it.'

In the autumn of '89 the band went back in the studio with Martin Hannett to record four new tracks, which became the zeitgeist-sharp *Madchester Rave On* EP. 'We gave Oakenfold the EP to do some mixes,' says Nathan, 'and he brought in Terry Farley and Andrew Weatherall. Those guys did mixes in conjunction with Paul. We then had this fantastic EP, with these three great dance remixes. They defined the genre for what was to come for the next couple of years.'

Although the band were happy with what they'd done with Martin Hannett, it was felt in the Mondays camp that it might be time to move on. Their US record label, Elektra, were putting together a compilation album to mark their fortieth anniversary, and asked all the bands from their contemporary roster to contribute a cover version of a track from the label's back catalogue. The album was titled *Rubaiyat*. 'All the choice stuff like the Doors, and Stooges and Love had gone,' says Nathan. 'Basically all we had left was this song, "He's Gonna Step On You Again" by John Kongos, who Shaun always described as "the South African cripple". I don't think he's disabled in any shape or form! Shaun absolutely loved it. Elektra gave us five thousand dollars to get this track recorded.'

'They sent us this big list down and loads of tapes of songs that had been in their catalogue and wanted us to do something,' says Shaun Ryder. 'At the time we were busy working on stuff for our new album – to us it was an inconvenience, it was pissing us off. No one else could be bothered, so me and Bez put a few of these tracks on. About third track in was "He's Gonna Step On You Again" by John Kongos. We heard it and thought we can loop that, we'll knock that out in five minutes.'

The obvious choice for 'Step On' production duties was the team that had led the Mondays on to the dancefloor with 'W.F.L.' – Oakenfold and Osborne. 'Step On', recorded at Eden Studios in London, marked Paul and Steve's transition from hot remix team to fully fledged producers. Rather than reworking someone else's tapes, the duo were now recording the band themselves. The new role didn't seem to faze the DJ. 'I think the fact that Paul had Steve Osborne as his right-hand man really settled him,' says Nathan. 'Steve was absolutely relishing it. Oakey wasn't out of his depth; he's confident, he gets on with things. Once he decided to do it, he got on with it.'

One extra-special new ingredient was added to the track's mix. 'Because all the house records had these great Chicago and Detroit divas belting it out over the beats, someone suggested we needed someone like that on it,' says Nathan. 'I'd met this wonderful, crazy black girl in Manchester who was doing backing vocals for Simply Red, called Rowetta. She was absolutely bonkers about Happy Mondays – she was like a million-per-cent fan of the band. I tracked her down and took her back to London. She did these fantastic, beautiful soul vocals on "Step On". We sat there at the playback of the mix, and it was one of those moments where everyone went "We've got an absolutely smash-hit record here!" I got on the phone to Elektra and told them. The A&R guy, Howard Hunter, said, "Well, I'm sorry, you can't have it, it's exclusively for our Elektra compilation and you can't use it." And I said, "Well, we're gonna use it." And he said, "You can't – we've paid for it." I said, "I tell you what, I'm gonna give you your five thousand dollars back." And that's exactly what we did. The record came out in the spring of 1990, and was bang in at number five.'

For Oakenfold and Osborne, going top five with your first band production was a major achievement. 'We'd taken a chance on Paul as a producer with "Step On",' says Nathan. 'It was unproven, but we felt confident in his and Steve Osborne's ability to deliver, and they delivered in a big way. It under-pinned everything we wanted to do, and gave us all the confidence to move forward and record *Pills 'N' Thrills And Bellyaches* in Los Angeles.'

# 8

# Pills 'n' Thrills and Bellyaches

Los Angeles is a long way from Hulme. It seems like a strange
choice of recording location for a bunch of lads used to selling
Es to squaddies somewhere outside Sheffield between takes,
but it certainly had its advantages. Firstly the choice was
practical. After the summer '89 jaunt with the Pixies, the band
were going on a ten-date tour of America's 'major markets',
spanning the main cities on both coasts, with a few Midwest
shows in between. They started off in New York, then took in
Boston, Washington, Philadelphia, Chicago, Detroit, then
headed into the sun for a final couple of West Coast dates.
Recording in LA made logistical sense. 'We were over there, we
had the opportunity,' says Nathan. 'I don't remember whose
idea it was. It was probably one of the band's, 'cos musicians
always want to go somewhere warm and funky to record.
Oakey came up with Capitol Studios, which is the house studio
at Capitol Records on Vine Street.'

'It was where the Beatles recorded, and Frank Sinatra,' says
Paul. 'It had a lot of history.' So not only were the Mondays let

loose in the sunshine of LA, they were based in one of its most iconic buildings. 'The Capitol building is world-famous,' says Nathan. 'It looks like a stack of pancakes, but it's actually supposed to symbolise a stack of 45s on an old mono record player, with the needle through the top. The studio was built in the fifties, as the likes of Nat King Cole, Sinatra and the Beach Boys recorded there. It had this amazing, fantastic musical heritage, and it was right in the heart of Hollywood.'

The only slight concern was the final date in San Francisco. 'We'd played our LA show on the Thursday night,' says Nathan. 'It was a good show, quite well attended, and we had Oakey out to DJ as well. We were going to be playing in San Francisco at a place called Bottom of the Hill on the Friday, then we were starting in the studio on the Monday morning. So we had to go to San Francisco the following day, do a gig and come back, settle in and start recording. But the band got wind that Soul II Soul were playing at the Universal Amphitheatre on the Friday night in Los Angeles. They got really excited, because Soul II Soul were riding high with "Back To Life" at the time. So the band decided that they wanted to go and see Soul II Soul on Friday night in Los Angeles. We had a gig in San Francisco, so obviously we couldn't go. Come Friday morning, we have to catch a plane at twelve o'clock to San Francisco, and none of the band would get out of bed. They'd all decided they're cancelling the San Francisco gig to go and see Soul II Soul. We've got this show to do, it's been sold out for weeks. So now I've got the band's agent, Mark Geiger from William Morris, on the phone to me and the band. I've got Tony Wilson calling me from Manchester, speaking to Shaun, everyone's trying their utmost to convince them they've got to go and do this gig. Eventually I get the promoter from the San Francisco show on the phone to me, he's freaking out, saying the guys have got to come. I said, "Look, I can't make them come. Speak to Shaun yourself." So I put him through to Shaun's room. Shaun gets on the line to the promoter, and says, "We can't come to San Francisco to do the gig, because the keyboard player Knobhead has an abscess on his brain . . . he's been to the dentist to get it sorted out, and the dentist told him he can't fly . . .'" And the promoter says, "My partner has had AIDS for the last seven years, and he still gets out of bed in the morning and comes to work!" And Shaun Ryder says, "Well if your partner's got AIDS, we're definitely not coming!" And puts the phone down. So we went to see Soul II Soul that night.'

The band were based at the Oakwood apartments, residential short-lease flats with a pool, tennis courts, and nice big cabana-style rooms, somewhere between Hollywood and Burbank. 'Oakwood apartments are cheap apartments that are rented out to young actors, to people in the industry,' says Paul. 'They're just over the side of the valley so they are a lot cheaper to stay there.' Budget or not, it was good enough for the Mondays, Simply Red and some bloke off *Coronation Street*. 'For years we've been struggling musicians,' says Shaun, 'and then we're leading this pop-star life in LA at Oakwood apartments. It was full of porno stars, Dirk Diggler, people like that, and funky bands. It was pretty cool. I think Mick Hucknall was out there at the same time, living on the same campus – him and Gaz our drummer were going to play tennis every day, while we were looking at the porn stars. Brian Tilsley was also there, trying to make it as an actor. He was roaming around Oakwoods in his porn thong leaf – the only guy in America that was shorter than I am.'

*

The surroundings, the timing, and coming fresh off tour were having a very positive effect on the band. 'It was a very creative and productive time,' says Nathan. 'The band had had some great success, a top-five record, they'd been the first indie band to play a ten-thousand-capacity venue, the Manchester G-Mex, two nights in a row, then filled Wembley Arena, selling thirty thousand tickets. They went from being a medium-size-theatre band to doing those kind of dates. There was an awful lot to be played for – the States were there to be won. Paul and Steve had a really great work head on them, in fact the whole band did. Shaun as well – he worked really hard on his lyrics. Everyone would like get up, get down the studio, get their shit done and then kick back by the pool for a bit, then go out in the evening. There was partying going on, but everyone was one hundred per cent focused on making that record as great as it could be. There was no moaning in the camp, no letting the side down.'

'At that time we were all pretty keen to get in the studio,' says Shaun. 'Partying and getting off in the studio came later. We were well keen on getting our hands in on what was going on, putting ideas in there. We were getting more of our own way on things. It was good. We were listening to loads of rap and hip hop, and then all your sort of "loved-up" stuff, mixing it in with ours, ripping great big chunks off everything. Everyone else was ripping the sixties off – we were ripping off what was going on at the time.'

The recording's dynamic was a natural progression from the 'W.F.L.' and 'Step On' sessions, mixing DJ culture with a live band, vinyl breaks with live sampled loops. The team of DJ, band, record deck and Akai sampler was a pioneering, fresh approach, as yet unexplored by many other artists. 'It was still reasonably early days of sampling, there wasn't the gear then that there is now,' says Nathan. 'The software wasn't available, it was all hardware, and you could only do a certain amount of sampling. I remember Steve Osborne cutting up tape and splicing it together, the old-fashioned way. They built those songs from the floor up.'

The sampling wasn't all from old vinyl, either. 'Oakey and Steve would work with the musicians in the band, get some grooves going on, sample it and then build it up from there,' says Nathan. 'Paul Ryder would have a bass line, and Mark would have some guitar chords, and Oakey would bring other ideas, some from records. Steve Osborne is actually quite musical and can play, so he'd get involved in the arrangement – they'd take eight, sixteen or thirty-two bars out of the track and make a loop out of that. Once you find the moment, once you've captured that, you loop it over. It's all about feel, isn't it?'

'It wasn't like working with a band in the traditional sense,' says Paul. 'Not being disrespectful, but they are not the best players out there. With the guitarist, Steve would sit there and play the line and he had to try to copy it – it wasn't a normal band. It was a vibe, a magical moment that's quite hard to put your finger on.'

'Shaun is probably the best I've ever seen at freestyling lyrics, doing improv lyrics,' says Nathan. 'The Mondays' sound was basically born out of funk, psychedelia, street smarts, and Shaun's exotic stories, his observations on everyday life – the mechanics of what makes people tick, and his insight into why they do things. Until that point he'd never written down any lyrics in his life – he carried them round in his head, or just put stuff on a tape recorder. But on that album, he would get down the studio late afternoon, at about four, five o'clock, listen to what was going on, do some freestyling on the mike, get some ideas down, get a tape of it. Then he'd go back to the Oakwood apartments, put his beat box on, and he'd sit there at his desk and work diligently on shaping his lyrics, getting his rhythms and all that stuff going on. He was very, very focused.'

And what lyrics they were. 'Being in LA was a huge influence,' says Paul. 'Shaun really soaked up his surroundings. He isn't the best singer in the world, but it's the way he put things together. He'd be taking chunks of ads or something random and putting that in. It worked.' In his more verbose moments, Tony Wilson enjoys comparing Shaun Ryder's lyrical canon to the works of Bob Dylan, which may be stretching it, but on *Pills 'N' Thrills And Bellyaches* Wilson may have a point. 'Kinky Afro', which the Factory boss describes as 'the greatest poem about parenthood since Yeats' "Prayer for My Daughter" ' – is taut, sharp and focused, a great piece of lyric writing.

Other tracks ably showcase this richly inventive streak. 'God's Cop' is about a particular Manchester irritant, James Anderton, the local chief of police – 'a Calvinist, Protestant, fucking religious nut', according to Nathan. 'At the time we had him on telly in the North-West of England, saying he'd had a visit from God, and he was going to clean up this ecstasy nonsense,' says Shaun. 'We had this lunatic bizzie running round with visits from God.'

'Holiday', meanwhile, started life as a loop from a Madonna track, and is about a regular inconvenience for a band on the road. 'That song is about Customs and Excise being a pain in the arse,' says Nathan. 'On the way out to LA, any time we'd go anywhere, we'd get fucking stopped and they'd go through everything. Shaun had this line – he'd say robbers don't dress like Bill Sykes! And drug smugglers don't wear Raybans. Real drug smugglers look like normal businessmen . . .'

Some lyrics were more obscure. You'd have no idea where the idea for 'Dennis And Lois' came from by listening to the words. It starts with 'We all learnt to box at the midget club' and gets less normal from there. Anyone? 'It's based on two real-life characters, this couple from Bensonhurst,' says Nathan. 'They are toy collectors, and big music fans. They'd go to see all these British bands' gigs in New York and make friends with them. They'd take you round to their flat and they had the complete collection – the flat was decorated in toy wallpaper, and the cutlery was toy cutlery and the furniture's all toy furniture. They're both about twenty-five stone each, they're huge . . . really lovely too. Every British band from that era knows Dennis and Lois, and that song's about them.'

While Shaun worked on his lyrics, Oakenfold and Osborne made sure the studio atmosphere was absolutely spot on, creating a relaxed but focused working environment. 'There was absolutely no pressure there whatsoever,' says Shaun. 'Everything we did seemed to sound right – we could just go in there and in five minutes we'd have this tune going. Within fifteen minutes I'd have the lyrics to it. Oakey could listen to a tune and know what was happening about it, and where it was going, if it was good. He was like the guru. Him and Steve were a great partnership. They could fit it together.'

Away from the studio, there was plenty of time to indulge in all manner of extra-curricular pursuits. The first night out clubbing was particularly memorable – Bez got chatted up by Julia Roberts. 'He didn't know who she was,' says Paul. 'She wanted to hang out with him but he blanked her! It was hilarious.' The movie star even offered to get her driving licence from her car to prove who she was, but by this time Bez was chatting away to her minder instead. Next time maybe.

'We were loving the music, and because things were going well it gave us a lot of time to party, without having any pressure on,' says Shaun. 'If things were going bad and we weren't getting anything done, and the music wasn't working out right, it would have been a totally different vibe, but everything was really going to plan. We were all taking E, we were constantly out partying.' Bez found time to indulge in his Toad-like approach to motoring, which included a stint driving down an LA freeway the wrong way. 'Bez loves driving,' says Nathan. 'The problem is he has an accident every five minutes! Bez and cars, anything motorised, it's an uncontrolled car crash, not waiting to happen, actually happening!' The rental cars only lasted a short while, though. 'They got took off us 'cos in the first week Bez had driven his car into about eleven different Americans,' says Shaun. 'Not into their cars – into them! Because they annoyed him.'

Bez wasn't technically a musician, but he had his uses in the studio. 'He was a very important part of the Happy Mondays,' says Paul. 'A lot of people may disagree, but to me he was a special part of the band. He brought something that was integral to that band – the vibe. The secret to the Mondays was the vibe. They were very loose in sound, and Bez was the vibe man. A lot of the time Shaun wouldn't be there – he sleeps all day and comes in at night. The others were all coked up, arguing and fighting, and Bez would lighten it up, because he's a smoker. The keyboard player would be arguing with the guitarist, who'd be taking his time trying to get the part right, and Bez would lighten the vibe.'

Following the LA sessions, Paul returned to the UK and played his first big outdoor gig – the main stage at the Glastonbury Festival. The Mondays were also on the bill, and churned out forty minutes of funk, with 'Wrote For Luck' and 'Step On' as crowd highlights. Alfonso Buller was on hand to holler 'Manchester vibes in the area!' before Paul went on, as he has at pretty much every Glastonbury ever since. 'I was really worried at Glastonbury,' says Paul. 'I was on between Peter Gabriel and Van Morrison – a really weird placement. The whole Happy Mondays and Stone Roses thing was going on; I think they thought we'll put him on anywhere, and it would work. It didn't work for me – the genre of the crowd those two acts brought, their musical taste, it was always going to be difficult to throw me into the middle of them. There weren't any dance tents at Glastonbury then. I played the kind of music I played at Future – the Cure, Happy Mondays, Stone Roses. I wasn't mixing so much, just fading in and out, more a vibe thing than a mix. The set-up was better than I thought it would be; it was a new thing for them. It wasn't that bad, but the records jumped. The crowd were a lot more open than I thought; if I dropped in the Rolling Stones, I'd get a bit of a cheer. Slowly I won 'em over . . . I dropped in Bob Marley, and people without realizing it were getting into it, listening and singing. I thought it was weird because I was used to Spectrum, where it was just full-on. I can remember ending up outside of Glastonbury; you hit the top field where all the travellers were. It was lawless. One of the tents had a sound system generated by five or six people on bikes, pedalling . . . we all had a go.'

A couple of months later, Paul was asked to DJ at what would become one of the most legendary gigs of the era – the Stone Roses at Spike Island. 'Being involved with Happy Mondays, I suppose I was an obvious choice for them,' says Paul. 'For me the Roses were always the proper band; as musicians they were always great. I wasn't DJing on stage; it was up in a tower. I remember walking for miles with my records! It was an island in the middle of nowhere; you parked miles away and just had to walk and walk and walk. It just felt like another gig at the time – there'd be a rave on every week-end, it just seemed like part and parcel of what was going on. I also played with the Roses at Alexandra Palace around the same time.'

*Pills 'N' Thrills* entered the charts straight in at number one, with a pre-sale of nearly a hundred and fifty thousand copies. The record was *NME*'s album of the year in 1990. Oakenfold and Osborne received a 'Best Producer' award at the 1990 *Q* magazine awards and a nomination at the 1991 Brit Awards, a remarkable achievement given that this was Paul and Steve's first band production. The band's live shows were steadily becoming more like a mass rave experience. The Wembley Arena show in January 1991, a three-day Brits tie-in that also featured James, 808 State, the Cure and Ozzy Osbourne (not on the same night, mind . . .), was particularly celebratory. 'Gary Clail was doing his shit on this old front-of-house desk, in the middle of Wembley Arena auditorium,' remembers Nathan. 'He was mashing it up on the sound system! Fantastic! Paul was DJing, the band were great. I remember just before the house lights came down. The venue was absolutely fucking packed to the gills, and they had this policy where they would only let about four thousand people in the standing area – the rest had to be seated, you couldn't go down into the pit. As the house lights went down, hundreds of kids went straight over the barriers. Security could do nothing – the place just erupted. I remember just watching Wembley Arena throb. Ten thousand is a lot of people at a gig . . . the whole place was bouncing. It was an amazing experience, seeing the Manchester crowd go to London.'

The band-plus-DJ set-up made a lasting impression on one young *Melody Maker* journalist. 'I was very much an indie kid, at the time,' says Ben Turner, 'but the Oakenfold remix of Happy Mondays' "W.F.L." had a real effect on me, it was a real entry point. It took me away from the Jesus and Mary Chain, bands that I loved, into this other area. The Wembley Arena gig was the first time I'd ever really seen live bands interact with a DJ. In the programme it had Happy Mondays, 808 State, Northside, then it said two hours of Paul Oakenfold. I remember looking at it and thinking "Where's this come from, how does that work?" I remember being on top of the roof, dancing to the records, seeing Paul Oakenfold being made into this star. It was the highlight of the whole gig. It actually interested me as much, if not more than watching the Mondays, who were the band that I'd come along to see. It was a big turning point. It was the first time I fell in love with the power of the DJ. Since then, I've had this obsession of trying to be in the booth and watch someone like him work. Every little detail intrigued me.'

For a brief moment, the Mondays were punching pop-culture weight in a league not seen since the Sex Pistols. It's no surprise who suddenly made a guest appearance, stage right. 'After *Pills 'N' Thrills*, I get a phone call out of the blue from Malcolm McLaren,' says Nathan. 'For me it was like getting a call from God – "Hello Nathan, it's God here!" Malcolm, who loves his history of London, was making a TV programme about the history of Oxford Street, with him telling tales from one end of the street to the other, illustrating these stories through music. He wanted the Mondays in it.'

The west end of Oxford Street, where Marble Arch now stands, has a rather grisly past. It's the former site of the Tyburn gallows, where public executions used to take place. The unlucky would be taken from Newburgh Prison in a horse and cart. At the east end of Oxford Street, where Centre Point now stands, there used to be a pub; they'd stop and give the condemned one last tankard of ale, before making the final journey down Oxford Street to the gallows. Malcolm, in his infinite wisdom, decided the Mondays were perfectly suited for the role of the convicts. And the music to accompany this last waltz? It's got to be a Happy Mondays version of the Bee Gees' 'Staying Alive'!

'And so, we think "great opportunity!" ' says Nathan. 'Shaun and Paul Ryder are absolutely massive fans of the Bee Gees, and if you know the lyrics to "Staying Alive", you can see that they're perfect lyrics for Shaun Ryder. We thought "fantastic, we'll probably even get a hit record out of it". So off they went to Real World Studios, Peter Gabriel's studio near Bath. Also down there at the time, making his album, was Seal, who they used to refer to as Otter!'

The band made the necessary disco shapes for four or five days, before encountering a major problem. Mark Day, the guitarist, couldn't get his head round the main riff. 'He's got great feel,' says Nathan, 'but he just couldn't do it. On and on and on it went, for days. Everyone was getting so frustrated. He just couldn't get the phrase at all. So it got a little bit stuck. Finally, he seemed to nail it. Then we went down to Eden Studios in Chiswick, where we mixed a lot of the stuff, to do the mix with Paul and Steve.'

At which point, Shaun decided to lose it. 'I was back in Manchester,' says Nathan, 'when I got this desperate phone call from Paul Oakenfold, saying, "You've got to get down here, straight away. I mean, now. Shaun is fucking freaking us out." I said, "What do you mean?" And he goes, "He's been sat in the studio, in the control room with us, for the last two days. He's got a ski mask on, and he won't take it off!" I said, "Just tell him to take it off!" He said, "He won't, and it's scaring us to death, we can't fucking work, we need you to get down here." '

Nathan jumped in his Merc and bombed down the motorway. 'Sure enough, there's Shaun, sat there on the couch behind Oakey and Steve, who are trying to work, he's got this fucking black ski mask on, looks like a fucking armed robber, swigging a bottle of beer. And I said, "Shaun, can I have a word, I need to talk to you." And he went, "All right mate, what's up?" And I went, "Shaun, you're freaking the fuck out of everybody! What's going on?" "What do you mean?" he says. "It's the ski mask, Shaun, why are you wearing the ski mask?" He goes, "Well, I've got to keep it on, Nath, if I take it off, me head's gonna fall apart! It's keeping my head together!"

'I was like, holy fuck. The boy's really gone out there. We finished the record, and it wasn't a great track – we hadn't nailed the feel of it at all. Shaun was obviously in such a weird space, and McLaren was absolutely, bitterly disappointed. He calls me up and just goes, "What on earth has happened? They're such an amazing band, a great song, how could you fuck it up?" And I was like, "I'm sorry Malcolm, we tried our best." We still went ahead and participated on the TV show, but I think that that experience really embedded itself very deeply for Paul and Steve. I think it really brought home to them how difficult it was going to be in the future. In tandem with this, Shaun had got very deeply into his use of heroin. You've got a guy sat in a ski mask chasing the dragon right behind you when you're trying to work . . . it's not good. I think that really wobbled them. Everything that we'd done up to then – the remixes, the single, "Step On", the album – had worked fantastically well. But of course Shaun hadn't been so deeply into heroin at those points either.'

'It was a nightmare,' says Paul, 'an absolute nightmare. They were all in a bad head space, stealing was going on; there were bad people in the area. It was just a really bad, bad time. They were arguing, there wasn't the vibe. As much as I like them, know they are good guys and still hang out with them from time to time, I knew the magic was gone.'

A year or so later, the band were putting demos together for their fourth album, and called on Paul and Steve to work on it, but following the ski-mask sessions, doubts had understandably set in. 'I'll always help them,' says Paul. 'I've worked with them since, but I felt I'd had the best times out of it.'

'I had ill feelings about it,' says Nathan. 'Paul and Steve's manager had got them a record label deal for Perfecto, an artist deal as well for some project they put together, a publishing deal . . . they became very cash-rich. Not to say they didn't deserve it, but they became cash-rich off advances, from the work they did on the Mondays album – that was the record that had made them and defined them. When I spoke to them, they said they couldn't start on this for another six months, because we're busy doing some other project for BMG, they had all these commitments. I thought well fuck that, you're only getting all this work because of *Pills 'N' Thrills And Bellyaches* – we're your band, you're our producers. I had a sense of resentment, I felt let down.'

Paul's reservations weren't purely due to work commitments, however. 'I remember Nathan ringing me up and saying, "You're making the biggest mistake of your career, they're going to be as big as Pink Floyd," ' says Paul. 'I said, "Not with the state of those demos they're not." They needed songs. You don't have any songs, and then they want you to fly all the way to the middle of nowhere, and then be in a studio and try to find a song? It's a very dangerous thing to do. We get these demos with nothing on them, a few beats, a couple of words here, and I'm like, "We can't go." It's the producer's responsibility. I said to Steve, "We can't do this, there's just no way." And believe me, we wanted to do it. We'd just come off a massive album – of course we wanted to do it! But there was nothing there. I said to Nathan, "Listen – I don't know if it was the pressure of Tony Wilson, but my advice is, don't go in the studio yet. Go and write a bunch of good demos. When we get the good songs, we'll go to the bloody moon and record it!" Then we knew we had them. They didn't have anything good to record.'

What followed was a disastrous session in Barbados, presided over by Tina Weymouth and Chris Franz of Talking Heads, who managed to scrape together a lightweight follow-up to the mighty *Pills 'N' Thrills*. Not that it was entirely their fault. 'It's not to say that if we'd gone to Barbados with Paul and Steve to make the album none of the things that went on would have happened,' says Nathan. 'They probably would have happened anyway.'

The idea of using Barbados as the location was to ensure the band's supply of heroin would be cut off. What the management and label hadn't bargained for was that Barbados was awash with crack. Oh dear. The album, aptly titled *Yes Please!*, was a nightmare to record: the infighting was spiralling out of control, Bez broke his arm twice, various vehicles were totalled, the band even nicked the studio's sofa to pay for crack. These weren't run-of-the-mill sessions for co-producer Tina Weymouth. 'We have met and worked with all kinds of freaks and weirdos,' she says. 'But always, when it came down to it, they turned out to be pretty normal people underneath. But when we met and worked with the Mondays, I realised that they were different. They were for real. They lived it every day. I never knew that people like that existed.'

By this point, an air of uncertainty, of implied threat, seemed to seep along the streets of Manchester. The Hacienda's glory days were coming to a slow, messy standstill. Gang violence had escalated in the city throughout the early nineties, following a series of incidents between rival gangs that began after police closed the Gallery nightclub in 1989, a popular haunt for the Cheetham Hill gang.

The Hacienda temporarily shut its doors in February 1991, after door staff were threatened with firearms. Tony Wilson issued a statement that said 'We are forced into taking this drastic action in order to protect our employees, our members, and all our clients. We are simply sick and tired of dealing with instances of personal violence.' The club reopened in May, complete with new airport-style security equipment on the door, but it was pretty much downhill from there. In June 1991, six bouncers were stabbed by a gang from Salford, who'd managed to bypass the metal detector. In May 1992 guest DJ David Morales got hit on the head by a flying bottle from the dancefloor. In June 1992 a group of Salford lads were refused entry to Justin Robertson's club night Most Excellent, only to return later in a stolen car, in which they proceeded to ram the club entrance. Goodbye, second Summer of Love.

'Factory hit its financial problems,' says Nathan McGough. 'It opened its new offices – it had a bridging loan with a German bank, interest rates were through the roof, they had gang problems in the Hacienda. The Mondays album became hugely expensive, costing about three hundred thousand quid. New Order weren't delivering the follow-up to their *Technique* album. There was no income coming in to the label, and the money Factory had made being cash-rich, with *Technique* and *Pills 'N' Thrills*, they'd spent signing other bands and stuff. They signed one for a hundred-thousand-pound advance, who didn't sell any records.' They also managed to spend thirty grand on a ludicrous designer office desk, which hung from a number of pieces of what looked like fishing wire from the ceiling of the new office. When I visited Phil Saxe a few weeks after it had been installed, the table was already an office joke, swinging gently, listing rather dangerously after having either been sat on by Bez on the day it was installed, or from being used as a makeshift bed for a late-night rendezvous between Shaun and a female journalist, depending on who you believe. I somehow doubt Tony Wilson's more colourful recollection – it would have been pretty gymnastic and highly uncomfortable – but full marks for invention, eh?

With all the designer desks, offices, unrecouped bands and undelivered albums, Factory were in deep financial trouble. London Records stepped in with an offer to buy the label for four million pounds, until London's Roger Ames found out that Factory didn't own any of the artists' back catalogue, even New Order's. Ames promptly withdrew the deal and signed New Order directly instead. According to Nathan McGough, this is what happened next. 'People were owed money,' he says. 'The Mondays were owed money from royalties – maybe twenty-five grand or so. Oakey and Osborne were owed royalty money. I'm assuming that they must have had some cheques coming through, because this is a while after. But Factory were having these problems. Tony Wilson's got a bee in his bonnet about Oakenfold and Osborne, because he says that every one of their creditors understood the situation, put up with it and gave them the time to sort their issues out. Oakenfold and Steve Osborne were the ones that petitioned the wind-up order on the company. I can understand Paul and Steve's frustration – they'd done good work, they've earned their money, they should get paid. But basically, that wind-up order, I don't know if that's the one that killed Factory or not, but if it is, then Oakey's the one that killed Factory. It's like killing the beast that laid the golden egg.'

Paul's recollection of the situation is understandably a little different. 'Listen, Tony Wilson earned around five hundred thousand out of that record,' he says. 'As far as I'm concerned, me and Steve did a good job – we should get paid. Tony Wilson's driving around in a fucking Gucci suit, in some Aston

Martin sports car ... it was all right for him. We were struggling – I needed the money like everyone else. We should have got paid! I don't make those decisions – the management advise you. Then the management and the lawyers say "We've spent six months waiting to get paid, the only way they'll pay us is to put in a wind-up order." Forget the romance, this is the reality – we've got to live. It was only twenty grand each me and Steve were owed. Do you think that because of twenty grand, we brought the label down? Come on! He spent thirty fucking grand on a table!'

Justin Robertson, who to this day is still owed money from Factory for a Happy Mondays mix, puts it like this: 'Everything that Factory did was more by accident than design. Everything was complete chaos. They had this ridiculous office – it was a monument to folly. If it hadn't been Paul asking for the money it would have been someone else.'

After the euphoria, the comedown. It was a messy end to a glorious, productive partnership, but it certainly wasn't the first great musical team to start out with a hit record and finish in a lawyer's office. What we're left with is the music.

'For me Happy Mondays were the first group from a guitar background that the new youth could relate to,' says Paul. 'They acted like any bunch of normal lads, rather than some stuck-up pop stars, which was exactly what house music was trying to stamp out at the time. "W.F.L.", then "Step On" and *Pills 'N' Thrills*, created a new form of music – it kick-started the whole indie-dance scene. Between us we created something fresh, something new. Something magical happened.'

# 9

# Even Better Than the Real Thing

'Oakenfold was the man who took U2 on to the dance floor. Sure we had been remixed before by other DJs, but until Paul did his mix of "Real Thing", nothing we had released had made any major impact in the clubs. He's a real pioneer, one of the originators of what we now know as the UK dance scene. Before Underworld, before Fatboy Slim, before Prodigy, Paul was working away in his brilliantly effective but understated way. Always curious about new ideas, never precious or elitist about his own. Like most originals his payoff is from simply doing what he loves to do.'

The Edge, U2

Following the success of *Pills 'N' Thrills And Bellyaches*, Paul and Steve were inundated with offers of remix and production work. The spacious, atmospheric feel that was first heard on the duo's remix of 'W.F.L.' graced many an Oakenfold/Osborne tune, from Massive Attack's majestic 'Unfinished Sympathy' to the lysergic Euro bounce of the Shamen's 'Move Any

Mountain', from New Order to the Cure to Arrested Development. The team were getting offered three to five remixes a week; it got to a stage where the pair were turning down more tracks than they were completing. This may seem perverse – why turn down work, particularly such lucrative work? – but the tactic has served Paul well. The average life cycle for a hot remix team is a few years at most; Paul Oakenfold has managed to retain pulling power as a name remixer for nearly two decades. His most recent remixes have included cuts for Madonna and Justin Timberlake. 'You have focus on doing them for the right reasons,' says Paul. 'I could have earned a lot more money if I'd done all those remixes. We could have made a fortune by just banging them out every other day. A lot of remixers would work with anyone, just to get the money. Some had three studios going at once; it really opened my eyes. But we didn't – we were really, really choosy.'

Paul and Steve began trading under a new remix team name – Perfecto. The name, incorporating Paul's initials, was also the title of his newly minted record company. The first Perfecto release, the Balearic classic 'Stories' by Izit, was released via London Records, but a new, improved licensing deal was soon struck with RCA, brokered by Paul's manager Brian Reza. Paul and Brian found office space in Chagford Street, in London's West End. 'I started a label because I felt there were no real dance labels out there that knew what they were doing,' says Paul. 'At the time there weren't many dance labels anyway. I had an idea that I could nurture new talent; that's what I really wanted to do. It was a great opportunity to sign and work with new artists, and to have my destiny in my own hands.'

The first Perfecto release via the new RCA deal was 1990's 'The Gonzo' by Lost, aka DJ Steve Bicknell, which also doubled up as the name of Steve's long-running and highly respected techno night. ''The Lost tune was a big underground record,' says Paul. Other early releases came from Jimi Polo, whose modern R&B sound met with limited success, and from Paul's old sound system installer and one-time mechanic, Carl Cox, who fared a lot better.

Carl had been given his chance to shine at Paul's Spectrum all-dayers at Heaven, but it was in the slightly later days of the larger-scale outdoor party scene that Carl really made his mark. 'People could see the potential from what I'd done with Paul,' says Carl. 'It was Sunrise who came forward for me. They asked me if I could sell tickets for them around Brighton, in the south coast region; that was my in, how I became associated with them. I sold a bunch of tickets, we'd put on buses that I'd drive to Sunrise, and I'd DJ. They put me on early, but even then people were just jumping, going mental. Every time I'd play, the crowd got into it, so I went up a few hours. Eventually I was playing at the end.'

The Midsummer Night's Dream event in Oxford was the one where Carl made the transition from warm-up DJ to top of the bill, king of the rave. 'I got on and played like a demon,' he says. 'All the promoters were there, and everyone was like "Who's the DJ?" My girlfriend at the time, Maxine Bradshaw, had these business cards with her and gave them all out. From then on it exploded. After that, Paul took notice! He was like "What's going on? He used to work for me!" Paul could see I was creating something fresh and new with the rave scene, so asked me into the office to talk about making a couple of records for Perfecto.'

'I said to Carl, "You're a rave DJ, you've got to focus on making rave records,"' says Paul. 'He didn't really know his direction. It was no good making something that didn't appeal to his audience. He focused, and he had a hit. We did really well with him.'

Carl had been playing a record called 'Roll It Up' by Success-N-Effect, a prototype for later drum and bass tunes, due to its use of the Winstons' 'Amen, Brother' breakbeat, known as 'the Amen break', which had first turned up on 1986's *Ultimate Breaks And Beats* bootleg album. Carl would mix this over another track called 'Daybreak' as his party piece. 'It rocked,' says Carl. 'When I had the meeting with Paul I gave him the conceptual idea of recording these tracks together, and he said "What about if I put you with a producer, and you do it?" I thought this was a great opportunity, so I went in with this guy called Martin Lascelles, who Paul found, and gave him the samples. The track became "I Want You (Forever)". That was day one in the studio! Paul was like, "If you tweak that a bit here, that a bit there . . ." On day two we did the tweaks, put a bit of piano on it, got the mix done; Paul comes back in and says "That's the one." It went out on Perfecto, and it hit all the charts. It was number one on the dance chart and went into the national chart at thirty-two. After two days! I wish I could make a record like that every week!'

The track started going off in Europe, then the call came in from *Top of the Pops*. This was slightly alarming for Carl. 'The whole record's samples – what am I going to do?' he thought. 'Paul said "Don't worry, it's fine, *Top of the Pops* wants everything to be live." I said "What, sing? You're joking!" So we had to find a black vocalist, in a week, to sing the line "I want you forever", and what I'd do was get behind the turntables, pretend I was doing all this stuff. We went to Pineapple Studios to rehearse, got a couple of dancers in doing their thing, got the singer in, started to build it up. Then we went to *Top of the Pops*, and on the day, one of the cameramen got a bit too close and whacked one of the dancers on her arm. The vocalist that I had, Beverley, had the flu, so we had to find someone else on the day – we did the rehearsals, and she just about managed to pull it off. The dancers were just fine, I did my thing, and the track went from thirty-two to twenty-one in the charts. It was the first time any DJ making a record got into the national charts, so that was another first for Paul and Perfecto, and great for me in terms of exposure. It was all timing – I was top of my field in the rave scene, we had maximum exposure on Radio One, the record came out and it was a hit. I was shocked. You need someone like Paul to drive you into the sense of belief that you can actually do it. That's what Paul did for me.' Carl went on to produce two more chart hits for Perfecto, before releasing his best-selling *F.A.C.T.* mix compilation in 1995, setting up the Ultimatum and Intec labels, and continues to spin around the world, another fine South London export turned global dance ambassador. There must have been something in the water round there.

Gary Clail, a former roofer and On-U sound system MC, was the other early Perfecto success, scoring a string of UK chart hits. 'Human Nature' reached number 10 in 1990, despite having its Billy Graham sample removed after a threat of legal action. It was a joy to see this most unlikely frontman bellowing his way through the track on *Top of the Pops*, but less fun was had behind the scenes. 'We were doing everything for him,' says Paul, 'he had mixes, he had Adrian Sherwood working with him, but he used to piss everyone off. He was just rude; he was always upsetting people. He had a fight with someone from the record company in Australia. You just don't want to end up working with someone like that.'

The RCA deal was to be short-lived. 'I think what happens with major labels is that they only want chart success,' says Paul. 'They are not really geared up for underground records. We did have chart success; Gary Clail did well, we had a big hit with Robert Owens' "I'll Be Your Friend". They'd let you get on with it, but a year later, when they looked at the books and saw that it wasn't really doing it, popwise, they changed their mind. Korda Marshall [RCA's A&R man] was great to work with, though. We got offered a better deal with Warner Brothers, and we went with that.'

The deal, through Warners' new subsidiary East West, included an office – Perfecto moved into the Warner building on Kensington High Street, which made it easier to keep an eye on things. 'We found that being an independent, you get to use the major label's marketing and sales team, but you're not completely part of the team. It was much easier being in the office – you'd walk up a floor if you wanted to speak to someone, which was easier than trying to track them down on the phone.'

For their next album project, Paul and Steve decided to work on Deacon Blue's fourth album, *Whatever You Say, Say Nothing*. This unlikely match led to a major sonic departure from the band's previous, bestselling work. The record was intended to invigorate the band's creativity with a fresh approach; unfortunately it didn't quite work out that way. 'We'd just finished the Mondays and we were approached by Sony to produce Deacon Blue,' says Paul. 'They were an out-and-out pop band, real cheese in some respects. I didn't want to do it, but their A&R man convinced me. He said "Look, just sit down with the band because they really want to change, to come up with more of an interesting sound." They were a really big pop band, they were selling gold, platinum albums, and I thought this could be a great thing to do, because it's not the obvious thing to do. We could completely change their sound. People would be able to see our production qualities, because we'd taken a pop band and made them more edgy. We got together with the band, and they were all like, "Yeah, yeah, let's do it." Great. So we get into the studio, and they'd just had their biggest-selling single, and they fucking changed their mind! I think it was the girl in the band who was going out with the lead singer, it was one of those clichés where she had his ear, and what she wanted was what went on. So we started off and suddenly, the first track we'd done it was like, this is great, we now need to go more edgy . . . they're all getting nervous, and I'm saying trust me, this is where we're going. Now, it's their record, we're just the producers. By the end of it I lost interest. It was becoming more and more pop. Obviously it had all of our sounds in terms of production, so the mix was a lot harder than the band were used to, but it was nowhere near where I wanted it to be. With the Mondays it was cool, they trusted us to get on with it and let us do our job, but I was running into all these battles with the band. In the end you just think, fuck it, they just ain't listening.'

Despite their initial enthusiasm, the band didn't really want to make any huge creative leaps or freshen up their sound. 'After a time, you get really familiar with the way that everything's played, and you get used to doing things in a certain way,' said Deacon Blue's Graeme Kelling. 'We worked with Paul and Steve on our last album to break that up. But in retrospect, we were trying to force ourselves into another jacket – a terrible-looking spangly one – and didn't realise that what we had was actually quite special.'

The new direction managed to alienate a large proportion of Deacon Blue's fan base. The band split a year later. It wasn't a particularly great experience for Paul, either. 'I was like, fuck this,' he says. 'I got really disenchanted producing other people's records and I was thinking I don't want to do this, unless it's something that is really worth doing. It's months out of your life. Three months in the studio with a band every day, six days a week does my head in. We got offered a few things, and turned them down. Poor old Steve – it would have killed him. He'd work for months on a project; some of which would just be shelved. I said to Steve, "Look, we can't do this." This was probably the beginning of when we started to move away from working with each other, because I ain't gonna spend six months of my life working on a record if I'm not into it. But it was Steve's only source of income, so he would go and do it.'

Remixing was an altogether more stimulating experience for Paul and Steve. Utilising the knowledge they'd gained from working with bands, the pair started to add live elements to their remixes, rather than work solely with electronics, like the majority of dance remixers. The track that really got a boost from this approach, probably the pair's most creative, influential mix so far, was Paul and Steve's reworking of U2's 'Even Better Than The Real Thing', the third single lifted from their *Achtung Baby* set. U2 had already commissioned one Perfecto remix, for 'Mysterious Ways', but the link between band and DJ was cemented when they met in U2's home town. 'I was playing in Dublin, and the band asked me to meet them in their studio,' says Paul. 'That's where our relationship started. I was really nervous!'

Managing director at U2's record company Island was Marc Marot, who would become Paul Oakenfold's manager a handful of years later. Marot had risen through the ranks at Island from its publishing arm, Blue Mountain, where he had impressed Island boss Chris Blackwell by signing dance hits like M/A/R/R/S's 'Pump Up The Volume', the Def Jam catalogue and Massive Attack. A natural lateral thinker, Marot created Island Visual Arts to exploit the label's celluloid copyrights, which included Traffic, Bob Marley at the Rainbow and Dame Kiri Te Kanawa's first performance at the Royal Albert Hall. A huge U2 fan, Marot pushed for the publication of a U2 songbook while at Blue Mountain, but was met with a stony response. 'Our sheet music printer told me to fuck off,' he says, 'and this was at the time of *Unforgettable Fire*! I felt there were enough U2 fans out there to warrant it, so I wrote out all the songs for the first three albums – all the guitar tabs, all the lyrics. The only way I could get the thing right was to go on the tour bus, with the Edge, with my guitar and my pathetic attempt at the chords and lyrics, and have the band take the piss out of me mercilessly for ten days! They'd call out "Come and have a look at this one!" That was my first real long-term stint with U2. It's those kind of things that builds trust between people – they took the piss out of me mercilessly, and I survived it.'

Trial by fire over, Marot ignored advice and published the songbook. 'We commissioned Anton Corbijn to take the photos, Rob O'Connor to do the design, and bought the print in China,' he says. 'Even though we were music publishers, we did something that music publishers never do, that is physically publish a book ourselves. After the first hundred thousand sales, and about the tenth reorder, Music Sales, the company who had previously told us to fuck off, came back saying "I think we've made a bit of a mistake here . . ." It was a fantastic moment.' Island chief Chris Blackwell took note, and started grooming Marot for the label's managing director job from the tender age of twenty-six, at least a decade younger than your average record company boss. When Marc Marot was twenty-nine, Chris Blackwell decided to sell Island to Polygram. Marot was the new MD, the youngest in the business.

The next U2 album was to be Marc's first big project, during a time when the band was in flux. '*Rattle And Hum* was one of their biggest albums; it was an eleven-million-selling monster, but it was poorly received by the critics,' says Marc. 'Personally I think they were wrong, but it was the first record where U2 took a critical kicking. The critics felt that music had moved on, and U2 hadn't – they'd rested on their laurels and followed a formula, following *The Joshua Tree*.'

U2 were in search of fresh stimulus. They wanted their new record to be 'forward-looking and forward-thinking and a complete about-turn', Adam Clayton reveals. 'We didn't really have any idea how we were going to achieve that. It was the beginning of the Manchester baggy scene in the UK, Stone Roses, Primal Scream and Happy Mondays, and it was confusing for us to figure out how to fit in. Those groups had a retro thing going on, which we were trying to stay away from, but they also had looped percussion and rhythm tracks and everything was becoming loose as people were getting turned on to ecstasy. We didn't understand that culture.'

'Dance music made us jealous,' says the Edge. 'It's wonderful to be in a rock and roll band, but it is limiting in so many ways. There are so many more possibilities with dance music as a form. That and the rhythm. It's also hard for a rock and roll band to match just the sheer excitement of being in a club and hearing really good dance music.' Dancefloor excitement? Looped, loose rhythms? Surely, after the success of *Pills 'N' Thrills And Bellyaches*, there's only one production team to turn to . . .

From the outside, it looked like the band purposely sought to dismantle the giant they'd created and rebrand their image, but Marc Marot insists it was a natural progression. 'The band never had a strategy meeting where they said "We're going to reinvent ourselves"; they simply felt it and did it,' he says. 'I don't think it was strategic or invented. They were working in Hansa Studios in Berlin, right by the wall, and this is what came out of it – something completely new. There was a really exciting movement going on in Berlin, and they were there right in the thick of it, literally as the wall came down. It informed and infected the record. When they came to me, their whole ethos was "Let's tear up the rule book and do something new", and that's where Oakey came into it.'

The label has a long, distinguished history when it comes to releasing world-class, rhythmic-based music, from foot-stompin' mid-sixties R&B releases to Bob Marley to Grace Jones. Island A&R chief Nick Angel had very broad taste, and 4th and Broadway, the label's dance offshoot run by Julian Palmer, was in rude health. The band had a solid, creative sounding board at the label. Chopping down the Joshua Tree would have petrified more traditional record companies; this was the label's biggest earner, and they were messing with the formula. Marc Marot's appointment certainly helped things along. 'In many ways my lack of cynicism and my naivety helped,' he says. 'I was of a "can do" mentality rather than a "can't do" mentality – because I didn't know what you couldn't do. So when U2 said they wanted to change, I thought it was the best thing in the world, whereas nearly everybody else in the record company was going "Oh my god, what are we going to do?"'

Island A&R Nick Angel was the first to suggest some reworkings for clubland. The supposedly po-faced, deeply serious *Rattle And Hum* U2 certainly weren't the most obvious candidates for the after-dark frivolities of the nightclub. The Pet Shop Boys' arch Euro-disco cover of U2's 'Where The Streets Have No Name' is a case in point – the camp humour embedded in the groove stems from the juxtaposition of the overblown weight of the original with the surface depth of Hi-NRG. Could the band handle the leap towards the dancefloor on one of their own releases?

'It was Nick that said "If we are going to do something different, let's really be radical,"' says Marc Marot. 'You look back on it now, and might think it's not such a radical idea to get Paul Oakenfold to do a mix, at the time It was – at the time U2 had never let anybody touch their stuff, unless it was under their direct supervision.'

The band weren't averse to the idea of dance culture; they'd even considered using dance production much earlier in their career. 'Before Paul Oakenfold, we actually worked with François Kevorkian in 1982 in New York,' says the Edge. 'We did three mixes with him around the time of "Sunday Bloody Sunday". I hung out with him in New York and he turned me on to some fantastic stuff. That was the first taste we had of the dance side of things. We also realised it wasn't like everyone had been saying, that disco was the enemy.'

'Working with François was the start of using name re-mixers,' says Adam Clayton. 'Around that time in the underground there was a lot of dub remixing going on, with the Clash and that kind of thing. It came from that – it seemed for us to be a logical thing to do. It was something we were interested in. François was a pretty maverick character. They were good remixes.'

Bono's love affair with dance started a little later. 'It was about the mid-eighties before I got all funky and into dance stuff,' he says. 'We didn't get rhythm until we went on the road with B.B. King. While everyone was doing drugs during the Summer of Love in London, we were in Memphis hanging out with the Muscle Shoals brass section and getting into rhythm that way. I guess it came together for us with *Achtung Baby*.'

Marc Marot and Nick Angel had been stoking the band's interest by continually sending them new music. Adam Clayton, in particular, received regular packages. 'Anything fresh and new that came along, we sent to Adam,' says Marc. 'Whoever was coming up – Pulp, or Oasis in their formative moments, anything that we thought was fresh and hot at the time, just to keep him informed.'

Nick Angel played Marc some of Paul and Steve's remixes, and they decided to take a chance on an Oakenfold/Osborne mix for U2. 'We thought Paul's work was strong enough to say "let's do it" – if the band didn't like it, we'd swallow the cost. So we commissioned Paul, but said if the band didn't like what Paul did, the record company would pay for it and we'd never trouble them again.'

If the album was the culmination of a new creative approach, it was Paul and Steve's mix of 'Even Better Than The Real Thing' that would really propel the band towards the discothèque. Steve Osborne recalls the band's enthusiasm. 'They were really interested with what was going on,' he says. 'They just got to a place where they wanted to experiment more with sounds and get out of the straight rock and roll thing. The brief we got was that they wanted to get into the club charts – that was their only brief, we were allowed to do whatever we wanted. When we were doing remixes for bands, we always tried to keep as much of the elements of what the band were about in the remix. We'd try to use as much as possible of what was there.'

Paul's focus wasn't on the broader U2 picture; he was concentrating on the groove. 'First of all I didn't know they were trying to reinvent themselves,' he says. 'All I brought to the table was the dance side of things. U2 were never dance, they never went into the dance world; this was their first adventure and I was there doing it. All I was trying to do was make a record work for the dancefloor. I felt the way to approach it was to build it around the riff and change the rhythm. We wanted to bring out the emotion and soul that was already in there. I took a rough mix to a club before we finished it; the reaction was really strong. We went back into the studio and changed a couple of things, then handed it in.'

'The first thing that happened was Paul delivered the mix to Nick,' says Marc Marot. 'Nick heard it once, then he and Julian Palmer burst into my office, kicked the door in and said "You have got to hear this." They put it on and I just laughed with pleasure, all the way through listening to it . . . I thought it was absolutely fucking awesome.'

'When everyone heard it, we thought "This is really it,"' says Adam Clayton. 'That was one of the most successful partnerships we ever had. It must be something to do with that song; it really suited what Paul was trying to do. There's a bit of Happy Mondays and Primal Scream coming through. Everyone loved the backing vocal.'

There were slight teething problems, however; the mix needed a few tweaks. 'The Edge rang me up and said "The guitars at the beginning aren't quite right,"' says Paul. 'I thought "it sounds all right to me!" But, of course, it's the Edge and he knows what he's talking about, so we went back in to have a look at it.' The Edge also asked for 'more Bono', according to Marc Marot. 'There wasn't much vocal; he thought if you put more of the lyric back in you'll have a bigger hit. And we did.'

The mix kept many original elements, but added female backing vocals, almost overpowering Bono with a viciously infectious hook. Surely that's a pretty bold move? 'My attitude was that they've employed me to do a remix that works on the dancefloor,' counters Paul. 'Bono is one of the very few rock vocalists who have soul. Bono's got soul, so his vocal sits really well on dance records – he can carry it. But what was really cheeky was putting female backing vocals on it. I thought it needed it, because it needed a lift on the choruses. I thought you know what, I'm going to get a vocalist in and I'm gonna try it; I'll run a pass with it and a pass without it and it's the band's call. And they loved it!'

The band certainly didn't mind Paul's tinkering. Their *Joshua Tree*-era image may have appeared a little solemn from the outside looking in, but within the band the spirit was markedly different. 'People had a preconception about U2,' says Adam Clayton. 'They saw us as some kind of stadium act that couldn't go there, but in fact that isn't really the way we see ourselves. We see ourselves much more as a kind of little rock and roll outfit practising in the garage. Dance was always something we were aware of and were interested in. We weren't that interested in rock being a macho thing; we're much more interested in it being a sensuous thing, so the dance side of rock – and *roll* – was always of interest to us. We were watching those movements and seeing how they did it. Sometimes the difficulty with dance music is that you sacrifice the song to some extent – there's always this tension, this conflict between what's just a good groove and what's a good chord sequence that tells the story of your song, but Paul managed it. It fitted in really well with the *Achtung Baby* project, which had definitely taken some influence from Manchester and what was happening in the clubs.'

The label were equally keen. 'So much so that I rang their manager Paul McGuinness and said "Paul, we've got a problem," ' recalls Marc Marot. ' "You know you said tear up the rule book . . . how about having two competing singles in the charts at the same time?" He said what tracks are you thinking of? I said the same track. Of course! Let's do "Even Better Than The Real Thing" versus "Even Better Than The Real Thing"!' It was a fairly ambitious scheme, even for a band with the stature and fan base of U2; eventually a compromise was reached, and the remix came out later than the original. What neither the band, label or remixers had planned was what happened next. The Perfecto mix charted higher than the original. For the UK public, Paul and Steve's mix really was even better than the real thing.

Although it may not have been Paul's main intention, the remix fitted comfortably into the band's reinvigorated persona. 'The reinvention had already happened with the album, but

Paul's mix accelerated and focused the reinvention,' says Marc Marot. 'We said that U2 can now be ironic, and it can be fun, which it never was before – it was deadly serious. Paul pulled it into really sharp focus, and helped U2 in a reinvention that has stood them in good stead right up until the present day.'

It was a natural step for U2 to ask Paul to bring the party to the live arena. 'It was the band's idea for Paul to tour with them,' says Marc. 'They make their own decisions, and they are very careful about who they have supporting them, and they became great admirers of Paul's work through the work he did for them. By Paul's remix of "Lemon", we'd got three or four mixes under our belt. The band completely trusted him.'

'What we liked about it was that we liked the idea of controlling the environment,' says Adam Clayton. 'When the audience comes into the arena, or the stadium, what a lot of people do is they have support bands, but they have just tapes playing in between. We loved the idea of having a DJ, who could perform a different sequence, depending on what the night required, depending on how the audience were reacting. We thought that made for a much more interesting experience, and it also put people in the right frame of mind for when our band came on.'

Paul became a regular touring support on the band's Zoo TV worldwide excursion. It took a little while to settle in – Paul and his DJ helper Colin Hudd still experienced the old roadie attitude from the crew for the first few dates, but with a word to the band that was swiftly sorted out – when the tour started rolling, Paul found his groove. His DJ set for these shows didn't heavily feature the trance anthems he's most known for; it was more like a massive version of Future, a real mix of rock and roll and all manner of party action. 'I did so much preparation for it,' he says. 'Every time we got into a new city, I'd go straight to the local record shop and find out what the biggest tunes were and have them ready to drop if I started losing the crowd. I had to keep them interested – they're a rock crowd. If they didn't like me they might start throwing things!'

The DJ got to get to know the band a little closer on tour. 'I found out just how creative, how open-minded they were,' he says. 'Me and Adam were always talking about new music; we'd end up in his room after the show, playing music, checking it out. I gave Edge a techno tape once; I put on it all these minimal techno records with all these really fucking weird noises and psychedelic stuff, I said "This is the real underground, check it out!" I think they liked the idea of being with someone who knew the underground scene.'

'U2 were totally organised; it was like a military operation,' says Gary Stonadge, who joined the tour as bass player for support act Big Audio Dynamite, Mick Jones's post-Clash outfit, and became friendly with the tour DJ. 'They had to be – they were the biggest band in the world, the whole focus was on them. They were great to Paul, and great to us; they looked after us really well. We were really disorganised, but Paul, on the other hand, was constantly working on tour. He'd be in his room with his decks, listening to tunes all the time, always working.'

DJing at this level was an entirely new climate for Paul. 'The shows were a big step up,' he says. 'I'd played Glastonbury and Spike Island, but I'd never experienced anything like it in my life. It was unbelievable. We were flying on a private plane, going through airport security through a special entrance . . . we'd have a motorcade on the tarmac, waiting to drive us. I was like a kid. Every night different stars would come to the show. We'd have parties with Jack Nicholson sitting over here, Johnny Depp sitting over there . . . Naomi Campbell was going out with Adam, so you had all the supermodels turning up to the shows. I DJed at Naomi Campbell's birthday party on the tour – I had Claudia Schiffer in the DJ booth, going through my record box!'

'I've worked with Paul since the days of Profile Records, since his association with Def Jam, through acid house, all these scenes, but there was nothing compared to this,' says Mickey Jackson, who started working as Paul's tour assistant at the Stockholm U2 gig on 30 July 1993. 'It was a tough tour, for nine weeks,' he says. 'It put Paul in a completely different league, and he stepped up to it. It was his turning point.'

For the football-loving DJ, playing at many of the world's finest stadiums was a massive buzz. 'Playing at Wembley Stadium was phenomenal,' he says. 'We played in a lot of stadiums, especially in Europe; I got to get into the dressing rooms and on the pitch at all these great stadiums. It was wonderful.'

The learning curve was steep but deep. 'How to build a set, how to work a crowd, the way he commands a room – Oakey learnt that from U2,' says his former agent David Levy. 'He was a real student of Bono, on the stage and of what went on backstage. He'd really work it backstage, socially. He learned consummate professionalism above everything else. No matter what is going on leading up to any particular moment, when Paul steps into the public eye, he'll switch. He learnt what it means to be professional, what it means to build a career.'

'The U2 tour was my first time working with a production that big, and it really opened my eyes about how to bring my music to a larger audience,' says Paul. 'It was amazing to see what a tight operation the tour was; everyone involved was extremely hard-working, totally on the ball. I thought this was how a large-scale musical event should be experienced.'

Paul also learned how to step into character, to be more than that DJ guy in the corner with his head down, nodding along to the tunes he's spinning. He's not a particularly imposing presence, physically – maybe five eight or nine – but once he hit that stage he soon learned how to make big shapes and command the space. He also learned staying power. 'I'd speak to the band and say "How can you go out there and play 'With Or Without You', night after night, and make it special?"' he says. 'I learned that you have to be in character, you have to try to give people the best night of their lives. Every night. You talk to any rock star, actor or pop star, they step into a role and play that person; I learned that from Bono – I thought I've got to do that, I've got to adapt to it in a professional way. Once you come off stage you can have a drink, relax and get back to who you are with your friends, but when I'm on stage I can play this person. You've got thousands of people looking at you, they are guided by your every move. When I'm tired, when I've just got off a plane to go to a gig, the people give me the energy to be who I am when I perform. You only capture that when you are in the moment. It's that split second where there are ten thousand people there, but you can also catch someone's eye and be one on one with someone. You are so there. If you can take that on board, you become so much better at what you do.'

To this day, Paul has a tremendous admiration for U2's frontman. 'In my opinion he's gone from being a great guy to just an overwhelming figure,' says Paul. 'They say that individuals can't change anything, and this guy has proven you can. At the time when I was hanging out with them, they were a rock and roll band, having fun with characters like the Fly and Mephisto, and having fun, as I saw it, with dance music. Then he found maybe his true path, what he's really meant to be put on this world for. When I last met him, I can't describe the warmth that I felt – I never felt so much warmth from any person I've ever met in my life. We embraced – you don't just go up and cuddle Bono, you know what I mean? – you felt so comfortable that you could, and he's so warm and strong and calm.'

U2's Adam Clayton recalls Paul's willingness to take on board his new surroundings, and learn from Bono and the band. 'Paul was focused,' says Adam. 'He really wanted to learn about America; he wanted to learn how to function in that bigger arena. It was exciting seeing someone who was quite clear-headed in recognising what they wanted to do, and how far they wanted to push what they were doing. There was an opportunity of being in these American cities, seeing what sort of an appetite there was in America for what he was doing, and how he could capitalise on it, I think he made the most of it. He was productive. He's got staying power – Paul Oakenfold delivers. He was good to have around.'

'Touring with U2 focused Paul's ambition, and it crystallised Paul's route to that ambition,' says Marc Marot. 'He spent a lot of time with five of the most hard-working people that I've ever met. I think that's partly what's informed Paul's work ethic, which is unbelievably strong. He talked with U2 extensively over that year about how they broke America. Their method was very simple. They went to America when nobody wanted them, they went back again when nobody wanted them, then they went back again ... then when a few people wanted them, they went back again. Then a few more people got into it ... until they broke. And that's what Paul did with dance music.'

# 10

# A Voyage into Trance

'Tales are filtering back of a scene in Goa, India, at the cross-roads of the drug trade routes, where the freaks get out of their heads in the jungle on cheap LSD and the brutalist electro of Skinny Puppy and Front 242. Something of this (dis)order must be created in this country, a tiny emblem in club culture and its tyranny of cool. Impossible? Who knows . . .'

Simon Reynolds, *Melody Maker*, July 1988

Ibiza wasn't the only outpost of the old sixties hippy trail to be undergoing a dance upheaval in the late eighties. Since the early sixties, when India decided to reclaim the Portuguese colony of Goa, the southern Indian state had been a haven for all manner of beatniks, outlaws, sun-worshippers and seekers of the mind, body and spirit. European and American travellers would marvel at the elaborate Christmas beach rituals, a blend of Hinduism and the after-effects of four hundred and fifty years of Portuguese Catholicism, ceremonies where the music played on, into the balmy night. The tolerant nature of the locals, the ability to live comfortably for comparatively little by Western standards, coupled with the widespread availability of charas, a good-quality hashish used in religious ceremonies that was still legal in Goa well into the seventies, made for an ideal breeding ground for boho colonisation. Legend tells of a late-sixties character named Acid Eric, who looked like a psychedelic Santa and would turn up at parties followed by beautiful women, eager to get their hands on his supply of the world's best mescaline. Equally legendary is Eight-Fingered Eddie, one of the original Goa freaks, who had a house on Colva beach, before moving on to Anjuna, centre of the later Goa scene. Eddie started to have informal parties on the beaches and in the jungle, ingesting acid and tripping out to psychedelic music before the Loft, before Spectrum and the Trip.

Spectrum and Land of Oz designer Dave Little saw the global psychedelic link first-hand when he first visited Goa at the beginning of the nineties. 'I just missed Paul Oakenfold going there, but I was hanging out with Alex Patterson and Youth,' he says. 'I reckon the whole Spectrum, E thing led to a hippy way of thinking. They went back on the old hippy trail, and that led organically to Goa.'

American DJ Goa Gil was the direct link from acid rock to acid house. Growing up in Marin County, he used to get the bus down to San Francisco's psychedelic mecca of Haight-Ashbury after school in the late sixties. He hung out with the Family Dogg, a boho collective who put on concerts at the Avalon Ballroom, complete with light shows, freak-out bands and posters that are the direct forerunners of Dave Little's Spectrum imagery. He worked briefly as 'equipment man' for the Hammond organ-led Sons of Champlin, who toured with Jefferson Airplane. Fed up with the speed freaks and rip-offs on the main street of the first Summer of Love, coupled with the double bummer of Nixon as president and Ronald Reagan as Californian governor, he headed to India, via Amsterdam. He was looking for Eight-Fingered Eddie, a path that eventually led him to Anjuna beach.

'We created a lifestyle that was the best of the East, and the best of the West,' says Gil. 'It was the best of the East, because we had the simple village life, close to nature ... we also assimilated the spiritual traditions of the East and lived this way. Best of the West because we had our art, our ideas and our music. And there, the two things synthesised with international input, because young people, or like-minded people, not necessarily young, from every country in the world, started coming there. It was all word of mouth. Everybody would gather there, and it just started to grow and grow, and more people came to know about it, and then it just got bigger and bigger over the years. The first parties were just with acoustic guitars, drums and flutes by a fire. And then some friends started to bring electric guitars and drum sets, even me, and we'd put them all together, and have jams on the beach every full moon, or Christmas and New Year.'

By the mid-seventies, Gil managed to get his hands on a batch of sound equipment that had been shipped to Goa, which he put together with a mixer he'd brought from America. He rented a PA and put it in a big space called the music house, which he lived in, turning it into a live venue. Every full moon they built a stage on the beach. DJs would play in between. This went on throughout the seventies; for Christmas 1977, the party went on from Christmas Eve until New Year's Day. There were tapes running all day long. 'One of the guys doing equipment for me was camped out at the stage, just changing tapes,' says Gil. 'We'd be swimming in the ocean, and dancing on the rocks out there, and then every night, a live music party. It was a pretty good scene.'

After a break at the beginning of the eighties, Gil returned for Christmas 1983. He'd been listening to emerging electronic sounds, 'all this electrobeat music which was the roots of techno and industrial. I started to get turned on to that. I saw the tribal and psychedelic qualities, and the futuristic qualities. I said "Man, this is it." We even started to play electronic dance music all night long, and have black lights and fluorescent paintings. That's how this thing evolved.'

Gradually, more electronic elements were added to the mix, by DJs including Fred Disko, Laurent and Ray Castle, alongside Dutch, Swiss, French and German visitors who brought new sounds to the area, on well-travelled and handily portable cassette tapes. Raja Ram, a flautist who played with sixties band Quintessence, started to have parties round his place in South Anjuna. Goa was a godsend for the connoisseur of out-there sounds; people would get stoned, drop acid, and share the weirdest, most far-out tunes they could lay their hands on. DJs such as Goa Gil and Ray Castle would splice, edit and mix on their Sony Walkmans; the locals would sell chai, trippers would stomp in the red dust and the music would play on. Beat matching is pretty hard on cassette, so the long, beatless breakdowns in the music that was beginning to be made for airing in this region had a practical purpose. Alongside Goa Gil, two French DJs, Fred Disko and Laurent, were some of the first to play electronic music in Goa, mixing in New Order and Blancmange with Cabaret Voltaire, the Residents and Eurodisco a few seasons before Paul Oakenfold and crew were discovering Alfredo's Balearic mix in Ibiza.

In the years that followed, parties became more organised and more heavily populated. A guy called Thornton used to run boat parties up and down the coast, carrying speakers into the jungle; Roberto and the Italian crew were doing their thing, as were Simon McCarra, and a large Israeli contingent. You'd see characters like Doctor Bubble grooving away, shoeless as usual, or electro DJ Tiga's dad, a face on the scene, with a young Tiga in tow. The police began to take an interest, and instigated upfront bribes, known locally as 'baksheesh'; a crackdown began on the parties, which lasted a couple of seasons.

The local government were embarrassed by the reputation for drug tourism Goa was steadily attracting, and sought to court a more upmarket clientele. Unfortunately, the infrastructure for mass Western tourism wasn't quite there, and the parties continued. By 1992 the parties were coping with an expanded influx of curious revellers, getting down to Hardfloor, Red Planet's 'Stardancer', KLF's 'What Time Is Love', Jam and Spoon, Harthouse and Eye-Q releases, mixed in with a few new tracks the Goa DJs were beginning to make. The sound of trance, rising from the embryonic electronic pulse of acid house, Belgian new beat, British progressive, and German and Detroit techno, had quickly become the predominant sound of Goa.

For someone like Goa Gil, this was more than just a musical trend. 'I'm basically using this whole party situation as a medium to do magic, to remake the tribal pagan ritual for the twenty-first century,' he says. 'It's not just a disco under the coconut trees.' The music became known as Goa trance, then the more general psychedelic or psy-trance, since the music was played, but not made, in Goa.

Paul Oakenfold had been first introduced to Goa via a couple of sources, while working with Steve Osborne, producing an album project in West London for INXS singer Michael Hutchence under the name Max Q. 'I got on with him well,' says Paul. 'He did look the rock star – I always felt he was in character all the time. He always looked great, always looked the part. The Max Q record should have been a lot bigger than it was.' Paul would hear early trance supplied by Hutchence's collaborator Ollie Olsen. Olsen was pioneering the trance sound with his Third Eye project, on albums such as *Ancient Future*. 'I'd met Ollie in Australia,' says Paul. 'He was very aware of what was going on. Ollie got Michael into dance music; he was producing psychedelic stuff. He used those sounds, and I quite liked the idea of taking a few of those sounds and using them in the context of what I did, but with a song. I thought "Let's do a psychedelic trance song, with that energy, but with a great song."'

Ian St Paul, Paul's Spectrum promotion partner, was the other crucial link that led Paul Oakenfold to Goa. Having left the UK after the ammonia incident, Ian headed for LA, then Goa, and came back with his usual pioneering, eulogising energy. 'The first time I went was on a two-week holiday with Ian,' says Paul. 'It was Ian took me into that scene.' Ian worked with Youth at Dragonfly Records, and was on a mission. His tireless promotion of the new sound had far-reaching effects – he turned on both Paul and Danny Rampling, who both gave the music prime-time exposure on Radio One, kick-starting the public's awareness.

Paul would get around Goa on an old Enfield bike, one time coming off it after taking a particularly tough corner; the bike went one way, Paul and his girlfriend Angela another. He saw a few other London faces there, such as Youth, but he didn't hang out with them much; instead he enjoyed the open-air parties, on beaches or in the fields. 'It was different to Ibiza,' he says. 'For a start the parties are all free, and they are outside, under the stars. It seemed a bit snobby – for example, you couldn't take photos. They'd shout "No photos, no photos . . ." You'd think "What's wrong with you?" It was strange; I couldn't figure it out. I went to about four or five parties in the jungle. I liked the energy in the music; I liked the crowd, I liked the way they dressed.'

Rich Bloor, who was soon to work for leading Goa trance label TIP, alongside Ian St Paul, Raja Ram and Graham Wood, also made it to Goa in the early nineties. 'I'll never forget my first party, at a place called Disco Valley in Vagator,' he says. 'Goa Gil was DJing for eight hours, invoking the Goddess, this mythical character. When you are discovering this new acid world, coming out of the London club scene, this crazy guy with rumoured Grateful Dead connections made quite an impact. He played all night and you'd get so out of it. It was so intense, completely away from the normal experience of going out clubbing, this array of freaks from all around the world, completely off their heads going crazy to this music. Because it's away from a club experience, away from anything marketed or planned, it seems more crazy, more wild and . . . just *more*. It's very tribal. The drugs make a big difference; everyone's on acid. When people are all on the same drug, and it's acid, it's a lot more intense. The senses are more alert. It's a far bigger drug experience; it goes on longer, you go further with it. It becomes like an acid meltdown, it's so off the wall. The London club scene had started getting really dressy, whereas in this other scene, people were making their own clothes. It was a self-expression thing. There were loads of beautiful girls, dressed really well, with their own style. People tend to think the scene is quite fluffy, rich fluffy people taking acid; it's not like that at all. It's a really mixed bag of people, with a very intense atmosphere. If you took people who thought they were really cool from the club scene, and dropped them into some of these parties it would completely freak them out. It completely takes you; you feel slightly unsure of your-self because everything's so unusual and out of your norm. You become so involved, you are immersed in this thing, this space; you are elevated; your feet don't touch the floor. It just feels a bit more outlaw.'

Future trance DJ Dino Psaras had a similar revelation. Dino cut his teeth as a house DJ at Daddy G's monthly night at Bristol's Thekla, alongside stints at his brother Andy's acid nights in his home town, Brighton, at the Pink Coconut and the Zap. As a young teenager he toured as warm-up DJ for Primal Scream's European *Screamadelica* tour, where he first met Paul Oakenfold, in the DJ booth of the Paradiso in Amsterdam. Dino first went to Goa in 1993, at a time when he was singled out by *Mixmag* magazine as one of the top twenty up-and-coming house DJs to watch out for. That was all to rapidly change. 'When I went to the parties in Goa, I completely gave up that music,' he says. 'I used to play techno and trance tracks in my set, but didn't know where to find them. Suddenly I found all these killers in one night. I'd been looking for this music for six years.'

Like Rich Bloor and an army of international travellers, Dino has strong recollections of his first Goa party. Not know-ing what was about to go down, he took the two-hour trip to the party via cab, and kept the driver waiting. It would be a long wait. 'I was lying in a hammock, and my brother said "You've got to come to the middle of the dancefloor, you'll never believe what's going on here,"' he says. 'It was mayhem. There were DJs with tape machines, speakers tied together with rope, and a dolphin washed up on the beach. There were beautiful people, all out of their brains; everyone was jumping, all on the same vibe. It was incredible – it had an energy you don't get in clubs. You don't see that anywhere else in the world. Everything about the place changed my life.'

For anyone who appreciated the more out-there pleasures of acid house, this seemed a natural progression, rather than the rather bland house offshoots that tightened their grip on clubland after 1991. 'After the rave thing, people reverted to cocaine, or were popping ecstasy listening to progressive house,' says Rich Bloor. 'It became boring, like a conveyor belt. Everyone danced the same, looked the same . . . there was no passion, flamboyancy or ad hoc things happening. These parties completely kicked the arse out of the club scene. They were far more crazy, there were far more freaks. It was so intense.'

'It was completely a continuation of acid house,' says Dino Psaras. 'At the end of the eighties, hardcore music went really dodgy – gangsters were running it, people with guns selling loads of pills. The music became double the speed, with really old tracks speeded up, double time . . . it was like Mickey Mouse. It was a breath of fresh air to go to Goa and hear all this music that was exactly like acid house, but a bit faster, a bit cleaner.'

Just as Balearic bliss winged its way back to London, the highs of Goa were soon to be imported to the UK. There were parties in disused bank vaults, in a former butcher's in

Smithfield Market, and a new night run by Ian St Paul, Andy and Dino Psaras and Mike McGuire, called A Concept in Dance, in a warehouse space underneath the Old Street round-about. There were no flyers, no big-time guest DJs, no media attention. Brightly coloured fluoro art lined the wall, en route to an art gallery exhibition. Everybody would partake in the acid punch.

Paul Oakenfold's interest in the music being played in Goa was heightened after hearing Dino spin at a new London club, The End. Dino met up with Paul, and played him tracks by Martin Freeland, a former techno artist who had scored a Summer of Love hit in 1988 with 'Urban Acid'. Alongside Simon Posford (Hallucinogen), Martin became an in-house engineer at Youth's Butterfly Studios in Brixton, a key venue for many early trance players, and began composing tracks such as the definitive psy-trance anthem 'Teleport' under the title Man With No Name. 'For me, he was the most talented one of the whole lot,' says Paul. 'I'd always try to get him to play shows with me. There were great times in that psychedelic scene; I used to go more as a punter, and then I liked some of the artists and music, like Martin's, so I started putting them out on Perfecto.'

The first Goa-influenced track on Perfecto was a remix package for Paul and Steve's 1994 'Rise' single. The 'Goa Pyramid' and 'Goa Sunrise' mixes are by Man With No Name and Ayahuasca, aka Dino Psaras. Paul's interest in the Goa sound led to a whole subdivision of the label, Perfecto Fluoro, developed specifically for trance releases, all displaying distinctive melodic hooks, ever-morphing harmonic filter sweeps, and an almost raga-like, modal quality that has similarities to classical Indian music. 'The main Perfecto label was more melodic and song-based, with things like Grace and BT; I wanted to put out edgier techno, so we formed Perfecto Fluoro,' says Paul. Man With No Name reissued 'Teleport', and the genre classic 'Floor Essence'; there were releases from The Infinity Project, Section X, California Sunshine, Virus, Johann and a band managed by Ian St Paul – Juno Reactor. 'They were like godfathers, they were the band,' says Paul.

Not all the scene's originators were happy with Paul's championing of the sound, however. 'Some of them were fine, like Raja Ram; I used to go round to his house,' says Paul. 'I just felt that a lot of them felt a bit threatened by me. I felt at the time that they looked at me as if I was spoiling their secret. I understand that when you have something special, the same as we did at Future and Spectrum, you don't necessarily want to make it more available, make it commercial, but that's what happens. Man With No Name is the only ever psychedelic trance act that's ever gone in the top-forty charts.'

Some of the Goa originals certainly felt uneasy about the sudden media spotlight, but perhaps were a little blinkered. As writer Erik Davis put it, 'techno is the sound of one world shrinking. The media tsunami that gave backwater hippies like Goa Gil DAT players and computerised music has also brought fax machines and MTV and journalists to their hideaway . . . you can't drop out and plug in at the same time. The underground is now networked, and you can't escape the feedback loop for long.'

There's no doubt that Paul Oakenfold popularised this sound, no more so than on 18 December 1994, when Paul's seminal 'Goa' mix was broadcast on Pete Tong's show on BBC Radio One. For the first time, the entire nation could hear the music blended to perfection. The mix wasn't purely notable for its use of the new melodic trance; it was groundbreaking due to its broad palette, fusing dance with film music to create an unforgettable atmosphere. It's way more than a stack of beat-matched records. Paul created an immersive sonic journey full of peaks and troughs, tension and release, a perfect headphone trip that manipulates its source material with edits, segments and cinematic interludes, including a touch of *Blade Runner* and a hint of Wojciech Kilar's *Dracula* soundtrack. First-hour highlights are numerous, including classics like Hallucinogen's electronic mantra 'LSD' and Man With No Name's 'Floor Essence' alongside Salt Tank's 'Eugena' and Paul's mix of Scorpio Riding's 'Dubcatcher'. After Goldie's 'Inner City Life', the second hour is more uptempo. The pedal's to the floor for a full-on fluoro trance workout, the wiggling acidics of The Infinity Project's 'Stimuli' blending with the ethereal tones of Dead Can Dance's 'Sanvean', before reaching a climax with 4 Voice's 'Eternal Spirit' and the Raw Canc mix of Man With No Name's 'Sugar Rush'. It's a well-worn cliché that the DJ likes to take his audience on a journey, but here, for once, the cliché rings true. The Goa Essential Mix went on to be the most requested mix ever on Pete Tong's show, such is its power.

'It was the hardest mix to complete,' says Paul, 'because of the arrangement, the keys, mixing in a lot of music that had no beat. It took months. The choice of tracks took three or four months, then I did a lot of research to find out what would work, keywise, from film music, that had the emotion and feeling I wanted to put across. I did that at the piano. Usually you are mixing beats, but this was all about key, mixing ambience, adding spoken word. A lot of it is in minor keys because it's more emotional. I mixed it all to a click track, then took that out when the mix was done. It was slow, hard work. I was on the verge of giving up at one point; I thought "Fuck this, this is a lot of work . . . why don't I just do a DJ mix?" But Radio One giving us a two-hour slot was a big deal, and to be creative, with no boundaries, was a really big deal, so that's why I wanted to take it to the next level. I was just trying to tell a story. The music was cutting-edge, and I've always thought that [film] score would work with my style of trance music. I think it really opened the doors for a lot of people, because it took the underground sound and played it on mainstream radio. Oakenfold fans weren't expecting to hear it; they were expecting to hear melodic trance, and I just completely banged it. Psychedelic trance was something that I was really into, and I thought it gave me a good vehicle to showcase what I can do.'

The mix was bootlegged heavily. Liverpool club Cream pressed up a large quantity of promo CDs. 'Typical Scousers!' laughs Paul when referring to the club where he was soon to shine. You get the feeling he may have had some hand in the bootlegs himself. 'They made shitloads of money out of it,' he says. 'I wasn't worried about the money – I wanted it out there. I thought it was a sound that people had never heard before; that was the idea, to do something new, fresh, and different.'

Although the Goa Mix never got an official release, Paul released a Perfecto mix CD entitled *Perfecto Fluoro* which acted as a companion piece to the Radio One Essential Mix. The double album is as broad as the Goa mix, featuring Björk and Terrorvision, alongside Ryuichi Sakamoto's music for the film *Merry Christmas Mr Lawrence*, Ennio Morricone's 'Miserere' and Samuel Barber's 'Adagio for Strings', mixed in with the trance stormers. It is sublime – a benchmark

Oakenfold release, transcending restrictions of genre and beat matching to deliver something truly unique.

Although there were the usual handful of trainspotter snobs muttering about the commercialisation of 'their' scene, the majority of the trance world welcomed the attention Paul brought to the scene with open arms. 'I remember Paul saying to me, repeatedly, "What you are doing is underground, and what I am doing is overground,"' says Rich Bloor of TIP Records. 'We were the underground, but we were also in business, so we were really glad that Paul's overground activities helped us out. It never really affected the underground clubber, as the underground never really followed the dance press, listened to Radio One, or cared about it. Some people were a bit snobby – like all good scenes, really – but Paul was involved for the right reasons. He had a passion for it, and this passion helped a lot of people so it was very positive. Between Paul and Danny Rampling playing it on the radio a lot, it meant I could go into the chain stores and sell the records.'

The widespread attention that was generated by the Essential Mix achieved concrete results for labels like TIP. 'Before that it was very low-key, a cottage industry,' says Rich Bloor. 'We were pressing up all our own sleeves, screen-printing them ourselves. I'd go round to the stores myself, with a bunch of CDs and a stack of records in the boot. We gradually started placing them, on a store-by-store basis, but after Danny played them on his show and after Oakey's Essential Mix, it all built up really quickly. When Paul got on board, he really turned everybody on. Between January 1994, when I started at TIP, and June or July, it suddenly became massive. We went from selling five hundred CDs to twenty thousand worldwide – we couldn't press them up quick enough! It became a big success story, very quickly. It was down to Paul being so on the pulse – if it wasn't for Paul, that wouldn't have been the situation. He made the scene more visible, and more credible.'

Dino Psaras, who went on to record as Cydonia with Steve Ronan for seminal trance label Blue Room, is also positive about Oakenfold's impact. 'The truth is, Oakenfold didn't need to do anything with this scene,' he says. 'He didn't need to put one of my tracks on his mix, or mix a Dragonfly compilation – it wasn't as if he was getting loads of money for doing it. In my opinion he did plenty, more than he needed to do. A few idiots had a bee in their bonnet about it, but they were just jealous. Paul helped me a lot – he wrote about A Concept In Dance and highlighted me as one of the DJs on the scene. Since that day I've been DJing worldwide, every weekend.'

The sound of the scene climbed ever-higher peaks in the mid-nineties. Simon Posford's tracks recorded at Butterfly Studios, such as 'Hallucinogen' by LSD, are timeless, transcendent slices of electronic music right up there with the acid classics. 'Everybody called him "the guv'nor",' says Rich Bloor. 'He's a very talented guy. I think he engineered or co-wrote about eighty per cent of TIP's "yellow" album.' New figures emerged on the scene – Paul Jackson, who'd worked with Andy Weatherall's Sabres of Paradise label; Nick Doof, the Infinity Project, Total Eclipse, and the first big Israeli act, Astral Projection.

Paul celebrated the success of Perfecto Fluoro with a Goa-inspired all-night free party in Ibiza. 'We organised a Perfecto party at Ku [now Privilege] with me, Sasha and John Digweed; it was the busiest party of the summer,' says Paul. 'On the same night we did a free Perfecto Fluoro psychedelic party with Man With No Name, Juno Reactor, Mike McGuire . . . Ian, Rich

Bloor and TIP organised it. We had to keep it so quiet – Perfecto was huge so if word got out, there would have been thousands of people there. By doing two parties on one night we managed to keep a lot of people away. The only way you could get to the party was with a map, and by stones that we painted! You'd have your headlights on, there would be a mauve stone . . . turn left at the mauve stone! It was an incredible party, fucking unbelievable.'

TIP's Rich Bloor remembers it well. 'It was at a place called Can Punta, one of the highest points on the island,' he says. 'There had been a few low-key parties going on for a little while, but that party was one of the first parties where a lot of people from all the different scenes came together. It was the biggest one. It was very much a community thing; we had a lot of help from our friends that lived in the north of the island, around San Juan. It was the young sanyasi kids, the children of the original sixties hippies who'd grown up in Goa and Ibiza, who painted the rocks and brought a special vibe to the parties. To get to it was a half-hour drive round the mountain, maybe longer. There's no road – you're driving across these bumpy, rocky dirt tracks. There were cars broken down halfway up the mountain! We had to get up there with this huge water truck, to water down the sand. When you've got all these people dancing in the heat, all these feet kicking it up, all the dust rises. It's unbearable; you have to have lots of water to spray on the floor to keep the dust settled. We built a stage up there, took all the live equipment, all these water trucks up and down this mountain. The sunrise was unforgettable, as was the sight of a beautiful girl swaying and meditating to the music, naked, on the edge of the mountain cliff, facing out towards the sun and the Med. The party had a massive impact.'

'Paul lives and breathes the island,' says former *Muzik* magazine editor Ben Turner. 'Privilege is a huge venue to fill, but he did it. The Perfecto free party has gone on to be one of those legendary events, quite important in Ibiza's dance history. Since then the likes of Sunday Best, and a lot of brands, have been doing free parties, and there's the Cocoon after-parties that go on now, with eight thousand people partying outside every time. Paul was the first big DJ to try that. He pioneered it, way before anyone else.'

The psy-trance scene took a bit of a battering in the late nineties; Rich Bloor remembers 1997 as a particularly hard year, as the media's attention had moved swiftly on, towards trip hop and big beat, which usurped the trance sound as the next big press buzz. The underground trance scene kept its head down, and slowly, the sound developed an enthusiastic new following worldwide. The Israelis took the English sound to another level, sharpening production techniques. Infected Mushroom were heavily influenced by Simon Posford, Domestic by X-Dream. Gradually new acts like Astrix and GMS took to the world stage. Infected Mushroom have sold over a quarter of a million records worldwide, a remarkable figure; alongside Raja Ram and Astrix, they are treated like rock stars in Brazil, where parties can be attended by as many as forty thousand. Brazil is currently the biggest magnet for trance – it's three times the size of India, parties can go on for three days, and the sound is merging with the mainstream – but it's only one of the current trance hot spots. Australia has a thriving scene, in particular the Earthcore parties, Israel is as strong as ever, if a little lacking in ideas of late, and there's vibrant scenes in Mexico, Greece, Russia, Yugoslavia, Portugal, Barcelona, as well as a revived energy in London, with the

Antiworld parties. Japan, however, is where it's really happening. DJ Raja Ram is treated like a pop star in Japan; he recently had four pages' coverage in *Loud* magazine for six months in a row. Although Goa trance has never been seen to be the most credible or fashionable of the myriad of dance subgenres, the scene that was whipped up by Ian St Paul, and broke through thanks to Paul Oakenfold, is in rude, expanding global health.

# 11

# Cream: Resident

'We'd spend Monday and Tuesday recovering, Wednesday, Thursday and Friday looking forward to Saturday. We'd live for the weekend. Every Saturday we'd travel to Liverpool to get our Oakenfold fix. It was like an addiction.'

Michelle Monaghan, Cream regular

'For four, maybe five years Cream was undoubtedly the place to be. I didn't feel like I had to be in London at any particular club. Come Saturday, it was all about Liverpool.'

Ben Turner, former editor, *Muzik* magazine, 2006

If you want to know what's happening in Liverpool right now, try this. Stand on the main road next to the docklands, away from Birkenhead, away from the river Mersey, away from the massive new sports complex that's sprouting up near the Albert Dock. Face inland. Look towards the city centre; you'll see an unusual site. The sky is filled with cranes, dozens of them. It's a visible, towering sign of Liverpool's recent optimism. The city is undergoing a facelift that would have been unthinkable, laughable even, when I lived there in the cash-strapped mid-eighties. There may be local doubt whether there's enough money or people around to fill these new pads, and the pace and scale of development even led to a recent UNESCO fact-finding mission, questioning the city's recently anointed world heritage status, but there's no doubt that Liverpool is moving up a gear for its year as European City of Culture. The down-town arcades near where the legendary old Probe record shop stood are now a gleaming new Cavern shopping quarter, which is a bit ironic for a city that bulldozed the original Cavern Club site in the early seventies to make way for a car park. Everywhere you turn seems to be the site of some new retail development. In the top part of the town centre, in the area near Chinatown, there's a string of new bars and clubs, where once the only entertainment was an irregular lock-in run by a gregarious Chinese landlord named Ernie Wu. If we're talking bar, music and club culture, then the European City of Culture tag is spot-on.

In Wolstenholme Square, near Duke Street, slap bang in the middle of this new after-dark economy, sits an imposing warehouselike space. Once a club known as the Academy, then later Nation, it is more commonly known as the building that housed the biggest, most successful UK club of the nineties. The club was so influential, it's no coincidence that its success mirrored the fortunes of the rapidly evolving city that's grown up around it. The club is called Cream. And there was no more successful DJ ever to play at Cream than Paul Oakenfold. Paul's two-year residency in the Annexe and Courtyard is the stuff of clubland legend, right up there with Larry Levan at Paradise Garage or Junior Vasquez at Sound Factory. The formative years at Future and Spectrum were groundbreaking, iconic, fresh, but it was in Liverpool, at Cream, that the DJ made his most indelible mark.

The seeds for Paul's two-year late-nineties residency were sown in the summer of 1988. The acid house boom hit the town with an avalanche of small, but significant, love bombs. An enterprising character named John – no last name, as requested – began throwing free, intimate, all-night acid house parties in Sefton Park, a large area of leafy greenery a few minutes from the town centre. Decks and lights would be set up inside a standard-issue two-weeks-in-Bognor caravan, pumping out Chicago house to a motley crew of ravers, vagrants and assorted misfits – anyone who didn't want to go home or go to sleep in Liverpool on a summer Saturday night. There were other sporadic acid parties dotted around the city, including one in part of the Wolstenholme Square venue that later became Cream, as early as June 1988. I recall returning to the city that summer and finding about forty wide-eyed converts gathered in the space that would soon become Cream, enjoying a strobe-lit, dry-ice euphoria, surprised that someone would come up from London to go clubbing, wanting to know all about Spectrum and Shoom. Most people agree, however, that it was the arrival of future Cream heads James Barton and Andy Carroll's night Daisy, launched in September 1988 at the State Ballroom, that truly kicked off the Liverpool acid house scene.

The State was a grand, imposing club space just round the corner from the town's two best-known sixties and seventies clubs, the Cavern and Eric's. Andy Carroll had played at the State since 1984, alongside Mike Knowler, a DJ and recording engineer who worked at the influential Open Eye Studios in the centre of town, recording bands on the emerging scene such as Big in Japan and Echo and the Bunnymen. Andy and Mike first teamed up as resident DJs at Sandbaggers in Southport, moving to a residency at the State in autumn 1984. 'In 1986 Mike went to New York,' recalls Andy Carroll, 'and he heard this new sound, the Chicago, jackin' house sound. He brought it back to Liverpool and it blew my head off. From then on me and Mike were playing house music at the State, blending it with Talking Heads, New Order, François Kevorkian mixes, the Smiths, all sorts. We had Citronic decks without varispeed, on a console unit . . . If you were trying to mix a track in, it was with your finger! Most of it was cutting, scratching and fading, that was the art – this was pre-mixing. We were playing what they later called Balearic in London, but at the time we didn't even know where the Balearic Islands were! We just lived in our little Liverpool bubble, doing this thing at the State, gradually introducing house music. We were mixing it up, playing these dubs, working it, making it happen.'

In 1988, Andy Carroll made his own trip stateside. 'I'd been going to Spectrum and Shoom in London, and I'd got to know Paul Oakenfold and Danny Rampling a little bit,' he says. 'Danny and Paul invited me out to Ibiza that year. I'd made a pot of money on my own, off my own back for the first time ever, so I had the choice – do I go to New York, where they make the music, or Ibiza, where they play it? So I went to New York for a month. I went to Save the Robots, the Tunnel Club, Danceteria. I remember seeing Mark Kamins DJ in a bank vault, seeing Kraze DJ, the guy who put out "The Party". I bought records from Vinyl Mania on Carmine Street. I was there every other day, so I befriended them. They were more interested in British electronic music than they were in their own music – I knew more about house than they did! I just started pulling stuff out left, right and centre that they weren't very interested in. I got to get into the basement, pulled some real nuggets out of there. I came back to Liverpool with a box full of dynamite and pushed the trigger. Then of course James Barton and his brothers started to arrive on the scene.'

A teenage James Barton funded his interest in music by going on trips round Europe, selling tickets, T-shirts and posters outside any major rock gig he could find. 'I funded my love of music by selling tickets,' he says. 'I saw Prince in Stockholm on his very first European date. I toured with U2 throughout most of Europe, saw Simple Minds, the Cure. I used to go to gigs and I'd listen and watch the band but I'd wonder how did they get those speaker stacks up here, how did they do that production? I remember going to Live Aid and thinking the same thing. I was a massive Clash fan, I adored the Jam, and in the mid-eighties we had all these great bands here in Liverpool. The greatest for me was Echo and the Bunnymen. I followed that band up and down the country. Then suddenly dance music, house music arrived. It was probably the first time I'd really heard a beat like that. There were some strains of dance music happening in rock records or electronic-sounding records, like New Order, and there was stuff coming out of Sheffield, which sounded new and different. But when Dave Dorrell and C. J. Mackintosh made "Pump Up The Volume", that fucking great record, suddenly it was like, boom!'

James first visited the State Ballroom aged fifteen. Soon he was regularly checking out resident DJs Steve Proctor, Mike Knowler and Andy Carroll. 'I used to go and watch those guys every Thursday night and they'd play a Cure record, they'd play a Bowie record, they'd play the Cult,' says James. 'They had a really lovely little vibe going on there. At the beginning I was a DJ groupie, but I probably didn't know it! Steve Proctor used to play from nine till twelve at a place called the Pyramid, and then he used to finish in there and walk two hundred yards round the corner and go on the decks at the State. I used to do that with him. Not with him directly, but me and my little crew of mates, we'd follow him, go to the Pyramid for the first few hours, listen to what he was doing there and then go round the corner to the State.' James's DJ fan worship would be mirrored week in, week out by Oakenfold fans at his own club, a few years later.

'James and his family had been going to State for quite a while,' recalls Andy Carroll. 'We had been playing a bit of music he liked, but suddenly he'd taken a trip out to Amsterdam, doing tickets, hearing house music, and suddenly it all made sense.' The idea of a new club night, the foundation of a scene that would eventually lead to Cream, was starting to take shape. Like Andy, James had been venturing south to London to check out the emerging acid house scene. He went to see Paul Oakenfold at Spectrum, and to Nicky Holloway's night the Trip at the Astoria, as well as a night called Daisy Chain, whose moniker James promptly filed away for later use. 'I couldn't believe this music I was hearing,' he says. 'I was going in and out of shops, seeing all the flyers . . . the artwork and the amount of effort that went into the marketing was phenomenal.'

James was keen to export this energy back to Liverpool, and was a little surprised that acid house hadn't already hit the city in a big way. 'On a Saturday night at the State the closest they'd get to house music was Salt-N-Pepa or "Pump Up The Volume",' he says. 'Weirdly, the big records in Liverpool at that time were Deacon Blue, and the Waterboys' "Whole Of The Moon" – kids on ecstasy, fucking waving their hands in the air, singing "you saw the whole of the moon"! That seemed to be the last tune every Saturday night at the State. A lot of people liked it; I hated it. I knew that there was all these other amazing records coming from New York, Chicago and Detroit out there, but no one was playing them much. Then I spoke to Andy Carroll and I said, "I'm gonna do this night." Andy said "Do us a favour, let me have a go" and pulled all these records out. He had the tunes.'

James convinced State owner Bernie Start to give him a chance running a night, known as Daisy, a shortened version of the name of the night James had checked in London. Reluctant to hand over a prime weekend slot to such an untried venture, Bernie let James have the venue on a Monday, one of the worst nights possible to start a new club. At around 11 p.m. on the first night, Monday 12 September 1988, Bernie thought his partnership with the teenage promoter was about to die a very quick death. The club was empty. Then seemingly out of nowhere, the crowds started pouring in, with DJ John Kelly at the front of the queue. Liverpool's first bona fide house music night was an instant success.

'It was really, really amazing,' says James. 'Suddenly we went from quite a negative, macho attitude in certain clubs in the city, to the whole thing becoming very colourful and fun. A lot of it was driven by drugs, but it was a revolution, a whole new genre of music opening up. People were being creative. I was seventeen, eighteen at the time. I just threw myself into it.'

The neon, day-glo acid house bug hit the city big-time. Soon the Daisy crowd wanted the new sound served up on the weekend. 'From about the second or third week of Daisy, people were just asking for house music all the time,' says Andy Carroll. 'We were still playing INXS and Talking Heads, but house music more or less took over the State. People were indulging in everything that went with it. When Steve Proctor moved down to London, we were playing on Thursday, Friday and Saturday night.' This wasn't such good news for Daisy. 'There were two problems for us,' says James Barton. 'First and foremost, it was on a Monday night, and kids wanted to party on a Saturday. But the main issue was ultimately the police.'

'When acid house exploded in Liverpool, the police didn't know what the fuck had hit them,' says Andy Carroll. 'They didn't know what ecstasy was, where the people were getting it from, what it was all about. They had everyone connected with the State under surveillance, from the club owner down to the cloakroom boy. I had my phone tapped. I used to do classic things like put the phone up to the speaker, ask them "Does this sound good?" Every time I came out of the club I got stopped and searched. I was also being followed. It was all too much for the police, and there had to be a scapegoat. They just brought things up in court – they objected to the licence, and the objections were eventually upheld.' Although Bernie Start appealed against these objections, the State Ballroom was finally shut down on 11 November 1989, an early acid house closure.

'We actually only got a few months out of it,' says James Barton. 'It was very controversial at the time, a thousand people going out on a Monday night. From a police perspective it was just about drugs. From my perspective, and certainly from people who were close to it, it was always about the music. The fact that people were taking drugs was just part of the lifestyle. But it made a few people concerned. The *Sun* had done its first acid house exposé, so the police were a bit nervous. But we'd kicked it all off, and it was hugely successful.'

After the closure of Daisy at the State, James was at a loose end. 'I didn't have a lot else to do, so I just did some one-off parties here and there,' he says. 'Then John Kelly said he'd got some friends that could get access to a club where there's a few parties going off, but no one's doing it properly. He said why don't we turn it into something?' With the help of Andy Carroll, a new night called the Underground was born.

Situated in a run-down nightclub called Nights Alive in Victoria Street, the Underground was less of a big night out, more an intimate basement drinking bar with dance music and close friends. 'It was a proper neon sort of gaff,' recalls James. 'We got some money together, closed down and then refitted the venue. We didn't spend a lot of money, but we fixed the toilets and put a concrete floor in. We made this huge mural on the wall which was sort of a copy of the Underground network with all the stations on . . . we had no money, so our whole idea was to ash-felt the floor, put paving stones in, put parking stuff in and give it a little bit of a warehouse vibe, something like the Hacienda. A lot of people said that it was the best club in Liverpool since Eric's. It was that good. It was mad, a real mixture of people. These loonbags were coming in from what we would describe as posh, affluent areas, and they were just completely having it off, mixing in with students, gangsters, scallies, and a lot of people from the suburbs. This was around the same time as the whole Blackburn rave scene as well. They were great, great times. What was interesting was how primitive our DJing was at that time. Although I started off as a promoter, because I loved the music I taught myself how to

DJ, so I went out and bought the decks and the mixer and sat at home and bored my ex-girlfriend to death by scratching records.'

James and Andy had by this stage formed a partnership called Hax Promotions, and were expanding into gigs, management and a record label, Olympic Records. The first signing to Olympic was veteran Ibiza DJ Alfredo. 'It became our business,' says Andy, 'we were in the thick of it all, promoting. We had Adamski, the Prodigy, N-Joi, Orbital, Mr. Monday – anyone that was making good tunes.' An early management success was the signing of K-Klass to Deconstruction Records, who instantly scored a top-three hit with 'Rhythm Is A Mystery'. 'K-Klass went from being unknown to doing *Top of the Pops* in a week,' says James Barton. 'That whole experience was fucking awesome. I used to love going on the road with them. I made sure they got good dates, made sure they had good lawyers and accountants. I really tried to make it for them. Everything was in place for them to be a much bigger band than they were, but they didn't continue to make great records – they made three or four really strong singles. They could have been as big as M People, the biggest Deconstruction act at the time; they could have gone on to sell a couple of million albums. The fact that we had a management company and a little record label doing pretty well opened up a whole new world, and I really liked it. At that time we really felt as though we were doing our thing for Liverpool. We really thought the lads in Manchester and London needed a little challenge. It was great for us to be up in Liverpool, which has this real rock guitar indie heritage, to be contributing to electronic music.'

The Underground started to hook up with an emerging

network of like-minded crews around the UK. Andy Carroll, in particular, was enjoying DJing and socialising out of town. 'We used to have Tonka sound system versus the Underground parties,' he says. 'The most legendary one was in Brighton, at the Zap Club. We went down with a full coachload, but ended up with about twenty-three people on the way back! Tonka were supposed to have a generator for the after-party, but apparently one of the guys from Tonka was too stoned, and left the generator in Cambridge. He had the PA but no gennie. There were different rumours about where the after-party was, with many dazed people wandering about, lost in a state of acid house after-hours confusion! It ended up in a council estate miles out of Brighton. The police followed the coach. It got to a point where suddenly there was only room for one vehicle of that size in the road, so when the coach stopped the police were blocked off and didn't realise what was happening. By the time they'd gone up to the front of the coach, everyone had piled into this house where the Tonka sound system had set up, using the electricity supply from the cooker point, as it had powerful enough ampage to power the system. There were people hanging off the rafters, there's a derelict pool in the backyard . . . it was madness, absolute madness.'

Despite its success, the Underground soon became another acid house licensing casualty. Although James, Andy and John Kelly were running the club, there were questions about who actually owned it, and the inevitable pressure from the police. 'All I know is we ran it from a promotional point of view,' says James Barton, 'but ultimately it was the police that called time on the Underground. Andy and Mike had already started at Quadrant Park, and when the Underground closed I went to join them.'

Quadrant Park was a large 'leisure complex' in Bootle. Mike Knowler booked the Quad for a Christmas dance in 1989, and took up residency on Thursday 11 January 1990. He became resident DJ three nights of the week, with Andy Carroll playing on Mondays and Saturdays. James Barton became a resident in November 1990, after promoting a bank holiday special in August featuring a live PA from LFO.

The club was huge. When you walked in, people would be dancing on chairs, dancing on the bar. DJ John Kelly remembers the buzz in the Quad as 'the same kind of atmosphere as a world championship boxing fight. When somebody dropped a record, it was like taking a penalty at Wembley. The club had an 8k sound system, but you couldn't hear the music for the screaming.' The management had established a 'members only' policy, which, alongside their 24-hour entertainment licence, provided a handy loophole in the law. It allowed them to open up the cavernous old snooker hall next door as an all-night rave. 'By the time I went there,' says James, 'their regular Saturday night was unbelievably crazy. The club would close at two, then everyone would go into the back room, and when I say back room, it was the size of a football pitch. There were like another five thousand people arriving from all over the country! It would go on until eight in the morning. Quadrant Park was the first proper all-nighter that I can remember.'

James and Andy Carroll were soon getting itchy feet, however. They were soon looking for a new town-centre spot. 'Quadrant Park was a great success, but one of the reasons I left was that we weren't in control,' says Andy Carroll. 'We weren't able to say how we wanted people to be treated at the door, or how things should be inside the venue, so that people had a comfortable night out, without queuing up for this, that and the other. We wanted to run it how we wanted – a club for ourselves. We wanted to fly our flag from the top of the mast and say this is a great night in Liverpool, we're all having fun, come and join us.'

Luckily, help was at hand. Local entrepreneur John Smith proposed launching a new club called 051, on a site in Liverpool town centre. The venue was formerly known as the Bierkeller, once home to the legendary mid-eighties psychedelic night the Hangout. James and Andy were one step nearer the club they'd been dreaming about. James pitched in with characteristic vigour. 'The 051 was Liverpool's answer to the Hacienda, our Hacienda. This was a purpose-built nightclub with a great sound system, all built around the DJ, all built around dancing. We hyped it to death. This was the pinnacle of four or five years trying to find venues where we could play our music.'

At first the hype and the legwork paid off. 'For six to eight months, it was amazing,' says James, 'but at some point I'd realised that the vibe just didn't seem to be getting there, because it was a big old concrete space. Because it was so popular, certain elements were getting in. I'd see fights happening in there. The doorman never helped the situation, let's put it that way. The owners became a bit greedy; they started publicising a night on a Friday night at a tenner, and because there was a massive queue outside, they'd put it up to fifteen quid at the last minute. In dance music you can't do stuff like that.'

A new face on the scene around this time was Darren Hughes, a psychology student from Chester. Darren had been introduced to James and Andy by Paul Roberts, from K-Klass.

'He basically made himself really busy,' says James. 'He'd come in the office nearly every day. He'd offer to help on things, or he'd put himself forward if something needed doing. He ultimately ended up just grabbing himself a phone and hanging around the office most of the time. And slowly but surely we started giving him jobs to do, a bit more responsibility. If me or Andy was out the office somewhere, or if we were on tour, he'd be in the office manning the phones and stuff.'

It was Darren who first let James know 051 wasn't working. 'I knew it was going wrong,' says James. 'I could see it every Saturday night – your mates stop coming, or your mates start finding excuses not to come. No one would tell me to my face. It was Darren who told me for the first time what I already knew. He said, "Look, it's fucking shit, it's full of dickheads, there's loads of fighting . . . get out of there, you're doing yourself a disservice." But I wanted to hang in there, I wanted to carry on.'

Darren took the matter into his own hands. He organised a twenty-first birthday party for his girlfriend in the back room of the Academy, a little-used venue in Wolstenholme Square. 'I remember us all having a real good scream,' says James. 'At some point during the night Darren said "Fuck 051 off, let's start doing something here." ' James wasn't entirely convinced. 'I was saying "If this doesn't work, I'm getting out – this is my last chance at creating a decent nightclub in Liverpool." 051 was coming to an end, I had the record label, I had the band. I'd had enough of nightclubs. I felt a bit bruised. Up until that point my reputation had been rock-solid in Liverpool, so I was a bit apprehensive. The last thing that I wanted to do was to try and do anything big.' But Darren Hughes's enthusiasm managed to win him round.

For the final party at 051, the first-year birthday party, Andy Carroll booked the DJ who would become synonymous with their next venture – Paul Oakenfold. 'Throughout the years I'd always kept in touch with Paul,' says Andy Carroll. 'I'd go down to London and drop into his office and say hello.' It was at the final party that James Barton met Paul Oakenfold for the first time. 'It was a bittersweet situation,' says James. 'We'd had guests at the 051 but not many really big ones – to have Paul Oakenfold there for our first birthday was a really big deal. It was also the last night that I ever went!'

After the major hype of 051, a subtler, more stripped-down approach was called for. The new venue was dark and empty; it hadn't had money spent on it in years. 'So me, Andy Carroll, Darren Hughes and a guy called Sam decided that we'd do a night based on good music,' says James. 'There was nothing else for us to sell. The only thing we spent any money on was hiring a really good sound system every week.' The new night was called Cream, and a club legend was born.

'At that time Cream wasn't a company or anything, it was just a name of a Saturday night in a back room with two DJs and two other guys putting posters and flyers up in town,' says James. 'It was all paid for by what little bits of money we had, from running the label.' The first night, in October 1992, was a pretty low-key affair. They booked London DJ Fabio Paras alongside local DJ Paul Bleasdale; Darren Hughes and DJ Paul Roberts's art student girlfriends made huge, whacked-out prints that hung from the ceilings. There was a red carpet and some plants at the door, to emphasise the freshly minted 'cream of the crop' vibe. 'It was friends and family,' says Andy Carroll. 'It was a great party with all the people we'd ever partied with over the years. It was like a lot of club nights – you start off with just your mates having a good laugh. The first week was a sell-out.'

Musically, however, the club wasn't quite up to scratch on opening night. 'Fabio Paras was a disaster!' says James. 'It was a bit of a fuck-up. Half the people in the club were people we knew. We were house boys, so to put on someone as dark and moody as Fabio, it just wasn't happening. I remember standing by the pool table thinking let's just grit our teeth and ride it out, but Darren refused to – he dragged him off!' Paul Bleasdale replaced him, rather appropriately playing 'Last Night A DJ Saved My Life'. The sound shifted, the mood lifted.

Cream's second night, with James, Andy and Paul DJing, was less of a success – the four hundred through the door in the first week shrank to around two hundred and fifty by week two. Although the turnout was disappointing, the dancefloor was still busy. 'I wasn't the type of DJ who would try to educate,' says James Barton, 'I was there to play big records. I played records for girls, and if the boys danced as well, then double bubble. There were less people, but it was still a rocking night.' 'After that it just built up gradually every week,' says Andy Carroll. 'It never stopped. It never went back, it just got bigger and bigger.'

Luckily for the Cream team, the Academy had a number of different rooms, allowing the promoters to expand the capacity of the night. A big turning point was Boxing Day 1992. 'At that stage we'd opened up another room,' says James. 'We absolutely smashed it, with about a thousand people. It was an amazing night. It was bursting at the seams. From that point on, it really kicked off.'

As the night grew bigger, James and Darren took more control of the business dealings. 'As a provincial DJ, I was itching to travel, see new clubs and meet new people, get out into the world,' says Andy Carroll. 'We'd been having a great time, and I was quite happy to leave the organising and the dressing of the club to James and Darren, because I was much more interested in the music. There wasn't much money in it at that point. I was making money DJing, getting offered more money to DJ out of town, so I said I wanted to get out and about. With a bit of foresight, everything would have changed, but I made my bed, I lay in it, and I have no regrets at all.'

James Barton was similarly broadening his horizons. Within eighteen months of Cream launching, he'd been offered an A&R position at Deconstruction records, home of K-Klass. The Liverpool crew had been informally tipping the label off about a string of dancefloor hits, since before Cream existed. Tracks like Hyper Go Go's 'High' and Felix's 1992 top-ten hit 'Don't You Want Me' were first heard by Deconstruction via the Liverpool connection. 'They were very clever in how they pitched the job to me,' says James. 'They said you can keep managing the band, you can come and work four days a week in London then come back to Liverpool for Cream. We can be Cream's office in London. I liked the idea of bridging the gap between what was the hottest dance label in the country with what was becoming the hottest nightclub. I was crawling out of Cream smashed every Sunday, getting back to London, and attending a nine o'clock meeting with the whole of BMG on Monday morning.'

By July 1993, with four hundred people locked out every week, it was time to stretch the Academy's expanding walls once again. The venue changed its name to Nation, and a major refit took place. The capacity took a giant leap from four hundred to eighteen hundred. A new sound system was installed in the main room. Darren and James went into business partnership with venue owners Stuart Davenport and Lenny McMillan. The venue reopened for the August bank holiday weekend, flying in David Morales and Frankie Knuckles for the night at a cost of over £5,000. 'It wasn't just about fees for those guys, it was also the flights and everything else. It was really expensive to do, something we'd never done before. But we wanted to make a big statement.'

With the venue expanded and refitted, the next step was to create a new Cream logo. 'Me and Darren loved *i-D* and *The Face*,' says James. 'We were into certain designers. We both loved what the Hacienda and Factory Records had done, not just the music, but also the design and everything else. Taking our first ad out in *The Face* was a big deal. It was *the* style magazine. I don't know which one of us hit upon the idea that we needed a logo, but Mark Farrow was the only person we'd discuss to design it.' Mark Farrow is a first-rate designer, behind the series of clean, minimal sleeves for the Pet Shop Boys, as well as all the artwork for Deconstruction. 'The only reference we gave him was the Nike swoosh,' says James. 'We didn't want to look anything like Ministry of Sound, which for us was very London, very authoritarian, a government-type logo. We wanted a clean, modern/industrial look, the look led by Peter Saville for Factory in Manchester.' The simple, Nike-inspired three droplets of cream logo Farrow created is now something of a design classic.

By 1995, Cream's premier-league status was a given. The club linked up with Deconstruction for their first mix album, *Cream Classics*, which included a mix each from Paul Oakenfold, Pete Tong, Justin Robertson and Graeme Park. The album sold over 250,000 copies, a then unheard-of amount for a dance mix album. The club was regularly locking out a minimum of a thousand people every Saturday night. Premier League footballers, pop stars and half the music industry joined the ever-expanding queue. 'It literally exploded,' says James. 'We struggled to cope with it, to keep track of it. It just completely fucking let rip.'

Paul Oakenfold was a regular guest during these formative years, playing alongside the likes of Cream residents and guest DJs Andrew Weatherall, Dave Clarke and Justin Robertson in the Annexe, the smaller back room of the club, whilst Graeme Park, Jeremy Healy or Pete Tong would spin in the larger main room. Justin Robertson remembers these sessions. 'The early days of Cream were very similar to what we were doing with Most Excellent in Manchester at the time,' he says. 'I remember me, Weatherall and Dave Clarke playing a lot of techno, weird electronic records and Wild Pitch stuff, and totally getting away with it. It was a bit of a "back to acid house" room, too – things like "Voodoo Ray" used to get battered. The crowd were really into it. It was intense and hot, and the crowd were really close to you. I remember Paul playing regularly. One birthday party Paul played with me and Weatherall. Me and Andrew were playing Richie Hawtin and DJaxx, being holier-than-thou about underground music. I remember Paul saying "I'm really gonna bang it tonight!" and lighting candles around his DJ box before he went on! His style of music had changed considerably – he'd previously played a lot of New York, Todd Terry-type records, and now he was banging out psychedelic trance, stuff on Dragonfly.' This was the beginning of the sound that would be the cornerstone of his residency.

The struggle to retain control of an ever-expanding Cream

took on a new perspective in November 1995, when student Leah Betts died after taking ecstasy at her eighteenth birthday party in Essex. The resulting media frenzy echoed the tabloid furore of 1988, and the resulting Graham Bright bill that followed. Conservative MP Barry Legg tabled the Public Entertainments Licences (Drug Misuse) Bill, which stated that drug use inside any nightclub would result in closure. Legg launched the bill at a press conference with Leah Betts's parents in attendance. If the bill was enforced to the letter, it could close every club in the nation. It was obvious, in the prevailing climate, that Cream needed a clear drugs policy to combat the threat of closure. Working with drugs support agency Lifeline, the accident and emergency department at Liverpool's Royal Free Hospital and the local council, Cream's Jane Casey worked hard to ensure the club had a viable, proactive drugs policy and that the licence was safe.

At the same time, darker forces were circling. Inspector Damien Walsh of Merseyside Police said, 'It is a well-established fact that more often than not, organised gangs, and therefore drug dealing, will enter a club via some of the firms which are licensed by the club owners to run their club security . . . there are overtures by criminals to take control of Cream. It's a jewel they would like to control.'

Cream didn't want to go the way of the Hacienda, which was to finally close during the summer of 1997 after scenes of gun and knife toting and drug-related turf wars. It could have gone the same way for Cream in February 1996, when twenty-three people were arrested in Liverpool and charged in connection with supplying drugs, allegedly inside Cream. Although Inspector Walsh later made it clear that the Merseyside constabulary were satisfied that the club was in no way connected, Cream had little choice but to work more closely with the police. 'It was a question of survival,' says James Barton.

These were difficult times, but Cream were determined to push things forward. In 1996 a new space called the Courtyard was opened, with a new Phazon sound system specially built by master New York PA designers Steve Dash and Phil Smith, the team responsible for the pin-sharp, booty-shaking sound rig at Twilo in New York. 'Every year we needed to make a big move,' says James Barton. 'In order for us to continue to be at the front of our game, we had to make the investment into what every DJ craves, which is a fucking great sound system. The Cream format was being copied all over, so we needed a change. We decided to create a residency, and ask the biggest DJ in the world to play every week.' Enter Paul Oakenfold.

'I played at Cream regularly in the early years, when the club was finding its feet,' says Paul. 'There was a higher rotation of DJs then, so I'd play probably four nights a year. Everyone was playing guest spots up and down the country, sometimes two or three times a night, and I felt I wanted to do something different. It was going against the grain, but I wanted a weekly residency. Every single week of the year. So I put the idea out there to all the big clubs – Ministry, Renaissance, Gatecrasher, Cream – and I got offers from all of them. I went with Cream, as I felt my working relationship with them was very good – they shared a similar vision. Instead of playing one week in Plymouth, the next in Glasgow, the idea was to create demand in this one club – if you wanted to come and see me, wherever you lived in the country, you had to come to Liverpool on a Saturday.'

To get to Paul, Cream first had to negotiate with his agent,

David Levy, at ITB. Well known and highly respected in the music business, Levy is the kind of meticulous individual who made sure his artists got exactly what they needed. 'The one thing I'd got to know about Paul's instincts by this stage is that they are very sharp,' says David. 'He had a complete vision; what I did was realise it for him, really. DJs and promoters hang out with each other every day and night, they get up to things together; to then try to do business doesn't always work. Basically Paul got to be the nice guy, and I got to do all the dirt.'

'I remember David saying that they were going to come at this like they would for any big artist,' says James Barton. 'The contract was thick. There were very particular things in there. How Paul was billed on the advertising was in there, obviously his fees were in there, although what he got paid has been grossly exaggerated! The extortionate fees that he was accused of demanding, he never demanded from us. But there were certain stipulations in there that people might find a little bit crazy . . .' The contract was around twenty pages long. Although standard practice for a rock and roll band, this was unheard of in dance music. The contract stipulated that he had to be met by a chauffeur-driven car at Stamford Bridge every time there was a Chelsea match on; if Cream couldn't get him to Liverpool by car, he'd get there by plane. If there were no flights available, they'd have to hire a plane. 'It never happened though,' says Paul. 'They were sharp enough to book the tickets three months in advance!' 'It was considered unspeakably arrogant at the time,' says David Levy, 'but it was a pretty innocent thing to ask for, really. There was a definite cheekiness to it.'

Cream had to make sure the technical aspects of the club

were spot on for the DJ. 'He helped put all the equipment together in the booth,' says James Barton. 'We had to supply an engineer, to make sure the set-up was just right. Paul came at it the way a touring band would. He had a roadie with him. We nicknamed him Bono! I think the whole experience of touring with U2 switched him on to how things should be done, and how well.'

It certainly made waves in the dance music press, an area of the media always ready to raise a questioning eyebrow towards a highly visible DJ like Oakenfold. There were murmurings in the media that Paul was getting a bit above his station, that he was forcing these demands on Cream. 'People were used to their little industry being the way it always was,' says Ben Turner, former editor of *Muzik* magazine. 'You turned up at a club, you'd be lucky if there's a beer there, the promoter might put some pills in your pocket and that's your night sorted. David Levy ensured that things were done differently around Paul. Paul was the first to really turn it into a full career, the first to have heavyweight management, the first to use a serious agent who would treat his bookings in a rock and roll way. When you look at that Cream contract, there were things built into it that no one had ever dreamt of putting into a DJ agreement before. When we heard about it at *Muzik*, we were outraged that any club would agree to it. I think it was a shock to James, a shock to Cream, a shock to everybody that a DJ would be demanding these things.'

James Barton was adamant they'd made the right choice. 'There were other DJs who we thought were big enough to do it, but we didn't think they'd be reliable enough or professional enough,' he says. 'I think a lot of people were particularly pissed off it was Cream and not their club that came up with the idea, or even if they did come up with the idea, they were never able to get to the finishing post with Paul. He had to be the most famous DJ in the world at the time, although Carl Cox was massive, definitely up there with Paul, and Sasha was certainly a huge DJ. Paul had everything; he was not only at the top of his game, but he was also highly professional. He was motivated enough to come all the way from London every week. A lot of DJs wouldn't have made it. They would have been playing in Nottingham, and given themselves an hour and a half to get here, or would have got stuck in Glasgow at some two-day party. It really mattered to Paul. Out of all the DJs we worked with, he had more of a plan than anybody else. The fact that he brought in an agent like David Levy at ITB so early on gives you an indication of how far Paul thought his career would extend. Paul was very serious about what he did. He treated it with the utmost respect. He loved it, he had fun doing it, but he always took it seriously. He realised that if he made the right decisions he would be very successful indeed at this. From the moment it was conceived, everything about it was one of the most professional things we ever undertook.'

'I got a lot of stick from the media when the rumour went round that I had this massive rider,' says Paul, 'but I'd learnt from touring with U2 that there's a proper way of doing business. Having a proper contract with Cream was the right thing to do. Even though it seemed long, most of what was in the contract would soon become standard throughout the industry. There was give and take on each side. I was allowed four weeks off a year, and I couldn't play within a hundred-mile radius of Cream. In return, I wanted to have a say in the technical side. Cream allowed me to get really involved. I had a say in the booth design, I brought a friend in every week who decorated the room with psychedelic artwork, so when we turned the black [fluoro] light on the whole place just came alive, it was electric. I chose who the opening DJ was every week, for continuity – I chose Paul Bleasdale, who was very good. All that went into the contract. I'm not the kind of person that would take advantage – anything I asked for in the contract, I could back up. I don't think I asked for anything that I didn't require; I wasn't saying "give me a case of champagne and I want fifty of my friends let in for free". I didn't want a booth full of people, I wanted the booth to be clear, so that you're focused. And that kind of thing never really happens – you look at a booth and there'd be loads of people in there. So I said they should build a little area beside the booth. That was for their good as well as mine, because it was a lot of their friends who were trying to get in. It was about getting the creative and professional side right.'

James Barton disagrees that Cream were forced into accepting unreasonable demands. 'I don't want anyone reading this to think we were forced into agreeing to this shit,' he says. 'We wanted this, we wanted to make a big statement about our club, about how important we thought Paul Oakenfold was, how important we thought DJs were. This was the next step up for DJs, a twelve-month contract, reams and reams of paper . . . it deserved the expense and the time and effort that went into it, because in our mind it was a huge fucking deal. It actually turned out to be an even bigger deal than we thought it would be, because Paul's residency has gone down in dance music history.'

Never slow to conjure up a story, the Cream PR machine went into overdrive for the Oakenfold signing. 'We knew Paul was a keen Chelsea fan,' says James, 'and it genuinely felt as though we were signing a number nine, signing a star player like Wayne Rooney to our stable.' In a move reminiscent of the Sex Pistols inking their short-lived deal with A&M Records outside Buckingham Palace, Paul and Cream set their sights on Chelsea's stadium at Stamford Bridge. 'The idea was hatched that we would have lunch, we'd sign the contracts with Paul and his agent, the sort of stuff you see in *Music Week* with all the big nobs round the table, and then go down to Stamford Bridge,' says James. 'So we went down there, I went into the club shop and bought the number-nine Chelsea shirt and had "OAKFOLD" printed on to the back of it! Everyone turned to us, Paul, his agent, journalists, photographers . . . I get the shirt out and they said "You've spelt it fucking wrong, you idiot!" The scary thing was that when we went back to the shop, they couldn't find the letters to do it again properly. They found them in the end, thank God. I think it was one of the most iconic photographs ever taken for Cream.'

'The shirt they used was massive,' says Paul. 'We were stand ing there on the pitch, holding on to this blanket!' The dance and trade music press lapped it up. 'I'd never seen something like it before in this genre of music,' says Ben Turner. 'You felt that, as serious as it was, they were poking fun at everyone else. It did wind people up, but to me that was the story that every- one wanted to know about. Paul always had a story – every year he came up with something that you couldn't ignore. And it was all masterminded by him, James Barton and David Levy. They created this whole ongoing story, which was great content for us. I remember getting the phone call when Oakey signed for Cream – they came to us for the exclusive, and for the next few years, if you wanted to know what was happen- ing in that story, you read our magazine. It was such a strong story, it helped us sell magazines. It became like a soap opera. It was like *CSI* – you have gotta keep watching.'

For the first year of the residency Paul played in the Annexe, building an intensely loyal following. His relationship with Darren Hughes was becoming particularly strong. 'Darren would be standing next to him all fucking night,' says James Barton. 'They'd talk before the set, Darren would be there throughout, then they'd go back to Darren's, and over a few drinks they'd talk about the night and they'd score it out of ten!'

'There was never a ten out of ten in all the time I played at Cream,' says Paul. 'I'm my own worst critic. In a lot of people's eyes there were unbeatable nights, but if a mix went slightly out, you've lost your ten out of ten. Being a Virgo, it's all about perfection, striving to be better. You push yourself every single week. It could be brilliant for other people, but for me and Darren, we knew we could get it even better. We were like brothers. We would analyse it on Monday, break it down, think about where it could go musically. I'd go to the studio and make special mixes. There was a tremendous amount of work that went into it during the week.'

'It was like a coach and a footballer,' says James Barton. 'That was one of Darren's best roles for Cream. They put so much effort into it, so much detail – you know, "Fourth record in, you dropped a mix, don't play this record again." They recorded every set.'

For year two of the residency, it was decided the time was right for a larger arena. 'Paul felt that although it'd been a great year, there was really nowhere else to go,' says James Barton. 'I think Paul had made his mind up to move on. Towards the end of the first year, a lot of people were thinking he'd leave Cream.'

'The Annexe was intense,' says Paul. 'It was one of the most intense situations I'd been in, verging on dangerous. It had a really low ceiling, it wasn't necessarily a small room because you had the whole back area, but there was so many people in there that at times it felt really dangerous. We were lucky that we had no problems with it.'

'Me, Darren and Jim hatched a plan to ask Paul to move into a bigger space, the Courtyard,' says James. Paul was hesitant at first. 'Whatever I do in life, I have to keep moving,' says Paul. 'I wondered where the challenge was – I've got to have a challenge. It was Jim that changed my mind. He said "Here's the challenge – you go into a far bigger room, you design it with us and we make the whole thing even better." I thought OK, this is a real step up. Let's do it.'

'On the first night a huge buzz was flying around,' says James. 'Everything had been prepared. I was in the DJ booth with David Levy, Paul Bleasdale was playing, people were dancing, but they were also waiting for something to happen. It was a bit like watching the support band, waiting for the headline to come on. What normally happens is that when someone like Paul Oakenfold, or Carl Cox or Danny Rampling, walks into the DJ booth ten minutes before they're due to go on, the crowd recognises them and they'd all go crazy. On this occasion, Paul sort of sneaked in, kept his head down. The Courtyard booth was quite high up, so he was able to stay out of sight. He was literally down on the floor of the booth while Paul Bleasdale's playing. Paul Bleasdale finished his set, and Oakey just put his hand up and put a record on the deck. I think he brought his tune down to about half the volume, just a rhythm track . . . the lights went down, the atmosphere started to build, and then after a minute or two of this rhythm track,

Paul appears, and puts on BT's "Flaming June". I just remember the tune kicking in, the lights kicking in, and then this almighty roar from the crowd. I was standing next to David Levy when it all kicked off and the crowd were going nuts. I turned round to David and said "Now they can say that this is the best nightclub in the world." People don't see what goes on behind the scenes, they don't see the struggles, the holes in the walls letting in the rain, the toilets blocking up. People were just in love or in awe of what was going on here. That's when I realised how big Paul was becoming. Now they can say that he's the best DJ in the world.'

From here on in, it was full-on Oakenfold mania at Cream, the like of which had never been seen for any other British DJ emerging from acid house. 'It was the move to the Courtyard that did it,' says James Barton. 'It was a bigger, brighter room, you could fit a lot more people in. That's when they started the Oakey chant! You know, "Oakey, Oakey, Oakey!" '

The level of intensity was phenomenal. 'The moment he put the needle on his vinyl, the place roared like England had just scored the winning goal in the Cup Final. It still gives me goosebumps just thinking about it,' says Cream regular Martin Heaps. 'It was so good that if we'd heard we'd won the lottery on the way down, the only thing we'd want to do was still go to Cream. Being an instant millionaire wouldn't have changed a thing,' says another Cream regular, Craig Docherty.

'Looking out into the crowd was mad,' says Paul. 'You'd see all these banners. I was locked into the music, right in the zone, but all around me were banners and a sea of faces. They'd come from all over the country, from Southampton, Glasgow, Ireland. I remember being told it was like a church; every Saturday night was like a church where you just religiously go for that vibe. And they all had their special places, their special spots . . . you would see them fighting for their spot on the podium! I'd always make eye contact. If you see a band and look at the singer, if the singer looks back at you it makes your day, so I would make a conscious effort to look into people's eyes, to recognise them when I played. It's a wonderful feeling! It was great just to see people happy. Sometimes I'd leave Chelsea, rush home, I'd have a car waiting for me, take me to the airport, jump on a plane, get to Manchester, come across, and fucking hell, I'd be knackered! That feeling made it all worth it.'

'It became a legendary thing, with a life of its own,' says David Levy. 'Everybody's off their tits on very pure drugs, he's playing this extremely messianic music, developing this whole arm stretch thing; kids would stand in exactly the same spot week after week . . . you realised people were religiously following this. *Mixmag* tried to interview me about DJ culture and I very cockily said, "Well, there's models and super-models, and there's DJs and super-DJs." The next month they printed it and that was that, the superstar DJ was born. Wish I'd never fucking said it!'

DJ fandom at Cream soon approached stalker-like pro-portions. 'There were male and female obsessives, tailing him to the hotel, handing over notes and teddy bears,' says James Barton. 'It was just like you'd expect for any pop or rock star.' 'It did get a little bit strange,' says Paul. 'I'd be brought presents, records, photos for signing. One girl would give me plants, flowers and clothes she'd made. She kept bringing me presents every week. She was a nice girl, but it did get out of control and I didn't know how to stop it. She climbed into the booth once, and the security grabbed her. I tried to get the security to go easy on her, but they banned her from the club. She started turning up at other gigs; it started to get really weird . . .'

Ben Turner made the trip from London every weekend. 'It was the place to be,' he says. 'It caused such chaos, such amazing scenes in the city. You'd got this Saturday-afternoon buzz that you only really get in the North of England when there's a big DJ in town. There would be police helicopters over the club, there would be armed police outside; it was all quite terrifying, but it added to the theatre of what was going on.'

'I was aware of the problems in the background,' says Paul. 'Cream knew that they had to work with the police, they knew that they couldn't have dealers and criminals running their club because they would have lost their livelihood. They were very conscious of it, and they worked quite tightly with the police to sort it out – they had to. I liked the edge that it brought to the night – it was raw and real. It reminded me of what we'd done at Spectrum and Future. It didn't really bother me. You'd meet a lot of villains, a lot of the wrong people, but it was just like when we met all of the football thugs at Spectrum. All of the West Ham used to go to Spectrum. They'd be pilled up and cuddling you!'

The London-based record community would also make regular trips to Liverpool. 'All the major record label people, like Stuart Dashwood, Paul Brown, the people signing the big dance records, they'd be up there with Oakey every week, seeing the reaction to that one special new record that got dropped into the set that week,' says Ben Turner. 'What was so special about it was that familiarity of the DJ playing the same records in a certain way every week, and then one record would get dropped and a new one would come in. That new record would explode at Cream, and everyone would start asking for it in 3 Beat. It almost became like the Pete Tong show, but in a club. You just had to be there.'

'What I'd learnt from watching Larry Levan at Paradise Garage,' says Paul, 'is that you don't play the records in the same order every week, you change it around, but you do keep playing them week after week. If you're playing a track six months in advance of release, like "Bullet In A Gun", you could create an absolute anthem. You create the demand, then other DJs want it, then the shops are after it. That's what I thought a DJ was meant to do – break records. For example I found a B-side of a CJ Bolland track called "The Prophet". The A-side was a funky house track, but I caned the B-side for about nine months and it became a huge anthem. The record company re-released it and it went top twenty. I was also A&Ring a lot of the tracks, so I'd tell the artists what to do. BT was signed to me, so I'd ask him to put a big ambient intro on his track to make it work for the club. I would have certain mixes of records that no one else would have, tailor-made to suit my style at Cream. Then we'd get the artists up to perform – we did this for "Bullet In A Gun", for Mansun – the "Wide Open Space" mix was huge. I'd done the remix specifically for that one room. These records may not have been a hit any-where else, but when they performed at the club, they were rock stars, because I'd been playing that record for six months!'

'The residency became quite a pilgrimage,' says Ben Turner. 'It was amazing to walk into the club and see the kind of impact he had. It was all built on rock and roll ideals – how the lights are all dimmed before the band goes on stage, how the sound elevates as the main act comes on – those were things Paul Oakenfold did before any other DJ, which are now quite commonplace. He did it first. You could argue that Junior Vasquez at the Sound Factory, or Sasha at Twilo were as important, or Danny Tenaglia's residencies, but from a UK perspective, in that era, Paul's residency at Cream was undoubtedly the big one. People in America may not acknowledge that, but in England that residency was very important.'

'The real reason the Cream residency became legendary was that he went there every week,' says David Levy. 'He really put the legwork in. Over the two years he did around eighty-five performances. This wasn't a monthly residency at Twilo, this wasn't Gordon Ramsay opening six restaurants and cooking in only one of them, this was Paul saying "I'm going to the North of England, I'm staying in the shitty Adelphi Hotel where the locks don't work, and I'm going to give you something no one in the world has access to." It was a very romantic idea. For the E generation, they'd never had a hero like that. I don't think anyone before or after has touched a nerve in quite the same way.'

To an irregular visitor, the benefit to the city of Liverpool of the combination of Paul Oakenfold and Cream seems obvious. Wolstenholme Square appeared to be little more than a shabby warehouse area near Chinatown in the mid-eighties; it's now surrounded by new bars and clubs. In a recent induction survey conducted at Liverpool's John Moore's University, 70 per cent of students listed Cream as their main reason for choosing to study in Liverpool. James Barton was made an ambassador of Merseyside in 1997; Paul Oakenfold became *DJ* magazine's number-one worldwide DJ in 1998.

'The main thing I loved about the Cream residency was the people,' says Paul. 'They were wonderful. The Liverpudlians are a great people. I can honestly say that it was my second home. The people had a unity about them that Londoners didn't. They had their dark side, the drug dealers, the villains, just like anywhere else, but they had passion, they were friendly, they made an effort to dress up. It was a really big deal for me. They really appreciated me coming from London every week, and they made you feel so welcome. I'd got that a little bit at Spectrum and Future, and I got that later at Home, but never like it was in Liverpool.'

'Cream had reached a peak by '97,' says Ben Turner. 'The Oakenfold residency was something that they actually really needed, which is probably why they gave Paul everything he ever wanted. It needed some kind of stability. They tried Deep Dish, they tried various people, it just didn't work. Then the Oakenfold thing happened, and that was it – it reached a new level. After three years of that, when he left, when it was Seb Fontaine as resident, that was when Cream as a club started to dip. There may not be one bigger player than the team, but Paul Oakenfold created a monster.'

# 12

# Bringing It All Back Home

During the second year of Paul Oakenfold's Cream residency, the club was hit by an unexpected bombshell that would significantly alter the DJ's future path. Darren Hughes, an essential ingredient to the Cream mix, decided to leave in June 1998. 'Me and Darren splitting up and him leaving Cream was a fucking big deal,' says James Barton. 'It probably didn't mean much to people on the street, but in our world, it was huge. We tried to talk him into staying . . . I don't think we did a very good job with that! It had been an ideal partnership for ten years, but there were a lot of problems between us, which ended up in court. Darren had already announced that he was opening up a new club in London.'

Paul was also looking to expand his DJ horizons. 'Cream wanted me to go into the main room for the third year of the residency, but I didn't like that room,' he says. 'I didn't like the shape of it. I've never really admitted it, but maybe I should have done another year. Looking back at it, I could have got another year out of it, but I'd spent two years, every single

Saturday night, going up and down the motorway. I was just tired. And having been travelling around all my life, I started to get the bug again. I wanted to go somewhere else. That's the main reason I left – I wanted to get back to travelling.'

Paul's feelings about leaving the club that he had made his own were decidedly mixed. 'I was sad that I was leaving,' said Paul around the time of his departure. 'It had obviously crossed my mind – had I made the right decision? Because I am leaving without a doubt the best room in the country, the best sound system, the best crowd. Everyone who's been to that room knows how good it was. I worked really hard at it and it had got to the point where I couldn't take it anywhere else. So I needed to leave it at its peak, so I could look back and say "Yeah, I really achieved something with that club." '

'The option for year three was to move into the main room,' says David Levy. 'It was a bit of a corridor. Don't forget, the Courtyard was more or less built to our specifications. It was always going to be hard to improve on that. The trek to Liverpool was also starting to take its toll. In the end Paul and I didn't feel that Cream could realise Paul's international ambitions as well as we could realise them on our own. So we basically pulled out at this point. Triggered by Darren.'

Paul denied he'd signed up for Darren Hughes's new London-based club. 'That's just idle gossip on the scene,' he said. 'I've not accepted any residency in London. I haven't signed anything.' This was all soon to change.

Cream had for some time been in talks with Ron McCulloch, a club promoter and entrepreneur based in Scotland, who'd started out as a DJ at a club called Reaction Dolly Disco in Glasgow in the seventies. McCulloch's Big Beat organisation owned the Tunnel Club in Glasgow, as well as a string of clubs and bars, even a microbrewery. Big Beat had recently opened a new club called Home in Sydney, Australia, and had major UK expansion plans. Cream held regular monthly parties at the Tunnel Club, and were seriously interested when McCulloch tabled the idea of buying a 50 per cent stake in Cream. 'The idea was that Big Beat would fund a global expansion for Cream,' says James Barton. 'We were talking about nightclubs around the world, merchandise, record labels . . . and a new Cream nightclub in London, at 1 Leicester Square.'

The proposed scheme didn't get off the ground. 'Basically, I wanted more involvement from James to take Cream forward,' says Darren Hughes. 'Gatecrasher was hot on our heels, and we needed to make a move, but James wasn't feeling the desire to open a club in London and branch out worldwide. Things weren't moving quickly enough for me.' Darren wasn't going to give up on the Leicester Square venue however – the site was soon to become the location for Darren, Ron McCulloch and Irish promoter John Reynolds's new venture, a club called Home.

This new set-up obviously affected Cream's main DJ resident. 'I knew for a fact Darren wanted Paul to play at the new venue,' says James Barton. 'That was a big downside. One of the things we agreed in Paul's contract was that if Bono or the Smashing Pumpkins come calling, or an Oscar party or a *Vanity Fair* party came up, and these are the sort of things that Paul used to do, we'd allow him to take a week off to go and do that. We were absolutely relaxed about that, because we knew that Paul was the best ambassador we could have had. We knew that Paul was in LA, Tokyo, Shanghai, Milan, or Paris, you name it, talking about Cream. So to lose that could have been a major blow. But there was another side. Paul's residency was the best thing that ever happened to us, but potentially it could have been one of the worst things that happened to us, because it was so big. We had a club that had three rooms, and Paul only played in one of them – the majority of people that were coming to the club wanted to see Paul. Towards the end of his second-year residency, it was in danger of becoming all about Paul; certainly some of the other rooms were suffering. We still offered him a third year, partly because we didn't want him to go to Darren at Home, and also because it was like we'd adopted him . . . he'd become part of the fabric of the business and the brand and the club and everything else. We didn't want to lose that. Initially, he indicated that he would consider staying. The talks sort of fizzled out.'

For the DJ, it wasn't simply a case of just leaving Cream and plotting up at Home, however. 'I didn't leave Cream to go to Home,' says Paul. 'I left Cream and said "Listen, I'm having a year off." I had done a year travelling and then Home came along. I thought, you know what, I want to live twenty minutes from a club and then have all my international friends flying in. It was really hard to get people from abroad to fly up to Liverpool.'

'I wasn't surprised that he made the decision to go with them,' says James Barton. 'I knew he would really get off on the challenge, because that's what it had been like with Cream. The temptation of the possibility of creating a huge new night-club and empire, based in London, was too much. I didn't feel any animosity towards Paul whatsoever. Paul was always very respectful, and didn't want to get drawn into the issues that existed between me and Darren. Paul tried to stay neutral. He dealt with it the right way.'

It was a major blow to Cream, but with a few years' hindsight, James Barton manages to remain sanguine about the split. 'Paul had given us two years, and we'd done great things together,' he says. 'On reflection, a third year perhaps wouldn't have worked. At the time, we'd already lost Darren – to lose Paul to the same organisation . . . you don't want to know how I felt about it. But the amount of times Cream has meant to have been finished as a result of something like this – it's about once every two or three years. I knew it wasn't the end of us. We just fucking went back to work.'

After seven months of contract negotiation, Paul signed to Home on a three-year deal, playing for three hours early every Sunday morning, with ten weeks off a year.

The dance media was all over the move. Expectations were a little high, to say the least; 'The world's biggest DJ comes home to save London's clubland,' declared *Muzik*'s front page. 'I want the challenge of making Home like a northern club,' said Paul. 'The challenge for me is to recreate what I had at Spectrum and Cream, and yes, London will be hard. Sure, Leicester Square can be tacky, but the music and the door policy will make Home work. It will be a northern superclub in terms of vibe; a creative, cutting edge nightclub, pulling an international crowd – the sort of people who fly from New York or Europe for the weekend. I hope that the north of England comes down and experiences it too. Let's put it this way, if I get half the atmosphere we had at Cream, we will have achieved what no one else has in London.'

Inside the new venue, Home more than made up for its tourist-heavy location. Eight million pounds were lavished on the seven-storey space. As with Cream, Steve Dash's team flew in from New York to fit the sound system. The restaurant at the top of the venue was chic city dining at its finest, looking out over the London skyline. There was a huge video wall outside, and TVs in the walls by the see-through lifts. Even the men's toilets were VIP class, featuring a huge glass waterfall. 'Peeing is believing,' remarked the press release, somewhat overenthusiastically.

Paul helped programme the DJ line-up, which included weekly residents Tim Sheridan and Steve Lawler, with Danny Tenaglia and the Chemical Brothers on a monthly basis. It was a solid line-up. 'We had a really international crowd,' says Paul. 'I was like, "Listen, book yourself into a fucking great hotel, come and hang out in the West End." You've got a high-end bar, you've got this fantastic restaurant with an amazing view, and a real jet-set crowd.' The private opening party, the day before the club opened to the public, was a top-notch ligger's beanfeast. Rod Stewart chatted to Ronnie Wood; the Prodigy mingled with Denise van Outen and Jamiroquai. Chris Eubank turned up in his lorry, while the Chemical Brothers were ultra-keen to meet newly famous TV chef Jamie Oliver.

The club opened to the public on Friday, 10 September 1999. Home avoided being swamped by passing tourist trade by asking clubbers to name the DJs playing that night. There were some initial teething problems – the sound system needed a tweak, and clubber Craig Docherty remembers 'the paint still being wet in the main room . . . I've still got the jeans to prove it!' There was a more pressing concern a few weeks into the club's life. There was a massive brawl at Home's door, outside the MOBO Awards after-party, involving around a hundred people. The police took a very dim view, and lodged a prosecution against the club, aiming to revoke Home's licence. The threat hung over the venue for the next eight months, but was eventually dropped. 'It was an event which turned pretty ugly,' says Ron McCulloch, 'but there were no arrests, no injuries. I've tried to put my finger on the problem. We haven't been able to get a working relationship going with the police, or gain their confidence.'

The challenge of creating a successful superclub from scratch, in turn-of-the-century London, was pretty tough. *Time Out*'s Dave Swindells, a London clubland veteran of many years' standing, was one of many to have doubts. 'I'm not sceptical about Home's success,' said Dave soon after the opening night, 'but there is a question mark about it also being cutting-edge. London is very volatile. Super-clubbing has gone out of the window – it's a '97 thing. There's been a reaction against it in London.' Club rival Ministry of Sound were predictably sneery: 'It's all a bit Planet Hollywood, with Paul Oakenfold as Sylvester Stallone,' bitched Ministry manager Mark Rodol. 'Ministry of Sound was a very dominant, aggressive presence in London,' says David Levy. 'It's no secret that Ministry's James Palumbo hiked the rent up by bidding for the space, just to fuck them. They ended up paying double the rent, because Palumbo kept bidding it up.'

Despite the daggers, by January 2000, Paul was cautiously optimistic. 'We're getting there,' he told *Muzik* magazine. 'We're finding our feet. We have got the regular faces who come down every week, and people from Cream who come down. I take time out after every show to talk to them, see what they think. I expected the criticism. It's London. It's Leicester Square. It was obvious that it was going to come. We just keep our heads down, just do our best and get on with it.'

Despite a string of good nights for Paul, the combination of the location, a strangely soulless venue, and the attentions of Scotland Yard plagued Home right from the off. It never really developed a loyal, regular fan base; ultimately police and council pressure proved too much to bear. In March 2001, Westminster Council revoked Home's public entertainment licence, using the Public Entertainment Licences (Drug Misuse) Act, which was set up following a drug-related death at a far less organised London night spot, Club UK. Scotland Yard's clubs and vice unit had mounted a series of undercover operations and found evidence of dealing on the premises – a lone dealer with sixteen pills in his pocket. Hardly a crime wave, but the police made the most of it. They even reported being offered free drugs. Ron McCulloch was livid. 'The decision is incredible,' he said. 'The police are making an example of us. Historically we have one of the best records of any club in the country for helping police do their job and having a hard anti-drugs policy. The action is undoubtedly unwarranted in my view.'

The police thought otherwise. A Scotland Yard spokesman told *The Scotsman* that the police drug unit had found that the Home staff weren't tough enough on drug users and dealers, compared to other clubs. Club owners were expected to hand over confiscated drugs and alleged dealers to the police; according to Scotland Yard, these were of far lower numbers at Home than elsewhere. Ron McCulloch disagrees. 'They compared us to Heaven, a club which is open four or five nights a week compared to our three,' he says. 'When our club is handing in twenty confiscated bags of pills compared to their eighty or whatever, you tell me who has a drug problem.' The drug unit's chief inspector, Chris Bradford, was obviously out to make a high-profile example of Home. 'Our actions should serve as a warning to other premises where there is a serious drug problem, that we are prepared to use all our powers to solve the problem,' he said.

After such phenomenal success at Cream, Home's failure was a blow to Paul. 'It was a fantastic idea,' he says. 'We had John Reynolds from Ireland, Ron McCulloch from Scotland and Darren Hughes from Cream – these were the best fucking three organisations, and then we had a club that, in theory, was in fact very similar to Cream . . . in the beginning, we had twenty-five coaches from all over the country coming to that place. It was just the location. I was never sure about the location – all the best clubs are off the main square, up back alleys. I was never comfortable with being right in the middle of town, in the bull's-eye. It was Ron McCulloch who talked us all into it. We were just fucked. We were constantly being screwed, the knives were constantly out. Ministry were really sticking the boot in; trying to find dirt on Darren. We were a big threat to them. Westminster Council were totally against it, they wouldn't give us a late licence; the venue had to close at three, while the Hippodrome up the road had a licence until six. We couldn't get the same licence as The End, because they come under Camden Council, in a different borough. We couldn't get a late licence, so we couldn't compete.'

Coming to London proved to be out of the range of many people's pockets. 'People started to not want to come to London,' says Paul. 'To come up to London for the weekend is very different from going to Liverpool for the weekend – it's two completely different prices. We were expecting a lot from people, to come down on a regular basis, on a coach, to stay in a hotel because they can't get home, and to pay West End prices. I think that was one of the things that was a big oversight. There were twenty-five coaches on the first night, but six months in, there were about three.'

'It was doomed to failure from the start,' says David Levy. 'It was such a nasty, negative experience negotiating the deal. They had their claws in Paul so heavily. It put a real strain on us. On the night before the opening, Paul and I went for dinner at J. Sheekey's in Covent Garden, and I told him what I thought. I gave him a Rolex and said "Wear this on your wrist, and every time you look at it, think of me, because I'm never setting foot in that club." And he said "Fair enough." Many people tried to come between us over the years, and no one tried harder than Home.'

The story of Cream had been one of a gradual, organic success, with sturdy roots slowly grown over a relatively long period. Home went into the heart of London's West End with guns blazing, waving a large chequebook, without building any real loyalty amongst its punters. 'It was quite transparent that Home was all about money,' says Ben Turner, former editor of *Muzik*. 'It was about Ron McCulloch bidding against Ministry of Sound for this space in Leicester Square, and paying through the nose for it. They never could find their way back from that. Oakenfold decided to go with Darren, rather than James, which in hindsight was a mistake. The cool kids didn't want to go to Leicester Square, it was the last thing in the world they wanted to do. The only bit that worked at Home was the View Bar VIP lounge. There were some amazing weeks on the dancefloor with Paul, but overall, it didn't really lock in to a regular audience. After Cream, where could Paul go in England? What else could he do?'

One thing Paul could do, in the aftermath of Home, was to enjoy a fine season in Ibiza. Summer 2001 saw Paul make his regular return trip to the white island for a series of Perfecto parties at Pacha. Guests included Timo Maas, Seb Fontaine, Carl Cox and Daniele Davoli. Season after season, Perfecto have delivered consistent, well-loved sessions in Ibiza, and have become one of the top draws for many a Balearic traveller.

On 24 August 2001, Paul headlined the biggest solo London gig of his career, a Channel 4-sponsored free party at Clapham Common. The channel had just acquired the rights to show the Ashes, cricket's main draw, from the BBC, and wanted to celebrate in style. They mounted a huge campaign in London promoting the fact, and announced that they would put up a huge screen in Clapham Common for the first England v Australia showdown. Paul had a friend at Channel 4's marketing department, who managed to book the DJ to play after the cricket for free, as a favour. There was only one problem. In the run-up to the event, England managed to lose the cricket series; it was pretty much over by the time the match reached Clapham Common. Channel 4 had made a commitment to screen the match, and had taken out advertising space all over town. The billboards were changed accordingly – instead of promoting the cricket on the big screen, Channel 4 now elevated Paul's DJ set to the top of the bill. There was a food stand, a reasonable-sized DJ area, a few toilets, a couple of policemen and a dog. A handful of security guards loitered round the front of the DJ booth. Everybody was expecting a couple of thousand people to take advantage of this warm summer's day, leisurely pitching up for some nice tunes in the park. Big mistake. According to the police count, around seventy thousand people turned up.

'It was fucking phenomenal,' says Marc Marot. 'It was one of the most gobsmacking moments. Channel 4 were completely

**Left:** *Paul head to head with Darren Emerson.*

**Above:** *Sharing a joke with Tom Rowlands from the Chemical Brothers.*

**Left:** *A hug from Sandra Collins.*

**Below:** *Paul and Fabio.*

**Inset:** *Paul, Hernan Cattaneo and Alex Patterson (The Orb).*

**Main picture and left:**
*Tower Records, LA.*

**Below:** *California and Shanghai – Oakenfold arrives.*

**Below:** *The record box that went missing.*

*One man and his bus, Area: One tour, 2001.*

**Left:** *Paul with Nelly Furtado.*

**Right:** *Paul and Dave Ralph cooling off.*

**Above:** *Promotional stickers for Bunkka.*

**Right:** *Oakenfold scores James Bond.*

**Left:** *An invitation from Her Majesty.*

**Below:** *Stirring up the crowd – promotion for a show at Narcissus, Bangkok.*

GREAT WALL

PAUL OAKENFOLD

Technics

*Paul in warrior mode, the day after the Great Wall of China event.*

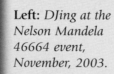

**Left:** *DJing at the Nelson Mandela 46664 event, November, 2003.*

**Right:** *Perfecto's Dan Rosenthal, Paul and LA club promoter Dean May.*

**Clockwise from left:** *Paul with Paris Hilton; at a video shoot with Brittany Murphy; Mickey Jackson, Paul and Trevor Fung; Paul in Marrakesh; memorabilia from Madonna's 'Confessions' tour.*

caught on the hop. By the time there were seventy thousand people there, this supposedly giant screen they'd put up looked like a telly. Paul's playing to a crowd the size of Glastonbury, and there's this little screen with a DJ set-up beside it with a small sound system. It was a riot.'

'I played at Wembley Stadium opening for U2, but the Clapham Common gig was arguably my biggest-ever gig in London,' says Paul. 'This was my gig, and it was free. No one in their right mind expected what went on. It was meant to be people sitting watching the cricket, with a bit of a party after. I was thinking "It's a nice day, we'll get maybe ten thousand," but the build-up was massive – they changed the advertising, so all over London I had these big billboard posters up. It became not just a South London event, it became a massive free party for the whole city. The people just didn't stop coming.'

Things got a bit out of hand at the end, however. Channel 4 had told the Clapham residents that they'd pull the plug at eight, pretty early for an outdoor DJ gig. 'The moment they put the Channel 4 logo on to end the show, bottles and cans started flying,' says Marc Marot. 'Unfortunately the hospitality area was directly behind the screen – we had to hide while vodka bottles were thumping on the roof, whacking into Channel 4 executives' cars! It was like Beirut!'

After the cut and thrust of clubland politics surrounding Home, there was something of a more positive, personal nature on Paul's mind – marriage. Paul and Angela Costa were married in Italy, on 20 September 2002. Paul and Angela met in the early nineties. 'I met her at Nicky Holloway's Milk Bar, next to the Astoria on Charing Cross Road,' says Paul. 'I was the resident there every Friday. It blossomed from there. We had a great time; we moved into a new property, Rosslyn House in Putney, in 1994. I proposed to her in Cape Town, then we got married in Positano, a really romantic town, one road in, one road out, not big enough for cars to pass each other. I hired Franco Zeffirelli's house there. Angela walked down the cobbled stone streets, on a Saturday afternoon, to this little church where we got married. All the people were clapping. It was really beautiful. We had all her family there, from Italy and Ireland, and I flew all my family over. It was great to have everyone around. It was a fairy-tale wedding.'

Mickey Jackson was Paul's best man. 'There are a lot of things that the best man sorts out,' he says. 'I've been away with Paul a lot and I know how he likes things done – it was like being on tour! It was a great wedding, a real occasion. We had about three stag parties! We arrived about four days before the wedding, which was great logistically as everyone had time to get to know each other, and we hung around for about four days afterwards in this beautiful place – we had our own castle. We all had a great time. It was really Paul's inner circle of friends and family at the time – no agents, no managers. He's a very private person. It was very touching.'

'It was a lovely wedding,' says Sheila Oakenfold. 'There was this church with a beautiful dome, and a beach there. They had a woman singing "Ave Maria"; it was magnificent. Sid did a speech, and Mickey Jackson did one. They'd do the speeches in English, and Daniele Davoli would translate them into Italian.'

'I was up all night writing that speech,' says Mickey Jackson. 'I remember I rushed through it – Daniele Davoli had to get me to slow down. It was all over the place, but I delivered; they got all the laughs and they got the sentiment. It was a great honour to be asked to be best man.'

'They kept calling me the beautiful mama,' says Sheila Oakenfold. 'Paul wanted me to do a speech but I said no, I'd start crying. So Sid did his, and then everyone was crying.'

With a new bride to look after, and the memories of Cream and Home fading into the distance, it was clear Paul needed a new challenge, and a new base. His thoughts turned to America.

# 13

# Trans-America Express

Paul Oakenfold's journey to America follows the ever-expanding path of acid house and dance music culture as they spread stealthily across the globe. The sound may have originated in Chicago and Detroit, but once it flew to Europe and subsequently bounced back across the Atlantic, a new core of house-loving cities, and a far broader audience, began to emerge. New York and San Francisco are generally acknowledged as playing key roles in the early development of this expanding, mutated electronic dance culture as it took hold in the States. Brooklyn DJ Frankie Bones' Storm Rave events, alongside Recess, Toon Town and the Wicked collective's nights in San Francisco, are some of the earliest examples of 'rave' culture in America. Many of these nights had strong transatlantic links. Frankie Bones first discovered the possibilities of large-scale trance dancing on the floor at Paul Oakenfold's Spectrum. 'I'm on my first E . . . and all this shit is going through my head – "you've got to bring this back to America"', he tells Simon Reynolds in *Energy Flash*. Over in

246

San Francisco, Doc Martin's Recess nights paved the way for Osmosis at DV8, where the Wicked collective, a bunch of British expats with strong links to Harvey and Choci's influential British sound system Tonka, made inroads with their full-moon beach parties. Mark Heley, a former journalist from London style bible *i-D*, arrived in San Francisco in 1991, hooking up with Preston Lytton and Diana Jacobs to promote the first Toon Town party in spring 1992. The knock-on effect of Spectrum reverberated on both coasts.

Less widely reported is a nascent dance culture beginning to take shape in Los Angeles. Once again, there's a direct link to Spectrum. After Ian St Paul's ammonia incident at Land of Oz, he headed out of London and ended up in LA, intent on spreading the acid gospel. He hooked up with Mark Lewis, a former classmate at Carshalton boys' school, who'd moved to the city of angels in 1986 and gradually became established as a DJ. 'I started DJing here in the middle of '88,' says Mark. 'I was working in a club called the Batcave in Marina Del Ray, and was introduced to two guys called Steve and John Levy that were doing a night called West Go West I filled in for them one night, then they said "You're from London, do you wanna play for us every week?" so I did. Then they started the Moonshine parties.' The Moonshine parties were legendary affairs; the first real flowering of an alternative LA dance scene. 'The Moonshine parties were amazing,' says Ken Jordan of LA-based dance act the Crystal Method. 'It was pretty basic – I remember this freight elevator, the smell of fish and a garbage bin full of beers – but most of all, there was a sense of wonderment. More than the music, more than the drugs, there was a real sense of community in the whole early LA dance scene.'

The Moonshine events soon developed legs. 'We were doing Moonshine as an illegal party when Ian St Paul came to stay with Mark,' says Steve Levy. 'We then started to run Truth, which was the first legal rave, at the Park Plaza. Ian was in the background, advising and mentoring me. He definitely had a hand in what was going on here. He'd kicked it off with Paul at Spectrum, then he was in the background with Moonshine and Truth, which had the same kind of impact over here.'

'There were a number of promoters operating in LA,' says Mark Lewis. 'Steve LeClare and Ritchie were doing OAP, One Almighty Party; there was Alice's House, Lost Angels, Gary Blitz doing nights . . . they used the same DJs all the time, which included English people like me, Michael Cook from Manchester and later on Dom T. There was something going on every day. The maximum amount of people for an '88, '89 party was about five thousand people, at Vertigo or the Shrine Auditorium. You'd play everything from downtempo stuff to Seal to Inner City to a techno track, whatever you were feeling. It was all new music to the crowd, so they were really interested in hearing it, whatever style.' One UK DJ Mark Lewis brought over was Carl Cox, who Mark had known from South London. 'I'd played at the Madhatter's Ball in San Francisco with Colin Faver, a party organised by Dave Dean, who organises a lot of clubs in LA and Orange County now, and also played for Mark Lewis,' says Carl. 'You had an English contingent in the house for the first time. Mark said come to the US, we'll be able to take care of you. I came in on a very low budget, two or three hundred dollars per gig. These people had no idea who the hell we were, apart from a few people that knew that we did parties and raves in the UK, but we all came together, and we knew the reason why we were there.

We gave them exactly what they came for, and it was awesome.'

By the time Paul landed in LA with Happy Mondays, the scene was thriving, adopted by young Hollywood lights including Charlie Sheen, Emilio Estevez and Judd Nelson, mixing in with a hardcore party crew. 'I remember Paul coming in town when he was producing the Mondays album,' says Mark Lewis. 'There was a little club on Pico called the BBC; they were notorious for doing after-hours, and we'd all end up there.'

Steve and John Levy's operation branched out from their successful party nights to form a record label. They hooked up with Ricardo Vinas, an A&R man who'd just left Capitol Records. They started the Moonshine music imprint, releasing home-grown talent alongside imported compilations. 'In the space of a few months, the label went from my living room to an office with twelve people in it,' Ricardo recalls. Moonshine's compilations included a tie-in with a London-based dance label, Journeys By DJ, run by Tim Fielding. The first Moonshine/Journeys By DJ release was a mix from Billy Nasty. The album went down pretty well on the West Coast. 'I must have listened to that mix about five hundred times,' says Ricardo.

'Journeys By DJ was born in the back seat of a car on the M6, coming back from the Hacienda in 1992,' says Tim Fielding. 'I was getting deeper and deeper into this awesome mix tape by Tony Humphries, and puzzling over why it was that my mates weren't buying our records, when they always snapped up my mix tapes. That's when it hit me – unless you're a DJ, you want your dance music ready-mixed, ideally by your favourite jock. The DIY spirit was in full effect, and by the time I got back to London I was on a mission. The only other label to be doing legit DJ mixes was DMC, who released them on cassette and vinyl to their subscribers. I set about being the first label to release DJ sets on CD. I phoned Billy Nasty for the first mix. We then put out mixes by Judge Jules, John Digweed and Danny Rampling.'

Journeys By DJ number five was a wide-ranging set from Paul Oakenfold. 'There was an immediate snag because he had been asked by Ministry of Sound to do a mix,' says Tim Fielding. 'But Paul being Paul, he quickly assured me that there wouldn't be a problem if there were two Oakenfold mix albums out that year – the Ministry one would be US garage-style, and the JDJ album would be another string to his bow. He was keen to do it because he kept getting recorded at clubs without his supervision, and figured the best way to defeat the dodgy bootlegs was to release a pukka version. The concept was to take the listener through a spectrum of music, and this appealed to his versatility and range. At the time he was into the Euro sound that was evolving into trance. You can actually hear that on the album, how Chicago house gave rise to Euro, and eventually became psy-trance. As much as any other DJ, Oakey was an integral factor in that musical evolution.'

Right before your ears, the evolution starts here. The mix slinks along from the house staples by Seven Grand Housing Authority and Roc and Kato, through DJ Pierre's hypnotic Wild Pitch anthem 'Generate Power', to Joey Beltram's 'Future Groove' all the way to Hallucinogen's classic Goa trancer 'LSD', mirroring dance music's flux, its rapid, fluid development.

Bootleg mix tapes of DJ sets had been big news on London's Portobello and Camden markets, so it was no surprise that the

JDJ releases were a huge success in the UK. 'By the time we came to Oakey's mix, it was obvious that DJ mix albums were worth taking seriously,' says Tim. 'We knew we could sell at least ten thousand by that stage. Oakey got paid what amounted to a few nights' pay, but it was clear he was not doing it for the money. He was doing it for the exposure, and to release a mix where he had full artistic control over the production. Coldcut's Journeys By DJ mix was the most critically acclaimed, but Oakenfold was the rainmaker. For an indie label, there's nothing like having a catalogue album like Paul's. It kept selling a few thousand a month; it was the biggest seller we put out. In terms of critical reception, he was such a big name by then that a lot of the dance music press were a bit blasé about it. But everyone had heard of Paul Oakenfold, so we got recognition from magazines like *Select*, and from the broadsheet newspapers, which we never had before. Some of the press were still not hip to the idea of DJ mix albums; they thought they were some kind of marketing gimmick, and there were plenty of tacky Ibiza compilations around to support their prejudice. In 1994 the big names like Renaissance, Cream, Ministry and Fantasia had started to up the ante. Paul's mix put us in that league for the first time. His album just kept selling. It introduced the JDJ brand to a range of music fans that we had been too marginalised to reach before.'

The success of the series in the UK helped open up possibilities in the States. Tim Fielding flew to California in 1993 in search of a US home for the JDJ series, and it was quickly snapped up for a tie-in with the Levys at Moonshine. 'Steve Levy knew Paul via Mark Lewis, and he loved the idea of an Oakenfold album,' says Tim Fielding. Levy came up with a new title to big up the deal, *Journeys By Stadium DJ*, and managed to license 'Lemon', a U2 remix, to bolster the set; some tracks were dropped, the Overlords' popular Euro trance anthem 'Wow Mr Yogi' was added, alongside that hardy Perfecto vocal anthem 'Not Over Yet', credited to State of Grace, after the Sean Penn movie of the same name.

Paul had already started to DJ in America, but his approach had been cautious rather than the full-on assault tactics he'd adopt after touring with U2. Early on, he'd played as part of a Hacienda/Factory tour with Mike Pickering, which was OK but no great shakes, and once at Twilo in collaboration with CMJ, which didn't really gel. 'It was packed, but I felt musically it didn't work,' says Paul. 'It went over their heads. I thought I'd sit back a bit and wait for when the time was right to go over and play more often. A lot of other DJs were playing in America, laying the groundwork – Carl Cox, Nick Warren, Sasha and Digweed; Trade were doing a monthly night at Twilo. They were doing their thing, but I felt when I was ready to play in America, I'd do it on my terms.' After the Journeys By DJ CD, and to coincide with his next US releases, the *Global Underground: Oslo* and *New York* compilations, it was finally time for Paul to start putting the touring miles in.

The first move was to set up some shows on the East and West Coasts, including LA. 'When we signed Paul we were very excited,' says Ricardo Vinas. 'We put together a deal with Gerry Gerrard, who'd become Paul's booking agent in the States. He's the Rolls-Royce of booking agents for that kind of music – all the big dance acts use him. Paul had been coming out to the East Coast, but he'd never played in LA.'

'At the time I didn't look after DJs,' says Gerry Gerrard. 'I was handling the Prodigy, Chemical Brothers, Underworld, and I'd also been working with Nine Inch Nails. I'd started to hear the buzz about Paul, quite late, because I'm in America, but when it finally reached over here I made attempts to represent Paul. I knew my artists were very much associated with DJ culture, and that by only working with rock promoters I was missing half the boat. So I figured if I brought in a DJ I'd be connected to both worlds.'

The first show was at the Viper Room, the infamous downtown rock and roll joint. 'Paul was known by this stage, a trendy name, but not necessarily a big attraction,' says Ricardo. 'I thought the Viper Room show would be a low-key industry showcase. I remember driving down on Sunset, making a left to go to the parking lot. There was a huge line going right down Sunset Boulevard. It went all the way down, around the block, right over to the next street. And I'm like, "Oh my God!" I was so excited. I went back around the block to take another look, and the cops gave me a three-hundred-dollar ticket, because I almost ran over people as I was making the turn on to Sunset. I was just buzzing at the amount of people that were there for Paul's show. It was a smash, and the fan base for Paul just blew up overnight. He became as big in America as he was in the UK.'

'They'd asked me to do four nights at the Viper Room,' says Paul, 'which I thought was quite funny, because you'd only ever see bands do a run of shows like that. It only held about ten people, so I could have done six nights! I only did one, but they said to me "why don't we do four nights in six months' time?" I didn't see it – why not do one night down the road in a place that holds four times as many . . . ?'

Paul achieved his US breakthrough state by state. 'I watched where Perfecto records were selling,' he says. 'First it was in Orlando and Miami, so I went there and worked it really hard.

The mistake a lot of British artists make is that they just play Los Angeles and New York, then go home thinking they've cracked America. The trick is not just to play the coasts. There's hardly a medium-sized town in America that I haven't played.'

'I've worked with a lot of other UK artists,' says Ricardo Vinas. 'Some of them love the idea of coming to play in America, but once they see that they've got to work for a fraction of the money they make in the country where they are already established, there's only so much that they are going to lose in order to do that. It's just a whole other dynamic. Paul was always very committed to playing in America. At the time he was giving up much bigger pay cheques for playing in the UK and Europe, but he went to small towns, to places that nobody ever heard of, places electronic music artists never really tour. He built a very strong fan base by doing that over time. That's one of the big reasons I think why his position is so solidified in America.'

Marc Marot emphasises the lessons Paul learnt from U2. 'Paul can't claim to have broken dance music out of Chicago and New York and all those areas, but as a pioneer of European dance going into America, he paved the way for absolutely everybody,' says Marc. 'He's played in a tin shed in Anchorage in front of thirty people, when at the same time he could be picking up tens of thousands of dollars for playing in New York; it's all about breaking markets and pioneering. He knowingly followed the U2 route. He said "You may not think you want me, but soon you will, and I'm going to keep coming back until you like me!"'

'It's like the elections,' says Gerry Gerrard. 'How do you become President? You get on the bus and go and shake hands

– you have to take it to them. Unless you have a huge radio hit, you have to do the dates, otherwise they don't really know about you. Paul made it in America through sheer hard work.'

The tours were also a great way for Paul to develop a countrywide network of US dance contacts to plug Perfecto. 'Paul was always breaking music twelve months before it came out on his label,' says Mark Lewis. 'He's very good at building a buzz. We would be fortunate enough to get the promos. Paul would cut ten or fifteen acetates, and give them to key people in the States; he'd have his core family in different cities. He was really breaking his sound.' One way of doing this was to record each set, and distribute them afterwards. 'I used to bootleg my own shows,' says Paul. 'I'd record them, then go to the local record shop, give them the DAT and say "it's yours". They then used to press up cassettes and sell them. When I was next in town, they would have heard of me. When we were looking to set a record up, we'd make sure the track would be on the mix tape. They were a very important part of breaking my career in America.'

Personal contact and incessant touring were the route to Paul's success in America. The first Perfecto West Coast tour featured Paul alongside Dave Ralph and Mark Lewis. It started off in San Diego, and took in Mark's club Logic in LA, San Francisco, a legendary session in Las Vegas and the Burning Man festival, in the Black Rock Desert in Nevada, which fell on Paul's birthday. 'Burning Man is the most hilarious experience you can ever have,' says Gerry Gerrard. 'You are really exposed to the elements – it's a hundred degrees out there, the wind and the dust gets up, you've just got to sit there and go through it. As long as you've got shelter, it's an amazing experience.'

Paul hired country superstar Willie Nelson's old tour bus for the journey to this acclaimed celebration of self-expression and self-reliance. The trip was pure rock and roll. 'Burning Man was unbelievable,' says Paul. 'Anyone's first experience of it is hard to put into words, that feeling you have. It's that feeling that makes it so special. Honestly, anything goes. Visually, it's crazy – I saw a red British double-decker bus out in the middle of the desert, you see people running around nude . . . You are completely removed from the world. Anything you think about could happen – nobody is a spectator. There are no rules. It's the craziest, most surreal place.'

Things took a more Hunter S. Thompson turn when the tour hit Las Vegas. Photographer Grant Fleming, who was along for the trip alongside Rowan Chernin of *Loaded* magazine, managed to get arrested in Vegas for trying to steal a gondola from the lake outside the Venetian hotel. 'There's a certain time outside the hotel where they allow you to hire the gondola,' says Paul. 'Of course Grant jumped in, started rowing it away, and the next minute the security guard was after them, rowing across the lake . . .' Grant Fleming filmed the tour, and turned it into a documentary called *Ready Steady Go*, which highlights the insanity of the global DJ trek, and features Paul alongside OutKast and Nelly Furtado, among many others. Unfortunately none of the performers involved signed release/clearance forms, the standard waiver that allows filmmakers to use such footage, so the film has never seen the light of day.

Despite occasional on-tour madness, the hard graft ethos Peter and Sheila Oakenfold had instilled in their son was paying off handsomely. Alongside the hectic touring schedule, Paul's next major mix compilations – *Tranceport*, and the *Global Underground: Oslo* and *New York* sets – were to once and for all seal Oakenfold's popularity stateside. By 1999, his global popularity was sealed. Paul entered the *Guinness Book of Records* in that year, as the world's most successful DJ. 'I thought it was a joke when they rang me up,' he says. 'I thought one of my mates was playing a prank on me! It didn't change my life, but it did mean something.'

The touring was certainly paying off; Paul's show gradually gained respect outside the club environment, reaching a wider audience that even the Guinness award acknowledged. 'Where it all clicked for me was at a place called the Mayan in Los Angeles,' says Gerry Gerrard. 'It's a converted theatre, a bit like the Astoria in London. The promoter brought in a lot of visuals; there was a whole show there. I look out across the audience, and they are all transfixed, all looking at Paul. I realised that there was no difference between this show and any rock band I've ever seen. They're standing out there, look-ing at him, not dancing, just kind of bobbing. I realised that the audience doesn't care how you make the music – as long as you've got the music, and you give them a visual aspect, it doesn't matter.' Paul agrees that the show was a turning point. 'The guest list had a lot of names on it,' he says. 'People like Demi Moore, Charlie Sheen and Drew Barrymore, a lot of young Hollywood stars, were turning up. We realised that people from outside the scene were starting to want to know what was going on.'

The Global Underground albums were released in a joint venture by Ricardo Vinas's Thrive and Seymour Stein's Sire/London imprint, gaining the series widespread US distri-bution. Unlike the majority of Global Underground albums,

Paul's GU sets were mixed live, giving them a more immediate, looser feel. The *Oslo* mix begins with a drum and bass workout before moving on to Cream anthems and Perfecto classics like Olive's 'You're Not Alone', before upping the pace on the second disc with progressive beats from Bedrock, to trance workouts from Astral Projection and Pablo Gargano. The mood is darkly psychedelic throughout, swirling and primal, managing to build a cinematic soundscape, without the 'Goa' mix's use of classical interludes or film samples. The Global Underground *New York* set is a bit more progressive, with less drum and bass, but for many fans, this is Oakenfold at his best. Three Drives on a Vinyl's 'Greece 2000' is the pinnacle here, a massive, moodily atmospheric trancer with a nagging hook that links directly back to the Age of Love and Jam & Spoon, adding a turn-of-the-century twist. The mixing is smoother than the *Oslo* CD, but retains a live edginess. Lustral's 'Everytime' floats into Miro's 'Paradise'; Talisman and Hudson's breakbeat fest 'Leave Planet Earth' segues into Albion's 'Air'.

*Tranceport*, Paul's 1998 Kinetic release, further helped cement Paul's sound stateside. From the spooky analogue bubbles and gated choral voices of the Dream Traveler's 'Time', to the driving pulse of Transa's 'Evervate', *Tranceport* is a solid, high-energy trance dance primer, a bridge between the genre's acidic past and its all-conquering future. The bar was raised even higher with the release of *Perfecto Presents Another World* in 2000. More of a studio set than the Global Underground mixes, *Another World* utilises a signature blend of spoken word, cinematic and classical touches – Lisa Gerrard's haunting vocal on 'The Host Of The Universe', 'Sanvean' and 'Sacrifice', Vangelis's 'Tears In Rain' and

'Rachel's Song' from *Blade Runner* – evoking a reflective, contemplative air. Tone Depth's 'Into Being' glides effortlessly into Chilled Eskimos' 'Take Me Away', slowly picking up pace with Timo Maas and LSG, towards Rabbit in the Moon's mix of 'Bullet In The Gun', undulating up and down, navigating dense, then open, terrain, all the way to Amoebaassassin's closer 'Piledriver'. CD 2 builds on the arpeggios of Jamez's 'Music', a fine piece of spacious modal electronica that Philip Glass would be proud of, through Salt Talk's wistful, happy-sad 'Eugina 2000', to the more unsettling tribal tones of Skope's 'Back To Front' and Tiesto's mix of Jan Johnson's 'Flesh'. The path clears for Vangelis and Lisa Gerrard, heading steeply upwards for Blackwatch's 'Northsky' and Delirium's 'The Silence'. It's a solid, invigorating set.

'The early Global Underground mixes were all live,' says Paul, 'but you're very limited when you are mixing live. I realised I wasn't getting what I wanted out of these compilations. You want more of a flow, you want the feeling . . . more importantly, people in their car, or at home, are listening a lot more closely. I realised I needed to go into the studio and build a longer intro, build a break section, re-edit. If there was a strong chorus, I'd double the chorus.' The extra attention was worth it. If the Global Underground and *Tranceport* compilations sealed Paul's reputation in America, this was the mix that took Paul to the masses. *Perfecto Presents Another World* is the biggest-ever-selling mix album in America, notching up over half a million sales.

In 2001, Paul embarked on the Area: One US festival tour, the brainchild of baldy techno dude Moby. Initially Paul's agent Gerry Gerrard resisted the idea of the tour, as it was mainly in seated amphitheatres. 'Since it was all about dance music, I thought this was wrong,' he says. 'It's ludicrous to have dance music played to people in seats. I said the only way Paul was going to do it was with his own tent, with his own line-up in the tent. The next day they called back and said yes. I was really shocked. The tent was quite small, maybe two and a half thousand people, but it worked. There'd be a line to get into the tent, just like at a club. Everyone wanted to see what it was about – it just blew up. It brought the nightclub experience to Middle America.'

The fifteen-city run started in Atlanta in July, and criss-crossed through the States, including dates in Washington, Chicago, Detroit, Los Angeles and Jones Beach on New York's Long Island. The tour featured Paul on the decks, plus live turns from organiser Moby, OutKast, Nelly Furtado, New Order, the Orb, Carl Cox, hip hop dons the Roots, and LA alt-metal band Incubus. It was a radical line-up for an American festival; like US radio, most stateside festivals tend to feature just one style of music on heavy rotation, like Ozzfest, Lilith Fair or the Warped skate tour. Moby took his inspiration from the one notable exception, Perry Farrell's Lollapalooza, and from European festivals such as Denmark's Roskilde or Germany's Rock Am Ring, where a wider musical spectrum treads the boards. 'I spent the last ten years going to summer festivals in Europe, and I never cease to be amazed at how eclectic the line-ups are – metal bands, dance acts, pop acts and genuinely strange and eclectic performers,' said Moby. 'You have the same people going to see every performer. It seemed so nice and harmonious. As time has passed in North America, it seemed to me that people's tastes have become a lot broader than they're being given credit for. I look through the record collections of my friends and they have punk rock and hip hop and dance and old blues and classical. I thought it might be time to do something for those people, to do something genuinely contemporary instead of just catering to one audience, like Ozzfest for heavy metal or the Warped tour for punk rock.'

This was a brave move – Lollapalooza went into hibernation in 1997, and few eclectic bills have graced the festival circuit since. For the American gig-goer, this might have been a genre-busting line-up; for Paul Oakenfold, veteran of Glastonbury, Spike Island, Zoo TV and countless festival shows, this was business as usual. 'Why not put on a festival that attempts to put a few Incubus and OutKast fans together in a DJ tent?' he asks. 'I take my hat off to Moby for trying to come up with something different, that actually reflects how people listen to music, rather than how radio programmers in this country think they listen to music.' Area: One turned out to be a highly successful blend, and was repeated in 2002 with David Bowie as headliner. 'It was very successful, it was the right time for it,' says Paul. 'It took dance music to the next level in America. I had my own tent that was absolutely rammed, to the point where they had to take off the sides and roll them up, because there were so many people trying to get in. It was a really good tour.'

The first Area: One tour cast Carl Cox in the role of Paul's support DJ, which he admits was a tough lesson. 'I was like "fucking hell, this is a reality check!"' he says. 'Paul had this amazing set-up. He had a booth completely customised for him, and so I went down there to do a sound check, thinking "This is lovely! Look at this!" I got my records out, and the guy goes, "Oh, you can't do that." I said, "What do you mean?" He says, "That's for Mr Paul Oakenfold. Can you just step away? He won't be very happy." So I said, "Where's mine?" He said "Well there's your turntables over there, and there's the stand that they're going on, and your speaker system we haven't sorted out yet." I felt smacked up! I didn't have any visuals or a DJ booth, just a table. Paul was already working on this rock level, he knew exactly where he was going.' It looks like Carl's learned from this – watching him backstage at his 'Carl Cox and Friends' arena at Miami's Ultra festival in 2007, as he surveys a heaving crowd listening to his guests Fatboy Slim and Danny Tenaglia, it seems Carl can't quite wipe off the broad grin that's taken up permanent residence on his face. He's got his DJ booth all right, alongside the best lighting technology money can buy. Like Tiesto, Paul van Dyk and many others, Carl Cox watched Paul build a network, up the stakes and pave the way for big arena shows, and followed on happily after him.

The only slight hiccup during the Area: One tour occurred when Paul had to face the perennial DJ nightmare – his tour manager forgot to bring the records to the show. OK, this may seem like an obvious thing for a DJ to bring along with him, but the combination of tour buses, taxis, side alleys and lack of sleep can occasionally trip up the most experienced DJ, or in this case, his tour manager. Most tour managers, however, would remember to bring the records when their charge is play-ing at such a big show. Especially when *Rolling Stone* magazine had come to do a feature . . .

'It was a very prestigious tour, we had our own air-conditioned tent, and there were queues around the corner every night,' says Mickey Jackson, Paul's touring assistant. 'This particular gig was at Jones Beach, which is about three hours out of New York. We have a saying – "no records, no show" – that record box is insured for something like a hundred grand. It was terrible. They offered to helicopter it in, they had a police escort lined up to bring it over, but this was at the last minute. It was too late.'

'I close the show, and we're ten minutes from me walking on stage,' says Paul, 'so I say to Ian, the tour manager, "Right, where's my records?" And everyone's looking at everyone else . . . I'm like, "please, don't go there . . ." There was no time to get back to the hotel and pick them up. So they wheeled me into the office for a big lecture. None of the other DJs would help me out. Then this guy called Liquid Todd, a New York radio DJ, said "I'll help you." He stood in. People were throwing things at him! They were booing him, but he still played on. And since that day, I've always helped him out. I get him gigs on Perfecto tours, I got him to do mixes on "Ready Steady Go", because he was the only DJ who stepped in and helped me. None of the others did, and they were friends.'

Although Paul's popularity was soaring in America, the outlook for the dance scene in general wasn't so buoyant. Senator Joe Biden forced a piece of legislation known as the RAVE Act through Congress in 2003, as an add-on to the Amber Alert bill, which concerned child protection. Echoing the UK's Graham Bright bill, Barry Legg's drug misuse legislation and the area of the Criminal Justice Bill that focused on parties, the RAVE bill – which stood for 'Resisting America's Vulnerability to Ecstasy' – enabled the authorities to prosecute promoters for the drug offences of their audience. There was overwhelming opposition to the act, which was passed without a vote or debate in Congress, and a heavily amended version took ten months and an administration change to become law. The effect on large-scale US partying was devastating. 'It killed it dead,' says Gerry Gerrard. 'They stuck it on to the Amber Alert bill, which meant that no one would vote against it, because they'd be voting against this bill about child protection. There's nothing wrong with the law as such – it says venues have got to be legal. I remember a party in an old warehouse in LA where it was pitch black inside, no one's stopping you going anywhere, and suddenly there's no floor, there's a hundred-foot sheer drop! There's nothing wrong with tightening that up, but the rave scene was never illegal on a wide scale – most parties were already in legal venues. They were trying to target the music. After the act came in, promoters just said no. They wouldn't touch dance music, because technically it meant they could go to jail for dealing, if somebody was arrested at their concert.'

'It certainly had a chilling effect on all of the promoters in America,' says the Crystal Method's Ken Jordan. 'They were much more afraid to do shows after that. Our friend Donnie was arrested – he was never convicted, but he was arrested. He had to pay out hundreds of thousands of dollars, just to defend himself.' Promoter James D. Estopinal Jr, aka 'Disco' Donnie, booked acts including the Crystal Method and Paul Oakenfold into the State Palace Theatre in New Orleans, gaining local celebrity status before being indicted under charges of violation of the 'crack house statute' and running an ongoing criminal enterprise. The charge carried a possible sentence of twenty years to life. No wonder the dance community thought twice about putting on large-scale events.

In a scenario that mirrored the UK, clubbing moved away from the rave and back to the nightclub, which is where it is at today, with VIP lines, table service and all that goes with it. The modern American superclub feels more like a distant relation to Studio 54 than Spectrum; a return to pre-acid house fiscal and social hierarchies. The wildness of the rave arena has been co-opted by business into a more sanitised experience, and, with the occasional exception, has lost much of its maverick spirit along the way. 'America has had this thing against dance music since the seventies, with the whole "disco sucks" campaign, everyone hating disco,' says Ken Jordan. 'That mentality is still there. The big clubs in LA are just bars with booths – there's no real clubs to go dancing in.'

'America doesn't have the culture we had, when we grew up in the scene,' says Carl Cox. 'They still see it as a very flashy thing – "we're into DJs with style, I've got my groupies, my car, my table service". DJing was never about that. Just give me the decks and I'll be fine; I don't need everything else. We brought it down from the highbrow point of view – it was about being in one club, where everyone was equal. It didn't matter if you had money or not, the music would bring us all together. In America, it has that stigma where the DJ has to be above everyone else. If Americans want to know why this music exists, they've got to get out of America and go to Europe, and see it for what it is. Burning Man is probably one of the only festivals that tells you the real story, because it's the desert, and it's up to you. That's what the scene was all about. America needs more parties like that.'

# 14

# Planet Perfecto

After the initial string of successful releases on Perfecto and Perfecto Fluoro, the label continued its run of hits with tracks like Grace's 'It's Not Over Yet', BT's 'Loving You More', Planet Perfecto's 'Bullet In The Gun' and Paul and Andy Gray's *Big Brother* theme, released as Element Four. 'We really started that whole melodic, progressive sound with Quivver, Tilt, BT, Grace, Perfecto Allstars,' says Paul. 'We had a really unique sound.'

'Not Over Yet' is an all-time classic Perfecto moment, the ultimate hands-in-the-air vocal anthem, whose longevity was recently bolstered by a spike-sharp cover on the Klaxons' *Myths Of The Near Future* album, as well as with Paul's rocky take on *A Lively Mind*. The track was co-written with Rob Davis and indie singer Mike Wyzgowski, and has been a hit twice over, reaching number six in the UK in 1995 and number sixteen when it was re-released during Paul's final Cream residency year in 1999. Paul remembers singer Dominique Atkins's input as key. 'She was great,' he says. 'She was a really hard worker; she'd be out there doing a lot of promotion. She toured with Michael Jackson; she was one of the best in terms of working the record. It was a massive hit for us – it sold over two hundred and fifty thousand copies.' Paul rates the Klaxons version, too. 'I really like it,' he says. 'They've kept the spirit of the song. It's a rock version of a dance record, rather than the other way round, and they've managed to keep the essence of what the song is all about. They've done a good job; there seems to be a really big buzz about them.'

There was one Perfecto signing that was less straight-forward, and tainted with controversy, that of Washington, DC resident Brian Transeau, also known as BT. A classically trained musician, who studied string arrangement and orchestration at Berklee School of Music in Boston, Brian first came to prominence with two singles on the Deep Dish label in 1993, 'A Moment Of Truth' and 'Relativity', mirror-ball symphonies both – sweeping, epic anthems that fitted perfectly into both Paul and Sasha's record boxes. Championed in the UK by Sasha, who flew him over to London, Brian soon hooked up with Paul and Perfecto for his first album, the innovative *Ima*. The album delivered the singles 'Loving You More', 'Embracing The Sunshine', and the Tori Amos collaboration 'Blue Skies', all massive floor-fillers, the blueprint for a much emulated dream house sound. Brian's second album for Perfecto, *ESCM*, featured vocalists Jan Johnson and T.H. Culhane, and was a move away from the euphoric dream house sound. It's darker, more experimental, musically more complex, a varied selection of electronica that gave birth to one of the all-time classic Oakenfold Cream anthems, 'Flaming June'.

Somewhere along the way, however, something seems to

have gone wrong. Out of all the artists that have worked with Perfecto, Brian Transeau seems to be the one who has the biggest problem with Paul. And it's not just a minor spat between record company and artist. Check these words from the November 2002 issue of *Mixer* magazine. 'I look at this incredible affection and respect that people have for Paul Oakenfold, who has not participated in a single piece of music that he's put his name on . . . Paul Oakenfold is a fuckin' hand puppet. He's a good businessman, but he is not a creator of music.' Say what?

Paul is genuinely bewildered when asked about this. 'I'm surprised he feels like that,' he says. 'I've helped him over the years, supported his records and talked him up. It's sad. We signed him, worked really hard for him; he did really well with us, but then his ego kicked in and he thought he was bigger than the Prodigy. He wouldn't listen. *NME* slagged him off big-time – he wanted to go over there and beat them up. He had no clue. The problem with Brian is that he's been on so many labels and had so many different managers because he just doesn't understand how it works. We spent a fortune on Brian's second record and it did nothing. So we dropped him.'

The comments about Paul's ability in the studio are based on hearsay rather than fact – BT has never been in the studio with Paul, so it's unlikely he'd have an accurate idea of what goes on. 'He's a much better pianist than me, a much better all-round musician,' says Paul. 'Of course he is. But just because you are a better musician, you may not have a feel, or a direction, an understanding of what a piece needs. I think what upset him was that we both do film music and I was getting offered really good films. That's where the jealousy started to come from. And then I think that he felt that his album should have been bigger. Marcy Webb, his manager at the time, explained to him how it works, and he fired her! He got really upset. It's just the way he is. He always used to slag the scene off, the parties . . . I was like, Brian, you can't say that, that's your scene! You make music for those people! But I don't hold it against him. It's his problem.'

The one person who should be able to see both sides of this argument is Richard Bishop of LA-based 3AM management. Richard represents both Paul and BT, so is familiar with the story. 'BT is an incredibly productive guy as a writer and composer,' says Richard. 'He's a guy who can't go through a day of his life without writing music. He's done a wide range of movie music, from *Go* to *Stealth* to *The Fast and the Furious* to *Monster* with Charlize Theron. He can sit down and write, and write quickly, and writes every single thing himself. BT's creative process is very different from Paul's, and he believes it is a truer role. I absolutely wouldn't agree with that, it's just a different role. They are different human beings and have different versions of what satisfies them creatively in their career. BT's satisfaction comes from creating and writing something, Paul's satisfaction comes from putting something together, putting a team of people together to make something that is really great and commercially successful. I think BT just wishes he has some more of what Paul has, in terms of the ability to do that. Ironically I don't think Paul wishes to have anything that BT has!'

Such petty spats are certainly not something Paul loses sleep over. 'He has a strange ability to put things behind him quickly,' says his assistant Dan Rosenthal. 'He shuts the door on them. He has a big heart and he's got as deep-rooted feelings as anyone, but he's got an amazing ability to put things under his belt when he needs to. A lot of people don't want to put their emotions to the side, because they feel like they're selling their soul. I don't think Paul sees it that way, he sees it as this is the only way to maintain at this level.' And hey, at least we got 'Flaming June' out of Paul and BT's time together, for which countless Cream regulars will be eternally grateful.

More straightforward was Paul and Andy Gray's theme tune for the *Big Brother* reality television phenomenon. The programme had already been a big hit in Holland when Paul was approached to write the theme, but was still a long way from becoming the global talking point it has since become. 'I was aware of *Big Brother* a little, because I'd known about the Dutch *Big Brother* series, and I had a feeling it was going to be a big deal, although I never knew it was going to be as big as it became,' says Paul. 'I was sitting there thinking we've got thirty seconds, we've got to do something that's a strong hook, that represents me and has got a distinctive sound. I sat there with Andy and I had this hook in my head. I hummed him the hook and we did it. It didn't take long – it was one of those things that just happened. I wanted it to be uplifting, in your face. I've been to the *Big Brother* house, and it's intense. The first thing you realise is that it's so small. The premise for the show is to be in people's faces, and it's cramped, so you're in my space. The music had to be smack-bang in your face, so it was riffs, it was fast, it was bam bam bam. It's not *EastEnders*.' The single, based on the thirty-second theme tune, became a top-five hit, selling two hundred and fifty thousand copies without a single airing on Radio One.

One question Paul has been asked a lot more than once is 'do you earn money every time they play the *Big Brother* theme?' The answer is a resounding negative. 'I wish I fucking did!' he grins. 'Everyone thinks I'm a millionaire from *Big Brother*, but that's not the way it works. We got about as much as you'd get for a remix, it was a pretty good fee, not great, but pretty good. Back in the day, the likes of Mike Post, who wrote the *Hill Street Blues* theme, or the guy who wrote the Channel 4 music, could get a salary out of it. What you got was called a repeat fee – every time it got played, you got paid. But they're smart – they don't do that now. They said, 'Listen, you are first choice to do this, but if you don't want to do it we'll send it to Fatboy Slim, and by the way there's no repeat fee.' And I felt it was a really good thing to do, because I had heads-up that it was going to be popular. It was very popular in Europe already, and I think they allowed me to do something that related to me. I'd been asked to do toothpaste ads, shampoo, and I didn't want to do things like that, but I thought this was the right thing to do. For me, it was cutting-edge, it was a new kind of TV. It caught my imagination; I wanted to be a part of something different and new, that changed the premise of a TV programme. Reality TV is now here permanently; in America there's channels that only show reality programmes. *Big Brother* started it – I'm proud of being a part of that.' Like the programme, the *Big Brother* theme marches on. The 2007 summer series was augmented by a mash-up version of the track cut up with Bros's 'When Will I Be Famous?', by bootleg specialists Joyriders.

Paul's knack of picking up emerging talent showed itself again when he signed Timo Maas in 2000. German DJ and artist Maas had previously released a handful of recordings on a variety of labels, including the UK-based Hope Recordings, but it wasn't until his seismic mix of Azzidio Da Bass's 'Dooms Night' that the public at large were aware of his bass-rumbling talent. 'Dooms Night' was one of those 'if all else fails . . .'

records, guaranteed to pack a dancefloor long before it was a hit, inducing cries of 'What the hell is *this*?' around many a DJ booth. The success of this booming analogue monster led to Timo's *Music For The Maases Volume 1* album, which rounded up previous mixes and remixes, and the *Connected* mix album for Perfecto in 2001. His first releases for Perfecto, 'Der Schlieber' and 'Ubik' (described by Paul as 'the best record Beck never made'), flitted around the outskirts of the UK charts. A curious, effective appearance on *Top of the Pops* in February 2002 helped Timo's Perfecto single 'To Get Down' enter the charts at number fourteen, helped along by the growing awareness of Timo Maas remixes for the likes of Madonna, Kelis and Fatboy Slim. 'To Get Down' is a driving, naggingly addictive piece of work, driven by Phil Barnes's riffing guitar and repetitive vocal hook. Timo's first solo album, *Loud*, followed a month later, with guest appearances by Kelis on 'Help Me' and Finley Quaye on 'Caravan'.

'I felt he was the most cutting-edge German DJ at the time,' says Paul. 'In all respect to Sven and Paul Van, Timo was a newer German sound and he did it extremely well. He was banging out loads of tracks – too many for my liking – but he was doing a lot of tracks, and we felt he would be a good signing. We thought we could develop his sound, so we could bring singers like Kelis, or the guy from Placebo in, to give him the potential to cross over. That was the idea.' As is the case for many DJ-based artists trying to break out of the world of the one-off twelve-inch, challenges arose as Timo and Perfecto tried to develop the sound across an entire album. 'With Perfecto, we sign records that are first and foremost for the dancefloor,' says Paul. 'But if you sign a great dancefloor record, it also has the potential to cross over into pop. You start spending shitloads of money, and it doesn't always work. It happened to BT, and it happened with Timo. "To Get Down" worked really well, but there's always pressure following a crossover hit. If you're a dance act, why do you have to have another strong pop record? You can still have another strong dance record. You don't need to go and do an album, you just go and keep on putting out singles and then when you've got ten singles, do a couple of remixes of the singles and put them on an album . . .'

To help this kind of situation develop, Perfecto had switched distribution to Mushroom Records in 1998. 'The reason why I chose Mushroom was because it was independent. I thought, great, I can just hire all the independent people who are good at what they do to promote the record. But we still found ourselves in this situation where everyone was saying we need a pop record. We don't want to be a pop label, we want to be a strong great dance label, and if our records cross pop, then great. Once you have a hit you're running around looking for your second hit.' Timo's album may not have been stuffed full of chart-conquering hit singles, but it's a substantial set nonetheless. His second album, *Pictures*, followed on Warners in 2005, with guest spots from Brian Molko and Neneh Cherry.

In 2002, Paul started a new offshoot from the main label, Perfecto Breaks. The first Perfecto Breaks compilation was from Lee Coombs, a respected DJ of whom Pete Tong once said 'If the [*Essential Selection*] show had an in-house orchestra, it would be Lee Coombs.' The DJ started spinning in 1989 around London and Cambridge, producing his first tune under the name the Invisible Man in 1991, started his own labels Paradise and Pumpin' Vinyl, and subsequently joined Justin

Rushmore and Abel Reynolds's flagship breakbeat label Finger Lickin' with 'Sky Juice' and 'Intensity'. His style has consistently mixed ultra-tight drum-programming skills with swathes of acid and electro-flavoured electronics, and has found favour with party heads worldwide. After Paul heard Lee's remix of New Order's 'Crystal', the pair hooked up. Paul was initially seeking a few of Lee's tracks to play out. They soon hatched a plan for Perfecto Breaks. 'It was a real honour for me,' says Lee. 'I'd always looked up to Paul from the start, and it was an ambition of mine to work with people like him. He said I could do whatever I wanted on my CD; it was great that he trusted my judgement and taste. I made the compilation that I had always wanted to make, where I was able to combine old tracks with new, and make a real journey with my own sound.' The album saw Coombs hook up with respected beat head Meat Katie for the track 'Two Men On A Trip', a gigantic tribal stomper, alongside a wide variety of textures including Santos' riff-driven 'No Ticket To Run', a rewiring of Joey Beltram's classic acid morsel 'Energy Flash', and Joe Smooth's all-time vocal anthem 'Promised Land'.

Labels like Finger Lickin' and widespread support for the genre from clubs like Fabric meant that by 2002, the timing was right for Perfecto's breaks offshoot. The album was a huge critical success, but as the breaks movement was still in its developing stages, it failed to make such an impact in terms of sales. 'It was a good idea, but never made a bean!' laughs Paul. 'I'd been putting breaks tracks on my compilations for ten years now, since the time of albums like *Tranceport*. I've always been into breaks; I love the rhythm, I like melodic breaks. It started to rear its head in a big way, so I thought I'd do a real cool series of albums by young breaks DJs. We had great, great reviews.' A second set, by TCR records' Rennie Pilgrim, was released, to similar acclaim.

At the beginning of the new century, two Perfecto acts scored big hits. Russian trance act PPK had a worldwide smash with 'Resurrection', and a new UK act, Dope Smugglaz, scaled the upper reaches of the British charts. Dope Smugglaz' excellent Radio One Essential Mix and singles 'Double Double Dutch' and 'The Word', sampling Malcolm McLaren and the *Grease* soundtrack respectively, pre-empted the trend for bootleg mash-ups by a good few seasons. The band were led by Tim Sheridan, whose first break came via a hook-up with Leeds sample-happy beatmasters Utah Saints, which was followed by a stint organising the launch of Kiss FM in the North of England. He formed Dope Smugglaz in the late nineties. Previously he'd endured a teenage stint in the army, where he learned a little about observation, body language, and tactics. That was fine, but the overall message seemed somewhat taxing. 'I spotted the gaps in what they were teaching, which was essentially ordered murder,' he says. 'I took every option you could that didn't involve killing people – cookery, strategy and stuff. I learned about music in there, and got into James Brown. I didn't want to be shouted at by blokes in moustaches, so I got out as quickly as possible. It was the time of acid house – I was destined to be this square killing machine, and I turned into this fantastic dancing machine! Acid house was an epiphany for me.'

Dope Smugglaz were a hot property before they signed to Perfecto. There was a lot of interest in the deal. 'We were the prey, a piece of meat on the savannah of Africa surrounded by a million different predators,' says Tim, in his usual florid manner. 'Paul was the only one who got on the train, came up to our local like a human being, sat down and talked to us like people. The rest of them didn't leave their office – they were still vultures on the branch. Paul had this belief – he knew that sampling, what we did in the underground, was the future.'

'I believed in them,' says Paul. 'I was really inspired by what they were doing, I got turned on by what they were saying. I believed in Tim – he's very talented. I felt it was something we could both spend time on, and that we could reap some rewards together. Not necessarily financial, but creative rewards.' Dope Smugglaz' first two singles were chart-stomping behemoths, but a later collaboration with the Mondays' Shaun Ryder, a cover of the Donovan track 'Barabajagal', failed to hit home. The band missed out in America, too, turning down the chance to sign to Madonna's label, Maverick. 'I turned down a lot of stuff because I was young and a complete fucking idiot, and attached to this crazy antique thing called morals,' says Tim. 'Maverick was a baby label then, maybe a vanity project. We ended up meeting Madonna, being lined up like when you meet the Queen. She said "Oh you are the famous Dope Smugglaz, I guess you think you are too good for us?" I just said "You are tired and over, love, O.V.E.R. over! And you look like Anna Ford." She sort of laughed ... Dave Beer was next to me and said "Fucking hell, you've just dissed Madonna ..." Then she walked off.'

As you can imagine, Tim Sheridan has had a fairly varied career when he's interfaced directly with the music industry, but he's as bright as one of his tartan suits, whether he's making records or not. He subsequently enjoyed a residency at Manumission in Ibiza, where he introduced electro to the Music Box area, before breaking away from the club to host nastydirtysexmusic with Smoking Jo, a free weekly beach party, which eventually landed Tim and Jo nights at Space and a regular party at Ministry of Sound in London. Recent nights at Turnmills have been similarly successful, with a similar mouthful of a name – his veryveryverywrongindeed night has residencies throughout the UK and in Ibiza.

It's not been an easy path, though. 'By the end of the Dope Smugglaz, I thought "fuck it, I've had enough, they are driving me mad",' says Paul. 'But I knew in my heart that he was a talented motherfucker. That's why our paths crossed again.' I'm speaking to Paul and Tim a good few years after the Dope Smugglaz, in the bar at Claridge's, as they plan a new collaboration or two. Round after round of vodkas slip down as Tim holds court, taking in everything from Pythagoras' theory of music to Alexander the Great, to the story of how he got his eye-rinsing new Vivienne Westwood coat for free. Paul is encouraging Tim to develop as a scriptwriter. If Tim does come up with a script for Paul to pitch in Hollywood, we are all in for a treat – he spits out more ideas per minute than Einstein on amphetamine.

It won't be the first time Paul has shown interest in stories. His interest in creative A&R stretches way beyond Perfecto. In 2001, he developed a series of audio stories for Galaxy FM under the banner 'Urban Soundtracks'. 'Because I'm dyslexic, I felt it was important to educate myself, as well as young people, about the classic stories, but told in a completely different way,' he says. 'The idea was to pick a classic story, then get a pop artist or film star in to read the narrative, and for me to put it to music.' The stories included Kylie Minogue reciting *Alice in Wonderland* and Keith Allen's take on Jack the Ripper, as well as a modern take on *Oliver Twist*, voiced by

Johnny Lee Miller over an eclectic electronic mix. Paul's version of *Antony and Cleopatra* won a Sony Award in 2002.

He's also keen on buying the rights for the odd book or two. 'Everywhere I go to DJ, I do radio, press or TV interviews before the show,' he says. 'When I'm sitting in a press conference, I ask them what their favourite books are, what are the most famous books in the country. Russia's full of fairy tales; I was getting books in China. I source the books and get friends of mine to translate them; I read them, and if it's worth buying the rights for the book, I do.' Dyslexia? What dyslexia . . . ?

# 15

# From Wheels of Steel to Silver Screen

By 2002, Paul was getting restless. The Cream residency was fading into memory, Home hadn't quite worked out, and in the first few years of the twenty-first century, dance music felt a little flat. The sheer thrill of acid house, the immersion of the senses, the visceral impact, was hard to find in mainstream clubland. The press decided to put the boot in, too, with a new, endlessly repeated media mantra – 'dance music is dead'. Even the dance press began raising an eyebrow and dropping the odd hint. *Seven* magazine's 7 November 2001 issue featured a smiley face on the cover, with cash signs in its eyes; the strapline asked 'Has It Come To This?' When the dance music media, particularly Ministry of Sound's *Ministry* magazine, begin to question the very existence of dance culture, you know something's not right. 'Whether you think dance music is happening or not, everybody involved should pull together when times are hard,' says Paul. 'What's the point in slagging yourself off?' Maybe the timing was right for Paul to leave the country.

'I don't like the negativity in England, it really pisses me off,' says Paul. 'I don't know why it gets to me, it's because I'm proud to be English, we're a great country, but all the moaning and slagging each other off is backward. People are fascinated by English culture, and when you are gigging abroad you really talk it up, but as soon as you step off the plane in England everyone is moaning. When that whole media thing blew up, I just let them get on with it. When *Ministry* slagged us all, I was like, "you fools, why are you slagging off your own scene?" And of course their magazine went under! It was understandable when the *NME* was slagging us off, because they didn't know what it was all about. Fair enough. But when your own scene are doing it . . . I didn't plan to leave England, but I had this great opportunity. I went to LA and quit one industry to start at the bottom of another industry. I like the idea of starting at the bottom – I did it when I first went to New York. Moving to LA wasn't a difficult decision. It was more of a challenge.'

Opportunity knocked when Paul flew to LA to meet movie director Joel Silver, to talk about scoring music for the John Travolta vehicle *Swordfish*. Paul had already delivered tracks for a couple of movies – *Shopping* and the remake of *Get Carter* – but flying in to discuss scoring a whole film was an altogether different matter. 'I didn't really know who Joel Silver was, until I walked into the office and saw all these film posters,' says Paul. 'I thought "oh my God, I'm really out of my depth!" But it was just right. We went through the whole idea for it. I thought I'm going to immerse myself into this. I could see a new career on the horizon.' Paul even got to go on the movie's set. 'They're shooting this scene at Frank Sinatra's house, forty miles outside town,' says Paul. 'There's John

Travolta and Halle Berry on set, it's a ninety-million-dollar movie, and here's me and my mate Mickey Jackson sitting in the producer and the director's seat, and they start to ask me what I thought of it! Mickey's looking at me as if to say "don't you dare ask me what I think . . ." I told them he was working with me!'

'If you've ever walked through a door and had everyone sing "happy birthday", it was like that, times twenty,' says Mickey Jackson. 'I was in shock. This was an actual live set. Joel Silver's come over to shake our hands, there's two Halle Berrys saying hello, the real one and her double, and Paul's sitting in the director's chair. They started showing us the rushes and asking us what did we think? I let Paul do the talking! It was typical Oakey – he didn't tell me where we were going beforehand, when we were on the way there in the limo. He just said he had a "serious meeting" to go to!'

The music Paul created for the film has the same slightly uneasy, built-up tension that drives many big electronic anthems, but adds a sense of claustrophobic menace that deftly underscores the action. 'I brought in Jan Johnson, Afrika Bambaataa,' says Paul. 'I wanted to use certain tracks that I felt would work, so I reworked them in the tone of the sound of the film. With certain pieces they wanted an orchestra, so they got in Christopher Young to help me as I'd never worked with an orchestra before. He came in and did a good job. I felt a little bit out of my depth, to be honest – there's a seventy-five-piece orchestra in the room. It's a little overwhelming. You're in Hollywood, on the Warner Brothers lot, where from being a kid you've known this is where they make films. You've just got to step up and think well I'm here for a reason. Because you know what you are looking for, which sound textures you want. I'm not a conductor or a classical musician, but I realised when I worked with Danny Elfman and Tim Burton on *Planet of the Apes* that you don't need to be. They bring their own conductor and orchestrator in, explain what they want, then someone writes it. There's very few people out there who do the whole lot.'

Ricardo Vinas was working with Paul around the time of these negotiations, having released the Global Underground compilations, played a key role with Perfecto in America, and later worked on A&R for Paul on his debut artist album, *Bunkka*. 'Joel Silver is not someone who would take a leap of faith on something he wasn't sure of,' says Ricardo. 'Paul had an up-and-coming vibe; this was an action film that was looking for a more electronic, progressive sound. The score was going to be a classic orchestral score by Christopher Young, but Paul sold them on scoring the whole movie, on how the electronic sound would give them an edge. It worked. It was a big step up for Paul. I think it cemented his desire to move here from the UK. He felt more secure about making the move, once opportunities like this were presented.'

Breaking into the movie business as a composer wasn't going to be easy. 'It's really hard to get an opportunity,' says Ricardo, 'because of the pressure, and because unless it's a real visionary director who sees music as a very intricate part of the story, it's a secondary thing. They're not going to take a chance on somebody that's new and doesn't know how to go about things, on any kind of budget, big or small. It is a very hard market to crack.'

'I got scared for Paul when he moved to LA,' says Gerry Gerrard. 'I call it the shark tank. You've got all these record companies, all these executives that want a piece of you. How do they do it? They stroke you. They say "you're the most amazing artist I've ever seen", they go on and on about how fantastic you are. It's completely insincere – they don't mean a word of it, and they say the same thing to every artist. Even if the artist isn't making it, they say it just in case they come back and make it later. It's all they know how to do. An artist can be very shrewd, have a good business sense, but some of them aren't great judges of character. I know Paul's a lot sharper than that, but I was still worried. In the first few months it blows you away, and I saw it within the first month or so, he's getting that LA attitude, and I'm worried. He's too busy to talk to me, there's more important people. But within two or three months he saw right through it. He's got his feet on the ground; he's certainly not susceptible to stroking. He soon realised.'

Paul's assistant Dan Rosenthal thinks that the LA move has had a positive impact. 'I think the main reason that Paul enjoys California is that even though there's jealousy, everyone's fairly creatively minded, so the energy is there – there's not as many people holding you back. There's more people that want to move forward, the same way you do. Paul really thrives on that. And I know a lot of people might think he's left his home, but Paul has as much pride about coming from London and being a Londoner as anyone I have ever met. I don't think he'll ever let go of that.'

Paul gave up all DJ commitments for six months, visited the *Swordfish* set, and soaked up the whole movie-making process. 'They didn't give me a specific brief,' he says. 'There were no restrictions. I just sat down and made the music, from ten in the morning until eight at night. It was a very civilised way to work.' Paul and Angela lived in hotels for the first few months, then a few more concrete offers came in, including work on Tim Burton's *Planet of the Apes*, *The Bourne Identity* and *The Matrix Reloaded*, which consolidated Paul's desire to live in Hollywood permanently. With the help of Ricardo Vinas, Paul and Angela started looking for somewhere to live. 'It was a brave move, coming to LA,' says Ricardo. 'Paul was established in the UK and he pretty much packed up and left.'

Ricardo scouted for houses. The first one Paul and Angela liked was in Mount Olympus, but the couple decided it would cost a fortune to get it done up how they wanted, so they opted instead for a smaller 1920s villa in the Hollywood Hills. Paul got to work on soundtracks, while Angela went to the Lee Strasberg acting school to study. 'I was lucky that I had Angela behind me,' says Paul. 'She didn't work, so she didn't have to quit anything, but she still had to give up her family and move abroad. It was a big decision to quit the UK, but I don't regret it. I had no friends, nobody here for me, but I had to make it happen.'

It doesn't matter if you are top of *DJ* magazine's poll, or the most successful DJ in the *Guinness Book of Records*; if Paul wanted to make it in movies, he had to start all over again. 'I'm bottom of the list when it comes to composing,' he says. 'I'm not Danny Elfman or John Williams, they are ten years ahead of me. But sooner or later, people will be looking for the new school, someone who brings an electronic score. I did *Swordfish* with a composer, but now I've got my own team. My game plan is to do high-profile cues – scoring scenes for a movie rather than the whole soundtrack. What I've learnt with films is that it's like music, there's a hundred films out every week, only ten per cent you know about. Even if it's a five-minute cue, you're attached to the film, they get you to do the red carpet, you're promoting it, you're involved in it. Then the director and the producer in the studio can see that you can do this, you can play the game. They've had their fingers bitten a lot with artists saying "this is my work, you can't change it" – in film you've got to work with the director, because it's the director's vision. If the director says "take that bit out", and you think that's the best bit, you've got to be flexible about it. Once they trust you with millions of dollars, if you work on a hundred-million-dollar movie, you've got to know what you're doing. It could take a few years. I'm in no rush. What I want to do is learn my trade, learn it in the correct manner, and work on credible movies.'

Jason Bentley, leading LA radio DJ and film music co-ordinator, worked with Paul on the Wachowski brothers' phenomenally successful *Matrix Reloaded* project. 'I got Paul involved in a couple of cues,' says Jason. 'He met the Wachowskis, they described exactly what they wanted, and Paul went away and worked his magic. It was a great opportunity for him.' Not that it was an easy ride. 'When I was doing *Matrix* with the Wachowskis, they were going, "wrong, wrong, wrong, wrong, wrong!" ' says Paul. 'I'm not precious, I was like, all right, I'll work twenty-four/seven. Tell me what you want me to do to make this thing work, and I will do whatever I have to. I flew in on the Sunday morning, I worked twenty-seven hours straight through the night to get the whole thing right, and went to bed on Monday afternoon. I was delirious.'

'The world of the composer is a whole different scene; in a lot of ways it's a pretty closed circle,' says Jason Bentley. 'It's hard to break into that. A lot of people think they can make it, but it's really tough. It's not something you can take lightly. A lot of dance producers have thought they can do it, and have failed. The studio system loves the name-brand composer, and don't take many chances. The pioneers like Tarantino are going to be the ones taking the chances, but as far as the mainstream, the effect of electronic music has mainly been to cut costs, as they can deliver a demo without having to record an orchestra. Not only do you have to be focused, you have to be trained in that area. I think you've got to spend a lot of time, maybe a couple of years, being a ghost-writer behind a leading composer, like Harry Gregson-Williams, who's helped Paul. I think you need to swallow your pride and do that for a while before you get a break. I wouldn't bet against Paul making it, because he's so resourceful and charismatic that I think anything is possible.'

Having collaborated with some major players along the way, including *Miami Vice* creator Michael Mann on *Collateral* and Danny Elfman on *Planet of the Apes*, Paul is making the move towards the big score. 'I've had the opportunity to work with some great people,' he says. 'I've had the chance to watch how these people work, to be in the studio with them and learn from them. With *Swordfish* I was thrown in at the deep end, I had my ideas, but I very much had to learn on the job. I wasn't shown the ropes, but it was a phenomenal way to start.'

Unfortunately, there was a marked downside of LA life. Paul's marriage to Angela suffered from the move to America. The couple separated and were ultimately divorced. 'We grew apart,' says Paul. 'I blame myself – I take the responsibility. I admire Angela for having the strength and the balls to move to America. She didn't know a soul here. I learnt that you've got to be strong to not let Los Angeles change you. I think she got washed away with it. She never wanted to be an actress until she went to LA. She did the right thing by going to college. She started getting her own friends; they're all going to school to be actors, so then they all want to go to parties and meet directors, producers. That's the route she chose. She'd grown out of the whole club scene, so she didn't want to come with me to any of the shows. Fair enough, I don't blame her – promoters generally ignore your wife or girlfriend, which I find rude. She went out with her friends and started getting more and more into other scenes. We started to not have things in common.'

# 16

# Bunkka

'I've always wanted to make my own album, but I was never comfortable with the idea of putting one out under my own name,' says Paul, lounging in his roomy suite at Claridge's, one of London's most stately hotels (decks on the sideboard, lobster and chips from room service: sixty quid). 'I'd done all these records under pseudonyms: IRS, Grace, Perfecto Allstars. It was Steve Osborne that convinced me I should do it. He kept on at me about it. It was a natural progression from remixing and production work, and I'd always wanted to do a song-based album. I kept putting it off, but eventually, I felt it was time to make that record. I didn't tell anyone I was doing it for over a year, because I didn't want the pressure. It took two years to make – I really agonised over it. At times I never thought it was ever going to be finished.'

The album was to become Paul's 2002 debut set, *Bunkka*. A song-based album isn't the most obvious starting point if you consider Paul's reputation as a top trance DJ, or the sound of the mix albums that broke him in America, but if you dig deeper, to those vocal anthems dropped at Paradise Garage, through Profile and Def Jam's verbose hip hop, Balearic hands-in-the-air classics or into the DJ's professed love of rock music, this kind of record begins to make sense. 'I wanted to make a record that represented my musical background,' says Paul. 'I grew up on pop music, I love guitar bands and I was very influenced by and involved in hip hop in the early days. I wanted to build from those roots upwards, rather than making a contemporary dance record.'

Once he had decided to make an artist album, Paul needed to sort out his management situation. He'd been a little stung by the failure of a huge internet-based deal that his manager, Ros Earls, and agent, David Levy, had tried to negotiate with Ministry of Sound. 'People got greedy,' he says. 'It was a five-million-pound deal, a great situation. It would have taken me to where I wanted to be. I'd have a residency online, so wherever you were in the world on a Saturday night, at a certain time you could go online and see and hear me. You could listen to the tracks, then click through and buy them. It was a good idea, and a huge financial deal. If you put five million on the table, everyone gets a bit starry-eyed. Ministry of Sound wanted it to happen, I wanted it to happen, but I felt it didn't happen because my management and my agent were fighting amongst themselves. It was just stupid, they were squabbling over who was getting what. They saw the commission on five million, and they were both trying to fight for it. That's how I saw it. David and Ros will always be my friends; I'll always have respect for the work they put in, but in my opinion the deal shouldn't have gone haywire. It should have happened.'

Like a lot of ideas around the turn of the century – the Dome, the millennium bug, Home – the Ministry idea was rather different on paper than in reality. Despite the doom-laden threat of millennium computer meltdown, there was a great deal of optimism about internet technology, a sudden frenzy of interest backed by large sums of cash. Unfortunately the ideas were way ahead of the science; broadband was a good few years away, and most internet pitches relied on it. The hype cooled as quickly as it had flared up. 'Times were changing,' says Paul. 'All I know was we were ahead of the pack. You need so much infrastructure to make it work. You have to have a really good partner; the deal just broke down.'

'That was the one time Paul and I really did fall out,' says David Levy. 'On paper it was a fantastic deal, but those times were heady. We were in the middle of a deal that would have made us all millionaires. None of us took it too well. There was a period of about three months where Paul and I weren't talking to each other, or if we did talk to each other, it was just to scream at each other, then put the phone down. Paul would be headlining Creamfields and there would be people on radio phones keeping us apart. Our friends and associates got so frustrated that my boss at ITB, Barry Dickens, had me write a letter to Paul, laying out the whole history of our relationship. The letter worked. We went into Barry's office like a couple of schoolboys, and Barry basically read us the riot act! We were both in our mid-thirties, both successful in what we do, and Barry just sat there and said "You two muppets need to leave this office when I'm done with you and sort this fucking shit out!" Because Barry is who he is – he's been an agent for real legends, like Hendrix and the Doors – we both respected him more than we were pissed off with each other. We sort of grinned foolishly and said "shall we move on?" Maria at ITB took over as Paul's day-to-day organiser, and over the next three or four years it became an amazing team.'

'We're cool now,' says Paul, 'but it was very upsetting at the time. I felt the idea, which was to be resident DJ in people's houses, globally, through the internet, was a fucking great idea. I still do; I've always felt sooner or later the technology will catch up with the idea.'

The fallout from the aborted Ministry deal led to Paul looking for new management. 'I was in a dilemma when I left Ros,' says Paul. 'I was going to sign with Paul McGuinness; he kept coming over from Dublin, we had meetings. Caresse Norman, who was Madonna's manager at the time, also wanted to manage me. I was like, "do I go with U2 or Madonna, or what?" Paul McGuinness didn't have an office in London, but it would have meant touring with U2 around the world. Madonna's management would have been very good for America. But what did they really know about my world? It was probably the hardest decision of my life.'

Marc Marot, who Paul knew through his mixes for U2, had just left his MD position at Island Records and was taking some time out. 'I heard through a friend that Paul was thinking of making a record,' says Marc. 'The mutual friend said to Paul "Why don't you talk to Marc, he might help A&R it." I was having a year out, thinking what I wanted to do with my life. Paul had been offered this huge Ministry of Sound deal, which wasn't very sound, and he wanted me to bullshit-detect it. It was right at the height of the internet madness. I looked into it, and began to understand that it wasn't going to work for him. He told me he was making a record and had some tracks to play me, did I think it would work . . . some bits didn't, but a lot of it did. Before I knew it, I'd got him a huge deal with Maverick for the album, and a huge deal with Mushroom for

Perfecto. Managing Paul wasn't something I decided to do; it was something that was thrust upon me. One day he said "I think you're my manager, aren't you?" And I said "I think I am!"' '

'Marc Marot went out and did his research,' says Paul. 'He went and bought all the DJ books, like *Last Night a DJ Saved My Life*, and read them all. It got me thinking – his background's in record companies and publishing, he's worked with NWA and Massive Attack . . . so I thought this is the best guy for the job. And I've never looked back.'

Paul had previously been working with Seymour Stein at Sire for his mix albums; Stein was perhaps the obvious first choice for the album in America. 'He's arguably a living legend,' says Paul. 'He signed the Ramones, Madonna . . . he came to see me in a nightclub at three in the morning, which for an older man was quite something – he was virtually falling asleep. That made a really big impression, so I signed to him for the mix albums. But the deal with Sire kind of imploded, then Sony, then Polygram wanted it.'

Heading the chase was Guy Oseary, the boss of Madonna's Maverick label. 'We were about to commit to London/Sire,' says Marc Marot. 'Guy effectively hijacked the deal.' The hook-up was fortuitous. 'I don't sign a lot of artists – I really try to focus on the few artists we sign,' says Guy. 'I'd worked with Madonna on *Ray Of Light*, signed the Prodigy and released the *Matrix* soundtrack, so Maverick was a pretty strong company for Paul.' Guy Oseary knew exactly why he wanted Oakey on Maverick. 'In terms of pop culture, everyone knows who Paul is,' he says. 'When that happens, you are a brand; you are one hit away from selling a lot of records. You demand attention. Paul's got that going for him – it was the thing I was most attracted to. I like the way he's built that up.'

Paul liked the idea of working with the young Maverick MD. 'He's got good vision, he sees outside the box, rather than just being some normal record company guy,' he says. 'He's a risk-taker, and I like people who take risks. It was good to work with someone my age, who knows what's going on. I just wanted to finish the record at my own cost, and then go and have a bunch of meetings. It didn't work out that way; Guy got wind that I was doing a record, we hung out, I liked the vibe, liked what he said, so I thought "this is it!" I was offered more money to go with another label, but went with Maverick, because of Guy.'

Although it was Guy who attracted Paul to Maverick, he already had a connection with label boss Madonna; he'd remixed her 'American Life' hit. 'I was already pretty close to her, because my US manager at the time, Jorge Hinojosa, was going out and sharing an office with Madonna's manager, Caresse Henry,' says Paul. 'The first time I met Madonna, I was on my knees in their office, sorting out my records. I look up and there's Madonna standing in front of me. I'm like "Oh, hi," and she just burst out laughing. It's the second time I've been on my knees meeting someone, I did that with U2 – for some reason I am always on my knees meeting these people! She was very polite; I learned a lot from her. The bigger they are, the less attitude there is. She's very charismatic. I've gone on to mix five, six of her tracks, I'm on her label, and I went on tour with her, the first support act she'd had apart from the Beastie Boys in the eighties. She doesn't do the day-to-day runnings at Maverick, she trusts Guy to do that, but she's extremely clued up, very aware of what's going on.'

The biggest challenge from an A&R perspective was focus.

'The hardest thing for Paul is that he has so many different options,' says Guy Oseary. 'When you deal with an artist that's only making a record, that's different to working with someone who has to do two tracks for this soundtrack, and has to do a remix for that person, or a tour in Brazil.'

The leap from DJ to remixer, from producer to composer, is a fairly large jump, and needed a carefully thought-out plan to make it work. 'Paul wanted to be more a film composer than a recording artist,' says Marc Marot. 'Being a recording artist was a means to an end. There was strategy involved. While Paul had done fantastic remixes and production, he's not known as someone who composes. Even though he clearly was a composer – look at the *Big Brother* theme, Grace, "Bullet In The Gun" – all things he'd co-written and put together. In 2000 there was one week where he was in the top ten twice, without his name on either of them – Element Four was in for the *Big Brother* theme, and "Bullet In The Gun" was in there as well. I said to him "This is part of your problem – if you would put your name on it and identify yourself, then people would begin to recognise you as a composer. Because you're not a group. At the moment you're working under the guise of five different things. Even when you do remixes, you do it as Perfecto, and as much as Perfecto is a valuable brand, if you wanna be a film composer, you've got to be Paul Oakenfold." So the idea of doing an Oakenfold album, rather than it being a Planet Perfecto album, came out of deciding we needed to do something to establish his credentials as someone who could write music.'

Making the leap from DJ to recognised artist was no easy task. 'The switch from DJ to artist was troubled,' says Marc Marot. 'Paul is known for a certain type of music. He's like an iceberg – the tip of the iceberg that pokes out of the ocean surface is what he's known for, which is trance, but if you look at what he's capable of, it's phenomenal – underneath the surface, there is a huge body of work he's capable of. That was the problem with making any record. He could go and do an Ice Cube track on one hand, then a track with Lisa Gerrard from Dead Can Dance or a Hunter S. Thompson track on the other. The difficult thing for me was to try and help make it coherent as a body of work. Paul's problem was that he knew he wouldn't be making a record that would satisfy the tip-of-the-iceberg people, who wanted trance mix albums; his view was "I do mix albums for that". It's one of those really weird paradoxes with fan bases, in that they want you to stay the same. But he's a human being – he wants to grow and change and experience new things . . . and why the fuck shouldn't he?'

The first track Paul turned his attention to on *Bunkka* was 'Ready Steady Go', a breaks-led, spy-tinged workout with vocals from Asher D of So Solid Crew. 'The idea of that track was to tie in with a movie, to get sync tie-ins for film and TV,' he says. 'I wrote that as a trailer for a movie that didn't exist.' The cunning plan certainly paid off. It's been used in movies from *The Bourne Identity* to *Collateral* to *Stormbreaker*, a couple of video games, including a Tiger Woods tie-in, on the TV show *Alias*, and on a handful of TV ads, including a long-running US spot for Saab. 'That track has been my biggest-ever record,' says Paul. 'It was in four commercials at one time. It's been in more syncs in movies than anything I've ever done.'

Curiously, it wasn't a big hit. It came out as a double A-side, coupled with the more immediate thrills of 'Southern Sun'. 'It's the strangest thing,' says Paul. 'Even Maverick admitted they should have had a hit with it. They didn't get it at the time.' 'I think we missed a trick there,' says Marc Marot. 'It's only in hindsight that it became the commercial beast it's become. Everyone played "Southern Sun" because it is easier, but it's "Ready Steady Go" that's proved to be the lasting track that's generating fortunes. That track is all over the place.' It's a very modern type of hit record, delivering across a wide range of platforms, rather than necessarily relying on single sales, radio or MTV play to get noticed. 'The problem at the time was that Maverick were thinking in a very linear way,' says Marc Marot. 'They were thinking old world, whereas "Ready Steady Go" is a new-world record; its success comes from synchron-isation. It became the theme for fashion shows, it was used at the Oscars. The irony is, that's why it was written – we did it to try to get into that world, we were aiming at Hollywood, aiming at television. First time out, Paul delivered.'

'I think "Ready Steady Go" will become the biggest record I've had, to date,' says Paul. 'I think it was ahead of its time. It's difficult to play in clubs, it didn't fit anywhere on radio when it came out, but there is something about that record that keeps going. It's still on commercials, still played at sports events to this day. It just doesn't go away. I've had other tracks that have sold more records, but they've come and gone. "Ready Steady Go" is still here.'

Paul's exploration of song-based tracks took him up a num-ber of strange musical alleyways he'd certainly not explored before. One song, 'Starry Eyed Surprise', sprang into life while Paul was watching the classic late-sixties movie *Midnight Cowboy*, a picture that features a haunting, mesmerising John Barry score. 'I was sitting here watching the movie, and I was like, fucking hell, that guitar loop's great! So I got out my guitar, played the line, and then in my mind I was going, bum cha, bum cha . . . so then I put a beat to it, and I started thinking, OK, now this is a rap record. So I went to LL Cool J, I went to Jurassic 5, to see if they wanted to do something on it. And then I was doing a show in Seattle, and at the time this band called Crazy Town had a number-one pop record with "Butterfly". I'd never heard of them. Suddenly I was hanging out with them, they are playing at the gig. I watched the frontman, Seth, aka Shifty Shellshock, and he was a white rapper, a rock white rapper. He's a bit rough round the edges; he's a Shaun Ryder. And I thought, fuck, that's not a bad idea! I said to him, "Listen I've got this track; what I want you to do, I'm looking for a lyric about a DJ, about parties, about having a great time. So it relates to me." So we did it. I listened to it and I thought, "Oh my God, it's too cheesy! It's a pop record, I can't put this on my record, I'm gonna get crucified by the dance media." So I played it to Marc Marot and [Mushroom records MD] Korda Marshall and they said it's a smash. It was top ten in twenty-three countries; it was top ten on both sides of the ocean. I didn't want it on the album. I was like, there's no way this is going to go on my album. And they said "yes it is". They did a deal with Capital Radio in the UK; for three months before it came out, it was a TV trailer for Capital Radio in London. It went straight in at number six.' It's still being aired as a Diet Coke ad in America, years later.

One timely guest on the album was R&B superstar Nelly Furtado, who makes an appearance on 'The Harder They Come', recorded just as her star went supernova. 'That track almost never happened,' says Ricardo Vinas, who took on an A&R role for Paul's debut artist album. 'I played Paul Nelly Furtado's video, talked to her manager and had a meeting set up,' says Ricardo, 'but within a few weeks of the meeting her career just blew up. It took a real effort to pin her down – we had a lot of cancelled sessions with her. Finally we managed to get her, at some weird time on a Sunday.'

What was needed next was a counterpoint male voice, which materialised when Bristolian rapper Tricky came on board. 'We had Nelly Furtardo on the track,' says Paul, 'and the lyric is about a relationship between two people. The guy doesn't want to know, and the girl's constantly chasing him. I was going to do the male part, which is more spoken word, but I was a bit uncomfortable doing it, to be honest. Tricky was perfect. There was a great vibe when we made that record.' The track conjures up a dark, hard, brooding swirl, the plaintive tones of Nelly Furtado offsetting Tricky's stoner growl and Paul's beat-heavy backing to maximum effect. Tricky's spot came about via a chance meeting with Marc Marot. 'Tricky was one of my artists at Island Records,' says Marc. 'I was in LA doing meetings for Paul, and I bumped into him at the reception of the hotel I was in. I ended up having a fantastic evening with him and two Californian gun dealers, who'd brought their wares to show him. There's a lot of dope around, and they are all getting these fucking great big guns out, each one bigger than the other! Tricky delivered what we needed. The track started as a kind of jam, and they only really got about fifty per cent of it, and we couldn't find a way of finishing the track off. Nelly Furtado was too busy promoting her own record; we could never get her back in the studio. So what we had was one verse and one chorus, and some scatting. Tricky's vocals were the binding that brought it all together, and turned it into the track that it became. It was one of those fantastic moments where Paul and Andy Gray did the mix – it just worked.' An accompanying video was shot at New York's Chelsea Hotel, which Paul remembers as 'a real good time'.

An army of vocal collaborators complement the album's mix. Jane's Addiction's Perry Farrell, a singer Paul has known for years, guests on 'Time Of Your Life'. 'Perry was very interested in electronic music,' says Ricardo Vinas. 'He's also a DJ. I thought he'd be the perfect artist for Paul to work with.' Carla Werner takes the vocal on the lead single 'Southern Sun', soaring high, lifting the tune skywards. Iceland's sublime Emiliana Torrini puts in an emotional performance on 'Hold Your Hand', while Grant Lee Phillips from Grant Lee Buffalo helps Paul get experimental on 'Motion'. 'He's a country rock singer, there's a lot of feeling in his voice. Few rock vocals really work in dance music, but Grant's voice does, because of the emotion he puts into it.' An old-school highlight is Ice Cube's vocal on 'Get 'Em Up', rhyming hardcore over a loop from *The Exorcist*. 'We'd circulated some backing tracks to movie companies that Paul was working on, but didn't think he was going to use,' says Marc Marot. 'The track that became "Get 'Em Up" struck a chord with the people who were making the *Blade* series of vampire movies, with Wesley Snipes. They suggested Ice Cube. The track ended up on *Blade II*.' *Rolling Stone* called it 'a poetic slice of hip hop and techno . . . a sound with a future'.

'Zoo York' is based on Paul's early adventures in the Big Apple. 'I remember hanging out in Times Square, years ago,' he says. 'It's about that sensation of chaos, being surrounded by so many people, pushing, rushing about, like some mad zoo. I push the strings on it, louder and louder so it's totally in your face. It makes it a bit on edge, which is the feeling I got standing in Times Square.'

Perhaps one of the least likely collaborators on *Bunkka* is
*Fear and Loathing in Las Vegas* writer Hunter S. Thompson,
inventor of gonzo journalism and all-round loose cannon. 'He's
a very important writer and I felt that he had something to say
to the youth of today,' says Paul. 'Clubbers around the world
always have one of his books on them, or they use quotes from
one of his books on flyers. I approached him with the idea of
doing a track purely because I was a fan. He'd never done a
record before.'

Persuading this undeniably cantankerous old scribe to record
on some DJ's first artist album wasn't the easiest of jobs. A&R
man Ricardo Vinas got to make the call. 'It took me some time
to get his phone number,' says Ricardo, chatting in a downtown LA coffee house next to the old Tower Records store.
'Paul was eager to hook up with him, and I initiated the dis-
cussions with a lot of people and their managers. Finally I call
Hunter S. Thompson somewhere out of state, I think in
Arizona somewhere. Some lady answered the phone and I
asked for Hunter, who came to the phone. I said hi, explained
who I was and that I was working for Paul Oakenfold, we're
looking for this and that, you know; there was silence on the
other end of the line. Then he just shouted "FUCK YOU!" and
hung up the phone . . .'

The second approach was a little less fraught. 'Eventually
Paul wrote to Hunter himself, sent him some records,' says
Marc Marot, 'and Hunter sends this great letter back,
saying "You are one of the most sincere artists of your generation! You are the soundtrack to youth!"' Someone close to
the great man seems to have changed his mind about the
project. 'It was his assistant, Anita, who became his wife,' says
Paul. 'She said to him that this was something worth doing.

So I called him a few times – I'd call him from England, at the time I came out of clubs, at about three or four in the morning, which felt about right. We talked about ideas, where it was going to go. We agreed to meet in LA; we flew in and he said "meet me at midnight". So I go over to his hotel at midnight, with a bottle of absinthe under my arm as a present. I'd read in a Johnny Depp interview that Hunter liked it. I walk in and there's Hunter, Keanu Reeves and Sam Shepard sitting there, all pissed! It was a jaw-dropping moment. So we recorded it right there, straight on to a DAT player. We talked about the Hell's Angels, about football, about politics. We even came up with an idea for the Hunter S. Thompson award, which would be awarded every year to a musician or writer. When he was talking I was trying to get him to move around, trying to get something out of him that I could write music to. We're working, then drinking . . . it was the first time I'd tried absinthe. Within half an hour I was practically on the floor; he seemed completely fine. The next minute, Johnny Depp was on the phone; Sean Penn came in, then Harry Dean Stanton. He had all these crazy friends; all the big actors loved him. Jack Nicholson and Sean Penn were at the bar. We ended up with something based around the idea of the American dream, called "Nixon's Spirit". He wanted to talk about being young and having dreams, and the way that society tells you as you get older that there are certain things you can't do. It doesn't matter if people don't know about Nixon, you can relate to it in a general way. We had a great couple of nights, an amazing experience.'

The sessions went well, but when it came to the question of cold, hard cash, Hunter decided to play his own unique version of hardball. 'Paul's got a female, Muslim lawyer in London, who was dealing with the album,' says Marc Marot. 'With

Hunter, we knew we were dealing with a volatile character, so we got the lawyer to write the most anodyne contract, really bland and in plain English. You should see the reply!'

I have. It's framed, hanging on Paul's office wall in the Hollywood Hills. It's a remarkable piece of work, a vindictive phantasm, raining insult after insult on the poor lawyer's head, each one highly graphic, many anatomically impossible. It ends describing which part of the lawyer's body he's going to stuff her head up once he's ripped it off, and what he intends to do with the corpse. The letter is cced to a most random selection – Bill Gates, Ted Turner, Paul Allen, Steve Jobs, George W. Bush – many of whom probably had more pressing things to worry about than how much Hunter S. Thompson would be receiving for his work on a Paul Oakenfold album. One day, this depraved masterpiece must see the light of day, as a fine example of the writer's more purple prose. But not here. You might be eating.

The lawyer went into shock. 'She was in tears,' says Paul. 'I sent her flowers. I just said "Give him what he wants . . . it's Hunter S. Thompson!" He agreed in the end.' This was to be one of Thompson's last public appearances. He died in Woody Creek, Colorado, on 20 February 2005, of a self-inflicted gunshot wound to the head.

'I thought he was really lovely,' says Paul. 'I kind of felt a bit sorry for him. At the end of the night I was holding him up, carrying him to his bed. He seemed real kind of run-down. I think he was also "Hunter S. Thompson", a character that he had to live up to. He was just obsessive, with alcohol and drugs, and you could see it was getting to him.'

Paul recorded twenty-nine tracks for *Bunkka*, some of which never saw the light of day. Some, like 'Faster Kill Pussycat', which was originally an out-and-out rock track, would emerge at a later date. A tune featuring Smashing Pumpkins' Billy Corgan didn't make the grade; neither did a nine-minute-long operatic track recorded with vocalist Summer Watson. 'She did a beautiful job,' says Marc Marot. 'The trouble was that part of the track samples Górecki's Third Symphony. Górecki is a living composer who uses religious texts as his libretto, and he wouldn't clear the sample because it took bits of the lyric out of context, even though it's in Estonian. It meant that this beautiful track couldn't make it on to the album, and we've never found a way of being able to do it. It's a shame, as it's one of the best pieces of music Paul's ever written.'

Reviews for *Bunkka* were mixed. Some fans predictably wanted an out-and-out trance album; some reviewers applauded Paul's bravery for attempting a broader palette. Despite this, helped along by the omnipresence of 'Southern Sun', 'Ready Steady Go' and 'Starry Eyed Surprise', *Bunkka* was a commercial hit, selling a million records worldwide. The success propelled Paul into a pop world he wasn't totally comfortable with. 'I thought to myself "how weird is this?" ' he says. 'There's me, Beyoncé, Destiny's Child and Justin Timberlake, all playing at some radio station show at Madison Square Garden. Mickey Jackson's being pushed around by security – understandably, we were trying to film it! We did "Ready Steady Go" and "Starry Eyed Surprise"; you've got all these twelve-year-old kids at the front all singing along. It was the strangest thing. I'm thinking, "God, I'm totally in pop world". And this is not where I wanted to be. First and foremost, I don't want to be a pop star. Second of all, I don't want to be in an area where I feel uncomfortable.'

Setting up stall with a song-based album was always going to throw up contradictions for someone known for dance music and the relatively anonymous world of the DJ. 'You don't want to be seen to lose your credibility, which plays a very important part within the scene,' says Paul. 'Everyone will call you a sell-out, straight away. Yet you try and make a fucking top-ten pop record – it's not easy. And on top of it, you find yourself in these situations that you don't want to be in. I had to go and do a radio tour in America and I'm sitting there on daytime radio, being interviewed; they don't know anything about me, they don't really give a fuck, I don't want to be there . . . but you've got to be there. Putting my surname on the record, and doing the press to promote it made me feel exposed. It was a long, hard journey, making that record. I went through a lot emotionally. When you are producing your own album, no matter how good it is, it's never good enough. When I'm producing someone else's record, I know when they need to stop: I can tell them when it's good enough. Now I've had to take advice from other people, which wasn't always easy.'

One of the more creative aspects of the album process was that Paul got the opportunity to develop his stagecraft, morphing from DJ into a live act. He developed his live sound alongside John Tonks on drums, who'd previously played with Tricky, and Tim Hutton on guitars and vocals, who has since worked with Groove Armada. Occasional guests such as Shifty Shellshock would drop by. Paul operated computers, keyboards and decks, and synced the visuals to the music. 'We did sixty shows,' he says. 'It's a very different thing to DJing. We pre-recorded all the vocalists on blue screen, and had them projected on video while we played along. You'd have Perry Farrell singing and dancing in front of the Eiffel Tower, or on the Vegas strip. I DJed for an hour to ease them into it, then brought on the band – we had a guitarist, bassist, and a drummer, with me doing what I do in the studio, playing keyboards, synths and Pro Tools. I ended up losing a fortune, but it gave me a real insight into touring with a band.'

A new vocalist began to work with Paul on a number of *Bunkka* live dates – a rapper called TC, also known as Spitfire. 'I was good friends with Shifty Shellshock,' says Spitfire. 'He took me into Paul's studio, some place off Sunset. Paul was so caught up with his whole vibe with work and everything that he didn't look at me the first time. He said to Shifty, "here man, here's a bunch of songs, a bunch of instrumentals if you want to write over them". And Shifty's like, I got better stuff to do. And I'm like, I don't! So I grab the CD, go to my house, record about three songs on it, bring 'em back. I didn't think he'd call me, but he did, like three hours later. And he goes, "hey mate, is this the guy that wrote those songs today?" I was like, "if it's the good ones, it's me!" Two months later I'm playing the Hollywood Bowl with him. I'm the only unsigned guy. He says this is your audition, to see if you're any good!'

Hollywood Bowl was the last place Spitfire imagined he'd end up, after years of playing in every type of band imaginable. He started off playing in a mariachi band in the Mexican neighbourhood he grew up in, just guitars, vocals and a bag of weed, then convinced a guy in a music store to give him lessons in exchange for washing his car twice a week, before becoming a music teacher himself, getting the odd session gig along the way. It wasn't an easy ride. At twenty-two, Spitfire was disheartened enough with music to give it all up and join the air force. 'I thought I was never gonna make it,' he says. 'So I join up, they ask me what job I want and the guy in the queue behind me says "You should be an airborne and weapons director, a surveillance operator." I didn't even know it was a flying position. Only two per cent of the air force fly; the rest are cooks and air traffic control, management and shit like that. So all of a sudden, my schedule of events included intense water survival training, land survival training, combat survival . . . I was like, "I'm game, why not, let's try it!" It was no joke – us, the Marines and the Navy SEALs, going through the programme. They taught me how to survive after you crash; we were out in the woods for a month, killing rabbits, and eating ants. They taste like lemon. It was kind of weird, I kind of got into it after about two weeks, I was all Ramboed out. Sitting there with my face all painted, with a knife, chilling in the woods; I had it down. They taught us how to hold our breath for five minutes, which is good to know, especially when I'm choking on stage.'

Things got a bit tricky post-9/11, mind. Spitfire thought he'd better find another way to make a living after being stationed in Afghanistan and watching friends die, and being shot at himself in a no-fly zone over Saudi Arabia. 'I decided to protest,' he says. 'I was asking too many questions, so they said I should shut up or be thrown in jail. The military told me I was crazy, said I had a "personality disorder", and sent me back to the States. That's when I decided I had to be a rock star.'

After Spitfire had been living in his truck in Malibu for seven months, Shifty Shellshock happened to hear him busking outside Starbucks. This led to work on Shifty's solo album, and a few short months later, to the stage at the Hollywood Bowl. 'Paul's been playing for an hour or so, and he gives us the nod,' says Spitfire. ' "Starry Eyed Surprise" starts playing, we walk out there, and Paul's looking at me, all weird. There's like twenty thousand people in the Hollywood Bowl. He starts playing it more, all these glowsticks break out, the whole fucking crowd lights up and starts screaming. I'm like, ahh shit! After a couple of minutes I got into it. Afterwards, Paul says "Good job mate, you're hired." '

About a year later, Spitfire got a call from Paul out of the blue. 'He goes "I want you to come to South Africa with me. Bono is putting on this AIDS benefit with Nelson Mandela. We'll do 'Starry Eyed Surprise' and 'Ready Steady Go', then we'll improvise a load of stuff. Write something over 'Ready Steady Go'." So I say the first time we're gonna play this live is in front of thirty thousand people, being broadcast to two billion people? He was like "Yeah man, I trust you." So we went and did it. We were hanging out all night before the gig; Paul took me all over Cape Town, up Table Mountain with Annie Lennox. I was like, "What the fuck's going on dude, it doesn't make sense!" It was crazy.'

'The event was called 46664, after Nelson Mandela's prison cell number,' says Paul. 'It was a really big honour. We played alongside Queen, U2 and Beyoncé. I'd been going to Cape Town for a few years anyway, and I really wanted to do something positive, for a good cause. It was me, Spitfire and Shifty, and we got a local guitarist in, because we were trying to bring in some of the African musicians. So right at the end, you know when all the performers all come out in a line, and they're all arms around one another, and you sing the last song? Well I can't sing, right . . . we went on at five o'clock – cut to eleven o'clock, the last song, they're like, everyone out, everyone out! I didn't know they were going to do that, so we'd got pissed. We were really pissed! So all of a sudden you've got Annie Lennox on one side, Spitfire the other . . . we start to fuck around, kick our legs up, and then I thought, this is going on TV all round the world, thirty thousand people in front of me, I'm pissed out of my head, on stage . . . I looked round, I've got Beyoncé there, Edge and Bono over there, and I'm thinking, "this is fucking unreal!"'

Apart from playing in front of thirty thousand people, Spitfire also got to guest on the official record that accompanied the event. 'There's Beyoncé, Bono, Eurythmics and Queen on it, so I called up Spitfire and said "Do you want to be on this record?"' says Paul. 'So I put him on, singing the chorus! Him and Bono, his hero! He was playing at Starbucks a few weeks before that!'

The collaborations kept coming for Spitfire. 'When I first started work with Paul, I went up to his house, with the huge, panoramic view, from the Pacific Ocean all the way to Glendale, and I said "Why do you do this? You're set man, you could retire and just do nothing." He said "I'd do this for free; this is what I do." We've worked on three movie soundtracks since. *Yellow* is a Spanish mariachi movie, so that was pretty easy to nail, then *Victims*, then some uptempo chase stuff for *Nobel Son*. I'd never done any music like that before; I was pretty shocked. I was like "Why are you letting me do this, you can hire anyone you want." Maybe it's because I'm cheap! I'm sure he wouldn't risk his reputation for a hundred bucks though. Me and him work.'

For Paul's record company Maverick, *Bunkka* was a success. 'Apart from record sales, how do you measure success?' asks Maverick MD Guy Oseary. 'He's probably one of the most licensed artists for commercials – "Ready Steady Go" has been used for more things than anything we've ever licensed. He's been a joy to work with. No matter where dance music goes, he's going to be part of it, because he's an innovator.'

Back in the UK, things took a decidedly regal turn in October 2003 when Paul got asked to Buckingham Palace to meet the Queen, as a 'pioneer of the nation'. 'Straight away I rang my mum and said "I'm going to have dinner with the Queen!"' he laughs. 'Little did I know there would be three hundred other people there as well! There was the guy who invented the transistor radio; Pete Waterman and the guy who produced the Beatles, George Martin, were the only other music people there. I really wanted to take my wife, but I couldn't, they wouldn't let you take anyone, so I turned up on my own. I was really nervous. The only other times I have been nervous like that was meeting U2, Paul McCartney and Mick Jagger. Paul McCartney invited me to his house and played me his new album, because I'd played a party for his daughters Stella and Mary. I'm sitting there with a Beatle, and he's asking me my opinion of his record! It was really weird; he was showing me all his guitars and stuff. I found him very interesting, and then the penny dropped who I was sitting with and talking to, and I started getting nervous, which was the wrong thing to do. I remember really desperately wanting to do something for him, but couldn't do it because the track wouldn't work. I turned him down and I really felt upset, because I felt like I'd let him down. It turned me off remixing a bit; it was really quite traumatic. I also had to go and meet Mick Jagger. He also played me his album after I'd done a mix for the Rolling Stones. I took my mate Giles because he's a big fan – I didn't tell him beforehand, we just walked in and there's Mick Jagger. I'm from South London and these are fucking legends! You don't expect them to be asking you your opinion about their music!'

The Buckingham Palace lunch was equally odd. 'I started

walking round,' says Paul. 'I bumped into Waterman. You've just got to have a few glasses of wine at that sort of thing, and start getting involved, otherwise you just stand there and you don't know who to talk to. Then you have your food . . . and I kept drinking. I thought "This is fucking great, I've got to have a look around!" How many times are you going to be invited to Buckingham Palace? When you meet the Queen she gets a whisper in her ear, telling her who you are and what you do. You get about thirty seconds – what are you going to say to the Queen in thirty seconds? One drunken night, me and my mates got together and thought right, we've got to come up with something that makes her think, that stands out from the rest. So we came up with some line, but of course I froze and couldn't get it out. I had this really creative thing going through my mind. I wanted to tell her about the book idea I had with children, how to help children who are dyslexic. I had it written down in my pocket, but of course it all went. Then I got talking to the guards – two of them were young, about twenty-five, and they'd been to my club. They started telling me about their job; I found it really fascinating, a lot goes on behind the scenes. I ended up staying there chatting and drinking. It ended at nine, and I was still in there at quarter past nine! By this time, I'm talking to the cleaner, anyone who comes my way, I'd talk to them! They were going to have to chuck me out of this place, they were literally turning all the lights on and I was still there, talking to the people who were serving the drinks, like, "Yeah, it's fucking great! Buckingham fucking Palace!" I was on such a high. I went on a bender that night. I went straight to the Four Seasons, sat in the bar, had a large champagne . . . I got on the phone, started ringing around, I was like, we're going out! I got home about six o'clock in the morning.'

# 17

# Thirst

With *Bunkka* successfully completed, Paul's thoughts turned to bringing the album to a live audience. 'We wanted to do something extraordinary,' says Marc Marot. 'We aimed to take a large scale show and put it into a thousand-capacity venue like Zouk in Singapore, the kind of show that you'd normally associate with Madonna or U2, and put it into venues where you are closer to it, where you can touch it. That was our motivation.'

Staging such a tour is understandably a major logistical challenge. Even for an artist with the global reach of Paul Oakenfold, who is guaranteed a sizeable audience, the costs involved in putting an arena-sized tour into a string of club venues would be pretty much impossible without some level of sponsorship. Luckily, help was at hand. In early 2002, brewing giant Heineken made it publicly known in the creative and advertising press that they wanted to form a megabucks tie-up with the music market. For many years a major player in global sports sponsorship, particularly in America and Australia,

Heineken saw a huge opportunity to tap into the youth market via music, one of their target audience's main leisure pastimes.

A couple of decades earlier, this might not have been so easy. In the late eighties, Neil Young drew up the battle lines. Neil's song 'This Note's For You' tells us that he wasn't singing for Pepsi, he wasn't singing for Coke, Miller or Bud. The song's video included a pastiche of Michael Jackson's infamous hair-on-fire incident, which took place when he was recording a Pepsi commercial, and it was initially banned from MTV for 'product placement'. Ironically the track managed to pick up MTV video of the year in 1989 after the station relented and put it on heavy rotation. In his keynote speech at the New York New Music Seminar in July 1988, U2 manager Paul McGuinness quoted Young's lyrics to illustrate the tough moral stance he and his charges U2 took against corporate sponsorship, berating such tie-ins as the antithesis of the rock and roll spirit.

Yet there's been a gradual shift in thinking since the late eighties. There may have been a few disgruntled murmurings when the White Stripes penned a Coke ad, and many a furious Northern Soul fan was outraged when the cream of the genre's rare gems soundtracked ads for Kentucky Fried Chicken, but the days when Jim Morrison threatened to trash a Buick on stage every night when he heard 'Light My Fire' was going to be used in a Buick Opel commercial seem well and truly behind us. U2 endorse Apple's iPod, even creating their own limited-edition version, on to which you can presumably download a bunch of Neil Young songs to sing along with. Seemingly every other TV ad draws on the depth and breadth of popular culture's songbook, from Delta blues to drum and bass and beyond.

In the twenty-first century, the era of the sweaty, legally dubious warehouse rave, where it was a fiver to get in and your evening's delight was provided solely by a fuck-off sound system, a couple of flashing lights and a cheeky half, feels like a long-lost, slightly hazy memory. Clubbing, once the scourge of national newspapers and constabulary alike, has been deftly assimilated into popular culture's mainstream, gradually shifting gear from what for many was a way of life, to merely one of many lifestyle choices. And yet dance music is everywhere. It may not have had the all-consuming, multi-platinum impact of hip hop, but as a soundtrack, as the theme tune for this lifestyle, via TV adverts, film scores and as the consistent background beat at the global shopping mall, it has become so omnipresent we barely give it a second thought. It would have been unimaginable, at the height of acid house, to imagine 'Voodoo Ray' or 'Strings Of Life' soundtracking a Pringles advert; now it is commonplace for an act like Basement Jaxx to agree for their music to be used in this way. Moby famously licensed every single track of his blues-vocal-lifting *Play* album for ad usage. Some hold out – notably the Chemical Brothers – but the ad companies merely employ soundalikes and produce a kind of Chemical Brothers-lite instead. As little as five years ago, most record and publishing companies rarely sent their music to advertising companies for use in soundtracks; now they are queuing up to get their music placed. And as well as TV advertising, corporate branding also started to make inroads in the music festival scene during the nineties. It didn't take long for the big-time sponsorship brands to realise the marketing possibilities of international club culture. And with the high costs of staging international dance events, such as Heineken's Thirst, sponsorship became increasingly inevitable.

'It's the way the music world operates now,' says former *Muzik* editor Ben Turner, who recently booked Paul to play at a Sony Ericsson event at the 2007 conference in Miami. 'When we launched *Muzik* in 1995, everyone was against working with brands,' says Ben. 'No one wanted brands associated with their events. We were all very anti that, in the same way that you wouldn't have had your music in a commercial in 1995, unless it was something so cool it was worth it. Now, it's a financial reality of making music. You don't sell enough records any more. I think it was when Dirty Vegas got their track on a Mitsubishi ad, which went on to break them in America, that things changed. From then on, everyone was scrambling to get their music on adverts in the States; now everyone wants to get their tune on *CSI*. Even the coolest festivals still have to rely on brands to cover their costs. It's just a financial reality.'

Capitalising on the opportunities presented by Heineken's high-profile overture to the music industry, Paul and Marc Marot responded by creating a concept for a high-end, global dance production, and presented their plans to the beer brand. The event was called Thirst. Over a period of nine months from September 2002, Paul took an all-singing, all-dancing Thirst audiovisual spectacular on thirty-six dates worldwide, taking in Ireland, Singapore, Hong Kong, China, Thailand, Japan, Malaysia, Indonesia, Brazil, Argentina, Chile, Mexico, Colombia, Holland, Dubai, Canada and many more. 'It gave me the vehicle to tour like a rock band,' says Paul. 'I had my own lights, my own visuals, my own production, and the selection of DJs I picked, like Daniele Davoli, Pete Tong and Hernan Cattaneo. No one wants to go into a club and see a parade of Heineken flags; that doesn't work, but there are alternative ways to do it. We managed to take this massive show into places it had never been before. I'd done something similar in the UK ten years before, on a college tour where we took all our own production, but this was on a much bigger scale. It really did take it to the next level.'

Thirst came about with the helping hand of one of Marc Marot's music business contacts, JF Cecillon, who is currently head of EMI Records' European division. 'Originally JF worked at Polydor in France, then Sega, then he set up his own music marketing and branding company called Music Matrix,' says Marc. 'His concept was that wherever someone like Heineken or Vodaphone needed youth branding or music branding, he could be the expert that would put the whole package together. JF, Paul and myself designed the platform for Heineken. Paul was deeply involved in it – if there were bits of it that Heineken didn't fully understand, Paul would fly to Holland to meet the worldwide marketing team to say "this is how it works".'

Paul's experience with music promoters and the global dance industry proved very useful. 'Even though Heineken has a central marketing department, in reality each market – and they are in every market in the world – has its own marketing team,' says Marc. 'It's all very well when somebody in Europe says we are going to do this worldwide concept – the problem is when you take it to South Africa or Hong Kong, the local Heineken marketing guy says "I've got a mate who is a promoter." But they may not be the right people for dance music – dance is a totally specialist market. And there's nobody in the world who knows it better than Paul Oakenfold. He knows the bad promoters, he knows the good ones and he knows the ones he'd never touch with a bargepole. We foresaw problems because suddenly we were being bombarded by representatives from Heineken markets all over the world, in over forty countries, all putting forward their preferred venue. It would have been the equivalent of trying to put on a rave in a totally unsuitable rock venue like Hammersmith Apollo in London, and getting a rock promoter to put it together.'

The concept for Thirst was more than merely your standard superstar DJ set. 'About four months before the show, there would be an activation period, through local media, through on-pack advertising and through marketing,' says Marc Marot. 'They invited bedroom DJs to submit their mix tapes, and would assemble local experts – a DJ, a record executive, people who knew about the dance market locally – to judge the ones that were coming through. In some cases Heineken were over-whelmed by the amount of feedback, in other cases it was relatively easy. There would be a whittling-down process, and Paul would judge the best entries, who would get to DJ on the night.' This part of the event was called 'Flavour of Thirst'. 'We went out to find tomorrow's stars today,' says Paul, 'but in a new way.'

'It was a brand-new experience,' says Kieran Evans of C-C Lab, the London-based company who put together the logistics and staging that got Thirst on the road. Kieran's background includes a prestigious film and music video CV, as well as a wealth of experience touring with the likes of the Grid and the Prodigy, masterminding the audiovisual backdrop for a host of electronic live shows. 'Paul was putting together his album and was thinking about trying to tour,' says Kieran. 'He wanted to do this tour in a very different way, trying to bring a live element back to the nightclub. Initially, there was a very ambitious plan for this, which involved shitloads of triggered vocal lines corresponding with 3D graphics. It was amazingly wishful thinking – when they looked at it in detail, they realised this was impossible. We couldn't do it, which is a shame, as it would have been like U2 on acid.'

Even with Heineken's big pockets, this early idea for Thirst was logistically impossible. 'They did the maths and realised that there was no way they could fund it,' says Kieran, 'but they still wanted to have a visual angle, and also some new, different elements, rather than it being just a straightforward Oakenfold DJ tour. Heineken were expecting some kind of big live music show, which they didn't get. Luckily, it actually turned into something bigger than merely a gig. It was a technically advanced visual show, plus the DJ competition, plus Oakenfold DJing. Nobody was doing that kind of show at the time.'

The tour was also unique in that it found the time to stay in each country longer than the usual overnight stop. 'Normally on a world tour, you'd go in, do the gig and then piss off the next day,' says Kieran. 'With Thirst, Paul was there for a couple of days beforehand, doing a whole pile of press, judging the competition and meeting the DJs. He'd hold DJ workshops in every territory, which, for a DJ of his status, was pretty fucking amazing. I remember being in Cork, in Ireland, for the first gig. We were in a shitty little back room of a pub and there's the number-one DJ in the world, surrounded by thirty gobsmacked teenagers, and he's showing them how to match beats. It was great. He was a leveller – in fact he was *the* leveller on the tour, because lots of people would stand back, and then he'd be the first to introduce himself and get people talking. He wasn't just being professional, he was being himself – he's actually quite a generous man and will give you the time of day. That was very striking.'

Initially the idea was that the DJ competition winner would get to play for the first fifteen minutes of the night. This was soon elevated to a much sweeter spot. 'Playing the opening slot didn't seem like much of a prize,' says Kieran, 'so it soon moved up so that the winning DJ would come on for fifteen minutes between Daniele Davoli and Paul Oakenfold, and provide a bridging gap between the two main DJs. Considering that these DJs were plucked from near-obscurity, from playing in front of maybe two hundred faces, to suddenly facing upwards of two thousand screaming people, it was a pretty amazing thing.'

As Thirst wasn't to be your usual run-of-the-mill night out, the staging of the event was crucial. Kieran Evans and the C-C Lab team built an impressive set that consisted of up to seventeen enormous video screens, bringing a stunning, retina-blasting spectacular to relatively small arenas. 'We got brought in partly due to my relationship with the Grid and the Prodigy, just knowing how to stage those events, knowing the landscape, the overall look and feel of the event,' says Kieran. 'It had to be reflective of contemporary dance music and also the scale and nature of the gig. We advised on that and planned the structure of the night, designed the lighting, designed the whole visual rig. There are different ways you can present dance music live. You can bring in a live band, but if you can't do that, what else can you do? The idea was to make Thirst one of the most visually spectacular shows you could ever see in a club. Let's wipe out all those rubbishy fractal-based videos you still see, and let's try and do something that has the production value of a U2 show, or potentially better. We wanted to do things with that level of production and skill, but in a much more intimate space.'

For three days before each event, before Paul was doing interviews and judging the DJ competition, the C-C Lab crew would scour the city and shoot relevant visuals for each individual show. 'We then had a unique library of material we'd created for each night,' says Kieran. 'It was a kind of mix-and-match thing. Paul had filmed visuals for his section of the show, and at the start of the tour stated very specifically that he wanted these visuals played at certain times in his set, but as he saw the whole show developing, and as he saw moments that we were bringing into it, he became a lot more fluid about how we used his set and how we used our stuff.'

As this was a heavily sponsored event, you'd think that Heineken would want their logo on screen every five seconds. Not so, says Kieran. 'The logo was not used at all during any of Paul's set,' he says. 'We basically told them that the way to do it was brand it at the beginning of the night, and then as the bigger-name DJs come on, slow it down to the point where the main visuals took over and there wasn't any branding at all. So when the main DJ comes on, he doesn't feel like he's whoring himself for a fucking drinks brand – basically it's his show. Heineken were very accommodating. I don't think that they would have been if he'd been an arsehole – he did so much press and PR, he did every interview that you asked him to do, so it made it easy. It was kind of you scratch my back, I'll scratch yours – if there's no logo throughout my show, then I'll be happy.' Considering Heineken were bankrolling the tour, this was a coup for the DJ. The brand weren't short-changed when it came to the main DJ action, however. Lush Perfecto visuals, starring a futuristic-looking Asian model called Jasmine, would ricochet around the venue in multi-screen sync, more often than not accompanied by Paul's preferred opening track, the UNKLE mix of Ian Brown's 'F.E.A.R.', a driving, beat-heavy symphony, full of string-tinged melancholy. 'By the time he came on,' says Kieran, 'the crowd would be totally in the palm of his hand.'

The tour wasn't all plain sailing, however. A couple of shows brought their own particular regional flavour. When the tour hit Hong Kong, the local underworld wanted a look-in. It was time for Thirst to meet the Triads.

'In Hong Kong, the Triads actually owned the event,' says Kieran. 'Unbeknown to Paul, the Triads took all our passes off us and then tried to extort us. The promoter had to pay an extra ten thousand dollars to get the event back under control. You had to have a working pass that corresponded with your passport, and if they didn't match up, you were out of the door. The cops were coming through the building after us, because we didn't have any passes. We all had to hide in a room because we were probably about to get thrown out and arrested. There was a very sweaty moment, when the guy from the agency and all the crew were just shitting themselves because of these Chinese cops. You could see them coming down the corridor. We were saying right, you go there, I'll hide here, we'll lock the door there . . . it was manic, we were running about like fucking maniacs! Then the Triad boss was paid the extra ten thousand pounds, and went and paid off the cops! And to appease the Triads, a Triad DJ was then put on the bill as well! MC Triad!'

'It was all over the shop in Hong Kong,' says Paul. 'I got really pissed off at that time – I thought "this is a disaster". But other than that, the tour was very well run, it was like a well-oiled machine. You get to the city, do radio, TV and press, judge the competition, then the next day turn up, soundcheck and you do the gig. It was so well run that there weren't any real problems.'

Well, not many. Security could be tight, to say the least. In Colombia the tour had a permanent armed guard. 'In Bogotá you don't just go out,' says Kieran. 'Everything has a ring of iron around it. We had these guards because everything was controlled by gangsters, so there was a ring of military police all the way round the place. You were driven through and had to keep waving your pass around. When we were filming the visuals for the show, we were given an armed guard because we were driving round at night. That was a bit mental.'

There were some slight border skirmishes when the Thirst show rolled into China. This wasn't the first time Paul had had problems in the country; 2003's Great Wall gig, which was celebrated with a highly regarded mix CD set, almost never happened. 'Paul was doing a big Asian tour, playing markets people don't usually go to, when the SARS outbreak happened,' says David Levy. 'The television news was full of stories about how it's not safe. People were dying left, right and centre, so we call Paul and say he should come home. He says "I'm not fucking cancelling, I'm here having a good time. I want to play the Great Wall of China!" So he stays out there. A few days later we call back and tell Paul it's getting serious, he should think about coming home. Paul just said "I've got a thousand face masks and we're taking them into China!" And that's what he did. They didn't catch SARS of course, and the gig happened.'

'We were in Melbourne before we went to China,' recalls

Mickey Jackson. 'There were six of us on the crew, and four decided to go, including Paul, myself and the Bear, the tour manager. We looked at all the press, tried to figure out how bad it was and then flew in to China to do the gig. When we got there we had a blessing from the local monks! We had six cameras with us to shoot it. It was a sell-out gig, right on the Great Wall itself. They only allowed about five hundred people in, although they'd sold about twelve hundred tickets; there were people trying to get in all over the place. It was cold, soaking rain. It was a four-hour drive; when we finally got there, it was freezing – all but two of the cameras shut down. It wasn't meant to happen. The organisers were saying the spirits don't want you here! But we did it. Paul even jumped over the wall, into Mongolia. We had to pull him up and bring him back. It was the first and last time they did a gig there.'

'It was a real challenge,' says Paul. 'I like the idea of taking DJing out of the realms of the nightclub. There wasn't a lot of people there, but it was a challenge setting it up and playing. You can't get more rural than that – it's an hour outside Beijing, it was pouring with rain, we're on the wall in the middle of nowhere! With Mongolia on the other side!'

SARS or not, the Great Wall of China gig was the first time any DJ, let alone one from the West, had been allowed to perform at such a prestigious site, and it caused a few repercussions, which came to light as Paul, the crew and his management got to the border patrol for the Thirst show. 'The Great Wall gig resulted in us getting banned in China,' says Marc Marot. 'When it came to do the Thirst tour, we had real problems getting back in. We had fifteen tonnes of gear, work permits, the full fucking monty – we'd paid the bribes you have to pay to get us over the border from Hong Kong to China.

We'd done the show in Hong Kong ... and then we got banned. We had to sneak Paul in as a tourist to do the first show. He wasn't allowed to play, he could only shake hands with people and judge the DJ competition – he couldn't professionally engage. We couldn't do the show. It's partly because the Chinese thought there was some kind of subversive movement going on, and they weren't in control of it. They made a spurious excuse that they were having a national party congress, and they didn't want any foreign agitprop going on within twenty days before it, or twenty days after it. They just dropped that on us on the border, where we had twenty crew and fifteen tonnes of gear. He did play in the end, and he's been back since, but it was a weird moment.'

Another strange night took place in Greece. 'One of the things about the tour was that if we couldn't do it in a nightclub, we'd try to find a different type of space,' says Kieran. 'In Greece the local promoter got us this theatre which was built for the Greek folk scene. It was made out of wood! It was absolutely rammed. We did the show and of course it's jumping, a good show ... then the video tech guy who was with me was saying "Is it me, or is this floor starting to kind of go up and down a bit?" The whole building started shaking! We were on the balcony looking down, and we could just see this certain area of the floor wobbling, where people were going absolutely bonkers. We were shitting ourselves; we just thought we'd better get out of there. We did make it through the night but it was a bit scary. Even the promoter was saying to us "How do I stop them dancing?" They did make an announcement, because they were going really berserk at the front, like at a rock gig ... they started crowd-surfing. It was just nuts. But we made it.'

*

By the time Thirst got to South America, however, the teething troubles had been ironed out, and the tour started to really come together. 'I think it's true to say that Paul helped open up South America for Heineken,' says Kieran Evans. 'In South America they thought he was God. We were playing Coldplay-size arenas; that's when the tour all started to make sense. The first night we played in Chile was in front of six thousand people, in this park just outside Santiago. It was heaving. We'd done about four or five dates, and it's a bit like rock and roll – the tour doesn't really start gelling until a certain moment happens. We'd had technical problems – the screen configurations weren't working out, the design wasn't completely working – so we changed the set-up, into this V formation, rather than simply being just a row of screens. It gave it a new dynamic. I had this idea when we were shooting the visuals, that we should maybe shoot the flag of the particular country. In South America there are flags everywhere, so Paul would have this section with "Adagio for Strings", some big number about forty minutes before the end. At the breakdown I thought "let's go to the flag". We put it up on the screen, Oakey's waving his arms in the air, and the crowd went absolutely fucking mental. People let off flares, they were climbing up the walls . . . Oakey turned round and saw the screen, put his hand on his heart and they exploded. The beats kicked in and we were away. Then we had to stop the show for a minute, because they'd built this separate stage, a high-up VIP guest area. The crowd in there were going so mad that the scaffolding holding it up was buckling with the strain, it was going to collapse. They had to clear the area and push everyone into the middle of the dancefloor, which made it even more mental. That was the point when it all clicked.'

Further chaos ensued in Buenos Aires. 'We couldn't move our kit to Argentina for the next gig in time, so we ended up pulling everything we could out of racks and packing it into hand luggage,' says Kieran. 'Even Paul had to help carry our equipment over. The next night we went to play at Pacha in Buenos Aires, which is a smaller club – its capacity is about two thousand. There were four thousand people there. We couldn't move, literally, none of us could move. The promoter Chino had another fifteen hundred people outside in a field, because he'd cleverly brought in some speakers, and he pumped out the show on screens outside. The whole area was just covered in people. It was absolute madness.' 'It was fucking unbelievable,' says Paul. 'It was on the verge of a riot! I've got a real allegiance to South America, it's like a second home to me. Last time I went back I played to sixty thousand people.'

Paul's love of Buenos Aires, with its phenomenal atmosphere at events run by Argentinian promoter Martin Gontad, led him into the path of South American DJ Hernan Cattaneo, resident DJ at the Pacha Buenos Aires night Clubland. Hernan's deep, tribal, progressive groove held great appeal for the South London DJ. 'I was the warm-up DJ for the night,' says Hernan. 'He heard me play and liked what I did, and he said "Would you like to come to warm up for me worldwide, on tour?" It was more than a dream come true for me, because, to be honest, it was not even something I was dreaming of . . .' Hernan subsequently became a Cream resident in South America, got his own radio show, released a fine Perfecto mix and a string of singles. 'I'd played in Argentina for years, and was doing really well there, but when I started travelling, everything changed instantly,' he says. 'I wasn't used to the "superstar DJ" kind of treatment, but it doesn't take long for anyone to start enjoying that!' Hernan has gone on to become one of the world's most respected DJs – yet another career fired up by Perfecto.

One of Paul's favourite memories of South America was being present at Diego Maradona's last game for Boca Juniors in Buenos Aires. He even got to meet him. 'It was amazing,' he says. 'It was the ultimate high. He was a real hero. They were playing in the equivalent of the Champions League, against a team from Brazil. I got invited into the dressing room before the match, got introduced to everyone, shook hands with them before the game. They'd never let you do that in Europe.'

Rio was particularly memorable. Paul decided to take the Thirst crew on a little trip. 'I got a bunch of us together at six in the morning,' says Paul, 'apart from Pete Tong, who wouldn't get up even though we were banging on his door. Lightweight! We drove all the way up to the Jesus statue, the Cristo Redentor. It was locked, so I paid the security guy fifty dollars to open it up. We took a big bottle of whisky . . . we were the only people up there when the sun came up. It was absolutely amazing. Then we played football on Coco Cabana beach; it was England v Brazil. We lost four–three, and this girl got two goals past us. I couldn't believe it. She was good.'

The main support on the tour was the pioneering Italian DJ Daniele Davoli, the man responsible for some of the biggest Italian house tunes of all time, including Black Box's 'Ride On Time', Numero Uno's 'Numero Uno' and The Mixmaster's 'Grand Piano'. The Italian's deck skills certainly helped keep the main DJ on point. 'At certain points Daniele would turn in one of the most amazing sets – he'd drop in loads of rock music, White Stripes bootlegs, his own bootlegs, and all that,' says Kieran. 'He'd keep Paul on his toes. Paul had to raise the bar – he'd think "I've gotta beat that now." The set Paul did in Argentina was just astonishing. It was supposed to be two hours long and he went on far longer. He pulled everything out of the bag. In Rio, Pete Tong was playing an amazing set – he really got the crowd going. Then Daniele came on; he'd been making all these bootlegs, and the crowd were totally having it. They weren't really dancing to the trancey stuff, so I thought "fucking hell, what's Paul going to do?" He came out and he played all this hip hop, he got out all the breakbeat action, trashed his old set, and just went for it. It was brilliant; it's moments like that where you appreciate that he is a really good DJ. He can read a crowd – he knows who the crowd is, what they want and when they want it.'

One moment on the tour came as a monumental shock. 'There was a particular part of the tour when we thought Paul was acting like a bit of a dick,' says Kieran. 'He wanted specific things done on the stage, with the set-up, and he was being very irritable, freaking out about the sound. The day before he'd been sweetness and light, and we'd done a pretty good gig, then the next day he was very different. It was like Jekyll and Hyde, we just couldn't understand what it was. And then it transpired that his dad had died.'

Paul had helped organise his father's birthday party during a break from the tour. 'He died on his sixtieth birthday, just before his party,' says Paul. 'It was awful. We'd hired a hall in Norwood, and got in all his friends from school, they were all coming from all over England. Two hours before the party started, he died, while they were putting all the stuff together at the hall. As the eldest son, as people were turning up at the party, I had to tell them the party's off, my dad's just died. And that's when I realised I had to hold it together, because of my mum. She'd lost it. My brother and sister had lost it, and I thought, being the eldest son, and this is part of what my dad instilled in me: it's my responsibility to look after the family. That's what you do.'

It was clearly a major blow for Paul; even now he finds it very difficult to talk about. There was certainly a marked change in Paul's outlook after his father died – he became far more fatalistic, living life day to day, not looking into the future. 'I never learned to take risks,' says Paul. 'My dad was always "save, save, save" . . . that's why I'm a risk-taker now. I'm going out in a blaze of glory. I want to take risks in life, and if it doesn't work, hey, I can hold my hands up and say to myself "at least I tried".'

'He was absolutely devastated when his father died,' says Sheila Oakenfold. 'It was very tough for us all. But he says he's in charge now . . . I say, wanna bet?'

# 18

# A Lively Mix

The *Big Brother* theme has consistently beamed Paul Oakenfold's music into British living rooms for what seems like for ever, as much a part of the show as a cat-fight before bed-time. In 2005, Paul stepped a little closer to the reality TV spotlight, moving from writing the theme to actually appearing in a US reality show, called *The Club*. 'They wanted to do a reality programme based on me, but I didn't want to do it,' he says. 'So I sold them on the idea of going to Vegas, this party playground, and doing a reality programme about a club, which I was a part of, alongside some other DJs. I appear in it, but I'm not the main story. It's all about what happens when this brand-new club, Ice, is set up in Vegas. It's about how they booked me, and my involvement in the club, the day-to-day runnings, everything that goes on behind the scenes when you launch a new club.'

*The Club* is an astonishing piece of TV. I have no idea why it wasn't picked up by terrestrial channels in the UK, as it's as addictive as crack. As anyone who has ever worked in a British club will tell you, after the first few nights the glamour quickly fades, and it's all mopping up, lost coats and doing the cash tills at four in the morning. An empty nightclub in daytime is a lonesome place; weirdly smaller than you remember, now that the lights have gone up, silent, smelling of stale beer and disinfectant. But not in *The Club*, no sirree – there's wham-bam action before every commercial break. There seem to be about twenty sponsors on board – every other shot is a flash of some beer or vodka brand. The staff go on group outings, play baseball, have pep talks before the night begins. The LA promoter/door person makes Jenni Rampling look like Mother Teresa. Best of all is the episode where UK club brand Godskitchen get to 'take over' the club's management in the dead of night, at the request of the owner, flying in heavies from England, busting locks and impounding computers. It's all very calm and professional, but it's cut so that everyone involved seems to be living out some deeply rooted *Scarface*-meets-*Casino* action fantasy. You can smell the tension. The producers worked on the US version of *The Office*, and it shows – it's so dramatic, it looks like a set-up. Nobody seems to be laughing much, mind, as Neil Moffitt from Godskitchen crowbars his way into the club. It's priceless, car-crash TV.

The behind-the-scenes stuff is best – oddly, for a series called *The Club*, the actual club footage is the least dynamic part of the programme. It's more exciting to watch the hugely expensive dry-ice machine break down than seeing it deployed over a heaving dancefloor. 'In a club there's a lot that goes on that you can't capture on TV,' says Paul. 'It's all in the moment. The storyline was a way to make it work as a programme. It wasn't set up though – what happened when Neil took over the club was for real. We had two million people watch it, which is not bad.' Since the series aired, Godskitchen have parted ways with Ice, but are moving ever upward with their expanded global links. Somebody, somewhere, please do *The Club* series two, with Neil Moffitt in the lead. The boy's a star.

*The Club* added yet another dimension to the fluid, lateral approach Paul Oakenfold adopts to promotion in the twenty-first century. He acted as a producer on the show, wrote the theme tune, released a Perfecto mix album called *Perfecto Presents The Club* and appeared on screen. 'Paul's career is built on multiple impressions,' says Richard Bishop, his American manager. 'Whether it's being involved in a TV show, doing a DJ gig or putting out an album, or having a track in *Collateral*, it's Paul's continued ability to stay visible that's key. *The Club* continued his visibility. I don't think it helped him particularly sell any more albums, but it was another piece of the jigsaw puzzle, and when you get all the pieces lined up together, that's when it makes sense.'

Paul's key role in American dance culture was confirmed in 2005 when his *Creamfields* mix album was nominated for a Grammy, in the newly created 'best electronic/dance album' category. A handful of dance music insiders had been petitioning the Grammy committee for a number of years for a dance category that recognises electronic dance music, just as rap and rock, country and R'n'B are awarded at the ceremony. The new category is an indication of dance music's health in the US – no longer purely an underground niche, the genre is now accepted and promoted by a broader section of the music business, an increasingly significant and familiar soundtrack. The days of burning disco vinyl at Kominsky Park and the 'disco sucks' movement seem to be gradually fading into the distance. Jason Bentley, the LA radio DJ who spins on the influential KCRW and KROQ stations, was one of the dance music industry insiders who pushed for Grammy status. 'Historically dance music has been defined by the recording academy in a very old-school, post-disco, R'n'B house definition,' he says. 'It hadn't really come to terms with everything else that had happened in the last ten to fifteen years. There was only one category, for best dance single. It had ignored a lot of the other artists, like Orbital, Aphex Twin or the Grid. Others, like the Chemical Brothers, were falling into the "best rock instrumental" slot. The categories desperately needed updating, and the thing about the Academy is that it's only as good as the participants. So a group of us formed a committee, wrote a proposal and lobbied for the category. We also lobbied for best remix, to recognise remix producers and engineers – giving the Grammy to the remixer, not to Mariah Carey – making sure those points were in order. It's been a major victory.'

Three compilation albums were assessed for the best album category – Paul's *Creamfields* set, Gabriel and Dresden's *Bloom* and Sasha's *Involver* – but Paul's won the nomination. It also took the flak – there were media mutterings about the viability of the creator of a mix album receiving the industry's top award, since, given the nature of a compilation album, the mix includes tracks recorded by other artists. 'I'm fine with the controversy,' says Jason Bentley. 'We made a very aggressive statement about who's part of our scene. They are not going to create another category for us any time soon, so if we were going to acknowledge mix CDs at all, it had to be as part of this category. In Paul's case, we are dealing with a DJ who had a strong hand in the production, by either featuring his own remixes or production of songs. This allows us to embrace the craft of the DJ.'

Paul's not fazed by the odd raised eyebrow when it comes to the Grammy selection. 'I think the mix album is part of DJ culture, and DJ culture should be embraced,' he says. 'We are taking what we do to the next level through the DJ compilation, where you remix, re-edit, rearrange, restructure and have your own records in the mix; it's become a new type of album. The committee obviously looked at Sasha's album and mine and felt they were both worth nominating for those reasons.' Paul's *Creamfields* mix didn't win the Grammy – the honour went to Basement Jaxx's *Kish Kash* album – but the nomination alone was a formidable achievement.

Further fresh juxtapositions emerged on Paul's 2006 artist album *A Lively Mind*. The album kicks off with 'Faster Kill Pussycat', an out-take from *Bunkka* co-written with Sneaker Pimps singer Kelly Ali, which ploughs a similar rocky, guitar-driven path as recent smashes from Deep Dish and Bodyrockers. The track features hot-right-now LA movie queen Brittany Murphy on lead vocals, best known for her role as Eminem's love interest in *8 Mile* and for a star turn in Frank Miller's noir comic caper *Sin City*. 'I was looking for a singer who had a strong voice and attitude, but had never sung on record before,' says Paul. 'I wanted someone from a completely different world to mine. Brittany fitted the bill perfectly.' Initially Murphy wanted the vocal to appear anonymously, but Paul persuaded her to opt for a credit and take the starring role in the moody accompanying video. It worked a treat – the single reached number one on the Billboard Hot Dance Club chart in America and number seven in the UK charts.

The album has a more measured flow than *Bunkka*; it's more uptempo throughout, more firmly focused on the dancefloor. Tracks like 'Save The Last Trance For Me' and 'Amsterdam', euphoric bangers both, would segue effortlessly into any trance-tinged Oakenfold club set, while 'Praise The Lord' and the T.Rex-riffing 'Switch On' have a breaks edge that would suit club or film alike. Vocalist Ryan Tedder restyles Grace's 'Not Over'; Ashley Winters continues Oakenfold's penchant for soulful rock voices. Ashley's band Bad Apples are signed to a new Perfecto offshoot Sound of the Renegade, and recorded with Paul in Studio City and at the Roosevelt, an old-school Hollywood dame of a hotel.

The album has such a strong dance tip that it was easily translated into a companion mix album, *A Lively Mix*, a widescreen reinterpretation of the album that got a lot of play on Paul's 2006 tour supporting Madonna. Overall *A Lively Mind* achieves a satisfying focus, with a couple of killer singles to boot. 'Sometimes the walls that appear when making an album are very hard to climb,' says Paul. 'Especially if you don't sing, but want vocals on the record – there's a lot more people involved, a lot more meetings and creative conversations. It's difficult to make an album that works throughout, but I think this record has a lot more balance than *Bunkka*. Everybody was expecting a dance or electronic record last time. This album is more comfortable in the electronic world than the last one, but it's still got a variety of flavours.'

Like *Bunkka*, *A Lively Mind* is stuffed to the gills with guest cameos. Hip hop legend Grandmaster Flash makes an appearance, which was a great honour for an old-school hip hop head like Paul. 'I've never been more nervous with anyone than I was with Grandmaster Flash,' says Paul, 'because as a kid he was my icon. He looked exactly the same as he did in the seventies, this tiny guy with a little leather cap on, a little leather jacket. It was a great honour. Meeting him was the pinnacle.' Representing the new school is N.E.R.D. auteur Pharrell Williams, who takes the mike on 'Sex And Money', another guitar-driven house stomper with a Bowie-esque vocal refrain. 'I first hooked up with Pharrell when I remixed the Neptunes' "Lapdance" for the *Swordfish* soundtrack,' says Paul. 'When we got together, I told him the idea was to bring in an artist and take them out of their genre, and do something completely different,' says Paul. 'I talked to him about what I did with Tricky and Nelly Furtado, when I took Nelly Furtado from pop and did a dark, filmic track. That's what made him think, "All right, I'll do something dance." He asked if I wanted him to rap or sing, and I said I wanted him to sing it because I didn't want a hip house track.'

Lyrically, 'Sex And Money' looks at the more glittery attractions of the high life, and doesn't much like what it sees. 'The tone of the record was very much my experience at that time, going through my split with Ang, my experience of Hollywood, the whole thing. I don't want to generalise, but in Hollywood there's a lot of girls who just want the guy for the money. So I thought let's make the track about what is current in the world, and especially in Hollywood. The guy wants sex, the woman wants the money. It's not just in Hollywood; I see it so much in London as well. It's everywhere, it's just that in Hollywood it's in your face as there are so many famous people there. The wider message of the track is about our obsession with celebrity, where it doesn't matter what you are famous for, just as long as you are famous.'

Not yet exactly famous, but loaded with star quality you

can't buy and a hollering set of vocal cords to match, is Spitfire, who guests on four album tracks, fresh from his role as live MC at the Hollywood Bowl and Nelson Mandela gigs. 'No Compromise' is a banging rocker, all thrash and thump, while 'Feed Your Mind' recalls Madchester's loping groove, with a Balearic-tinged 'Sympathy For The Devil' backing vocal worthy of Thrashing Doves. 'Spitfire's great, he's like a young Anthony Kiedis from the Chili Peppers,' says Paul, clearly enjoying his A&R role. 'He's like Eminem meets Johnny Cash.' No pressure, then.

Another collaborator Paul started working with during the *Lively Mind* sessions was an old associate, Gerald Z Morse, known to one and all as Zeo. His knowledge of electronic music-making runs as deep as you can get; Zeo was the original marketing director for the Fairlight, the first-ever commercial sampler, back in 1978, a cumbersome piece of studio trickery that cost sixty grand. He demonstrated the Fairlight at the AES convention in New York, giving up a space next to him to one Roger Lin, who was desperate to show his new drum machine. 'You had the first digital-system sampler and the first drum machine in the same room,' he recalls. 'As you can imagine, it went nuts.' Zeo soon travelled to the UK as a Fairlight rep, selling the first-ever sampling equipment to a number of British-based studio heads like Trevor Horn, Peter Gabriel, Blue Weaver and Daniel Miller. He started picking up remix work from Chris Blackwell at Island Records, which led to mixes for Donna Summer and Earth, Wind & Fire. Zeo plotted up at Zomba studios in West London, working with Sydney Youngblood and D-Mob, and met Paul through Danny Rampling. The first record they worked on together was a mix for Ofra Haza. Zeo took a lot of time out to teach Paul about

studio technology, but the partnership was short-lived –
the studio wizard was deported after being spotted by the
Home Office appearing on *Top of the Pops* on Boxing Day
1989. 'They said I had to pay a year's worth of back taxes –
which I'd already paid in America – so I bailed out. I lived in
Amsterdam for six years. They didn't care!'

Moving forward to the twenty-first century, Paul and Zeo
are back together, this time working on film music. They met
again through LA-based DJ Mark Lewis. Paul and Zeo's working relationship has changed a bit since the days of acid house.
'I used to be his mentor,' says Zeo, 'but the tide has turned.
One thing I learned was that I couldn't come back after so long
and expect to do what I used to do with him. Paul is a filter –
as he gets older he'll get classier and classier. For a guy that
basically, you know, comes from the south side of the tracks
down there, that guy is one of the classiest, most cultured
gentlemen. He's my mentor now.'

The first job Zeo was given was to build Paul a studio in his
house. 'I put this huge list together, thinking they were going to
go out and buy it,' he says. 'They went out and got it all
sponsored! I was really impressed.' This isn't surprising – Paul
has developed strong links with the technological side of the DJ
industry over the years. He had a hands-on role in the design
of Pioneer's groundbreaking CDJ-1000 CD deck. 'I was asked
by Pioneer to do some of their showcases at a trade show in
Earls Court,' says Paul. 'From then on, I got involved with the
early stages of developing the CDJ-1000; they spoke to me and
Roger Sanchez. The Pioneer guys from Japan came over; we sat
down and talked through how you could make it a lot more
DJ-friendly. I knew about CD DJing through a friend of mine
called Alan Jell in Hong Kong, who was one of the first DJs I

knew to use CDs to mix. Because of his location, he didn't have the access to vinyl that we had, so everything was on CD. He'd always said CDs were the way forward, and I tended to agree with him. I liked playing vinyl, but it was always easier to play CDs. They were easier to carry! Pioneer brought a prototype over, and I said "change this, change that", then they came back and we worked and worked on it. It was sturdy and very comfortable – it was very much like the Technics turntable – it had the wheel which was like the deck, it had the movement and the varispeed. Originally this was very stiff, but we changed it. It became a very well-designed, user-friendly machine. The rest is history – it's now the industry standard.'

The CDJ series of CD mixers has helped facilitate a new technological approach for dance music. 'The technological changes over the last few years have made things change in the scene,' says Paul. 'It's becoming easier to make music, and cheaper to produce. Cheaper and faster – you don't have to cut an acetate every time you want to play a new tune. That's why the CDJ has become so popular.'

Paul supported his second artist album with a number of dates, of a more DJ-based variety. 'It was a lot more comfortable,' says Paul, 'because I thought if I'm going to do it, we'll do it this way. There was a lot of pressure from the record company to fit me into the mould of a typical band, but I'm more comfortable touring like this.' Tour dates included a European trek supporting Madonna, the first act to support her on tour since the Beastie Boys in 1985. Just as Paul learnt from his time touring with U2, this stint left a lasting impression. 'I've learnt a lot professionally from Madonna,' says Paul. 'I saw why she's at the top of her field – you could see her determination in the rehearsals. For one gig she arrived a bit late, but she was rehearsing as people were coming in. The message I got is that if you want to be at the top, you have to constantly work at it. It gives you a kick up the arse to see someone work like that. It's easy when you've been doing it for that long to turn around and say "You know what, I don't need to rehearse this"; but the fact that she still does is what makes her so good. That tour was a real good shot in the arm for me, a real morale booster. Very rarely do you see that – when you're up there, you've still got to work hard to stay up there. That's what I saw with her. It was relentless. I thought "how can I take that and then put it into my world?" And then you think, well, when you are on that long plane trip and you get to the hotel really tired, and you've got to do a soundcheck, that's when you do need to make it. The difference between Madonna and everyone else is she makes that extra effort. The day you don't soundcheck, that's the day it'll all go wrong. The placement of the monitors could be wrong, the levels could be wrong. There's the little things – I jump up and down next to the turntables, so you know it's not going to jump when you play. That's why we soundcheck every gig. I took that organisation, the professional side, into my own world.'

Following the worldwide success of 'Faster Kill Pussycat', *A Lively Mind* was nominated for a Grammy in 2007. Paul even got to invite his mum Sheila and her partner Sid to the ceremony, who were chuffed to be sitting near Madonna, Queen Latifa and Samuel Jackson. 'Getting the Grammy nomination for *Creamfields* was great, but this was even better,' says Paul. 'With *Creamfields* I did all the remixing, re-editing and rearrangement, but it wasn't all my work in that I didn't write the music. I never thought I'd win this time, I believed Madonna would win it, quite rightly as it's a good record and

a big-selling record, but the nomination really meant a lot.'
Paul's mum was a bit put out, though. 'He gets on well with
Madonna, doesn't he?' she says. 'You'd think she'd let him
have a turn . . .'

# 19

# The Minister of Entertainment

Miami, late November 2006, a week before Thanksgiving. Paul Oakenfold is headlining a unique event at Miami's cavernous dance club Space, the first-ever worldwide live broadcast for the booming internet concern MySpace, with an estimated audience of a hundred million or so. It's a big deal for both the company and the DJ – if this works, we'll be seeing a lot more of this kind of thing in the near future. The dream of a global digital residency Paul first took to Ministry of Sound at the turn of the century may well be within reach. Broadband may still be in its infancy, but given the onward, upward path of number-crunching computing power and the size of potential audience, the possibilities of a regular MySpace gig are more than enticing for this global-thinking DJ.

For many British dance industry players, Miami means one thing – the yearly Miami Music Conference, which takes place each March. The place is awash with industry hopefuls, schemers and established talent each spring; it's almost impossible to walk down the street along Ocean Drive without bumping into a dozen dance luminaries. In November, it's a bit more sedate, but the MySpace event is attracting a fair amount of attention. A two-seater biplane buzzes along the shore above South Beach, a busy strip of beachside cafés, bars and hotels slap bang in the middle of the Art Deco district, trailing the message 'MYSPACE PRESENTS PAUL OAKENFOLD @ CLUB SPACE'. The effect is somewhat diminished when a rival flight follows two minutes later, heralding 'DANNY TENAGLIA 11/24', but it's impressive nonetheless; you don't get many Ministry of Sound aeroplanes dodging traffic above Elephant and Castle.

Paul's staying at the Victor, a glam deco haven right next to Casa Casuarina, Gianni Versace's old mansion on Ocean Drive. The hotel exudes the rococo splendour of the jet set; a marble-floored palace more understated than the go-go fifties gleam of the Raleigh's amoeba-shaped swimming pools, or the monolithic design statement that is Ian Schrager and Philippe Starck's Delano, formerly the only place to hang during the Miami conference, now being smartly superseded by the trade-mark quiet sophistication of places like the Victor. You can only book three days minimum, and a suite like Paul's is around fifteen hundred dollars. A night. In the lobby there's a fish tank full of jellyfish, a mural of docile, grazing pelicans, and Paul Oakenfold and his US agent Gerry Gerrard discussing tonight's gig. Business as usual, then.

Darkness has fallen by the time we get to the hotel. There's a palpable sense of possibility, of imminent party action around South Beach, once night-time sets in. A sea of neon flickers to life as every bar, club and hotel gets ready for the night. The stars come out, in the sky, on the sidewalk. There's a doorman in the Victor's lobby now, not your average meathead, more a polite greeter who nonetheless would turf you out on your ear if you were rude enough. Your name's not down ... *sir*. Decade-old, watered-down Euro-trance fills the lobby, way too loud, which seems a little out of place in such a shrine to quiet sophistication, but it seems like even the more sedate elements of Miami hospitality are gearing up for the night.

Paul springs up, ready for business, record box in hand, wondering where the driver is. We slip into an oversized Ford Expedition SUV. The windows are tinted so dark the driver can't see his wing mirrors, and has to wind down the windows every time he wants to see behind him, which rather defeats the object. He asks Paul what he'd like to drink at the club, rings ahead and flinches when he finds out that the details haven't been adequately sorted. So much stress over a couple of drinks.

We arrive outside Space in good time, and marvel at the giant satellite rig that's been set up by the back door. 'If a bird shits on that, we're all in trouble,' grins Paul. We're whisked into a VIP area to the side of the heaving main floor, a marqueed outside area. DJ Sandra Collins is filling the night air with the drifting sax motif from 808 State's 'Pacific State', blended over a crunchy, tech-y, electronic backbeat, giving the loop function of the Pioneer CD decks a proper workout. Unlike Paul, Sandra managed to show up to this worldwide live broadcast about five minutes before showtime, but any panic doesn't seem to have affected the eager-to-please, smiling, hospitable crew, who are on hand with the largest bottles of Grey Goose vodka I have ever seen.

The affable, well-respected New York DJ Jonathan Peters, Sound Factory resident par excellence, pops by to say hello. I ask him if he's nervous playing to such a large, global audience, but the broad grin he shoots back denies any butterflies. A gyrating flock of podium people take to the stage in front of the DJ booth, done up head to toe in stretchy white ghost sheets like some trance Hallowe'en nightmare, goofing along to a wobbly remix of Moby's 'Go'. The three dance arenas that make up the club are monitored by giant overhead video screens that are relaying the action from the sweeping rostrum camera that hovers over the crowd, from the bar areas, even the toilets . . . one minute you're minding your own business, the next it's beamed out live over the dancefloor and into a million living rooms. The wonders of technology. A startling trio of surgically enhanced post-op transsexuals come over and introduce themselves. The security are all wearing 'Space – who needs sleep?' T-shirts. It's going to be a long night.

Soon Paul's moving towards the booth. A line of Space security surround the stage, lifting what seems to be the entire decks, CD and mixer set-up off the stage. There's a low-pitched hum, whistles, catcalls. The surplus equipment and bouncers are removed, leaving the DJ alone to start his set. The tension mounts and the beat kicks in. Here we go.

A sea of oversized, sabre-like glowsticks are cutting the air above the crowd, trailing a warm orange glow. Luke Skywalker would be proud. The silver-capped six-foot trannies of Miami stalk the stage in vicious heels, unleashing a stream of giant white condom-shaped balloons with overblown panache. After a costume change, the dancers sport macho Charles Atlas body stockings and spangly Mexican wrestler masks, spraying each other with high-pressure dry-ice guns. The DJ keeps his head down, concentrating on bringing in the next track. As muscle dancer number one leaps off stage, crowd-surfing in eight-inch red high heels, a silver ticker-tape parade worthy of 4 July showers the floor. There's cheers and waves as energy levels reach new highs and the music steps up a gear. A *Blade Runner*-meets-*Fifth Element* dominatrix hits the stage, vicious-looking miniature laser beams attached under each of her fingernails, flashing bright red light over the heads of the jumping dance space. The DJ climaxes his set amid thunderous applause, and smiles under a warm, clear Miami sky.

Paul seems introverted after the show, running the events of the night through his mind. He found it a challenge playing to the two audiences tuned in to his set – the crowd in front of him and the many more listening and watching at home. By the time we get to the hotel he's perked up though, and indulges in yet another round of Grey Goose as Gerry, Sandra, her boyfriend Vello, my wife and I take turns in shouting at each other, taking the piss, getting into headlocks and jumping up and down on Sandra's bed until the new day dawns. It's been a successful night.

Four months later, Paul is back in Miami for the conference. We're speeding past the city's sprawling technoscape, over an endless purple neon lit bridge, away from South Beach, heading downtown for yet another engagement, in a leather-seated Range Rover. Paul was initially just playing one night at the conference, the Perfecto party at Cameo with the full crew – Hernan, Sandra Collins, Kenneth Thomas – but as is always the way with this relentless, workaholic party starter, more and more gigs were added. Paul's now playing every night of the conference, having performed with members of the Florida classical orchestra in front of twelve thousand at Miami's Bayfront Amphitheater Park the weekend before. Tonight it's the Sony Ericsson 'Night Tennis' event, which delivers exactly that – a bizarre mix of UV lights and a neon court, in a shed venue that certainly ain't Wimbledon. Once the playing arena is cleared, Paul fires up a set of trance-led classics, dropping in Eurocentric versions of 'Born Slippy' and 'Missing', oblivious to the fact he's had a mere three hours' sleep.

Back at the Ritz Carlton hotel, Paul's right-hand man Dan Rosenthal is fielding a consistent stream of calls, despite the fact that the DJ is booked in under an assumed name and he hasn't told anyone he is there. 'He's not here right now,' says Dan, rather unconvincingly, as you can hear the Oakenfold belly laugh bounce around the room in the background at club volume. Dan's been working for Paul for three years now, having previously studied film, completing an internship under *Evil Dead* and *Spider-Man* director Sam Raimi and working for Paul's old US A&R compadre Ricardo Vinas at Thrive. The first instruction Paul ever gave to Dan was 'you've got to keep up'. You somehow get the feeling he's been on his toes ever since. 'Paul has one of the most unique brains that I've ever encountered,' says Dan. 'He will literally give me a list on let's say Wednesday of twenty-five things to do. Then he'll go out on Friday night, and stay out partying, all night, and then in the wee hours of Saturday morning, he'll recite the list back to me! I'm sitting there, looking at him, wondering, how does that register up there, after forty-eight hours without looking at a piece of paper? Paul understands that we're all human, but in his world, there's very little room for mistakes.'

You don't get the impression that this is a nightmare employment situation, however – Dan clearly loves his job. 'Paul is a great communicator and a very likeable person,' says Dan. 'He doesn't add nonsense to anything, he really gets on with it and he does it in a very personable way. He really enjoys the exchange with people; he listens a lot, and has respect for people who listen. He's also a great judge of character and once you are trusted, you are trusted. He's incredibly loyal, and that's reciprocated. Of all the people I've met through Paul, I can't say there's a friend of his I haven't liked. People would take the bullet for Paul, not that they need to, but he attracts that type of appreciation from the people around him, that type of loyalty.'

Paul's in an expansive mood, telling tales of DJ triumphs, disasters and global mishaps. He recalls a gig in Cuba, where he smuggled the decks in. 'We said we were en route to somewhere else, we were on holiday and this was the equipment we travel with, and they believed us,' he says. 'That was hard work. They dance to a three-four rhythm; it's all about the hips. We tend to dance to a four beat. The younger crowd got it, but the older crowd didn't, they complained! That was tough.' Paul's most surreal gig was a beach party in Mumbai, the Bollywood capital, where Paul played with one deck and a cassette player, and if he turned the monitor up the sound system would cut out. His scariest gig, apart from the time in Chile where a rather keen fan had to be rugby-tackled by Paul's management before she knocked the whole rig over, was probably the Sony PlayStation launch in LA, where Paul was meant to play on a thirty-foot-high tower which was swaying in the breeze. The fire marshals put a stop to it, relocating the gig in an underground car park, which was so packed you could hardly breathe. He's had a few scary flights, too. He watched with horror as gasoline trailed out of the tank on take-off between the Dominican Republic and Costa Rica. He was in a typhoon on a plane heading for Tokyo airport, where they had to abort the landing. Another time, on a private jet flying over Mexico, one of the engines went. 'You can fly a plane with one engine,' he says, 'I found that out, but I didn't know at the time! Then the promoter leaned over to me and said "I don't want to scare you, Paul, but the propellers have just stopped." I found out that planes can glide in to land, too!'

Talk turns to current projects. There's a handful of Perfecto albums to be scheduled, with Dutch DJ Em Jay, Jan Johnson, Bad Apples and Spitfire all gearing up for release; Perfecto are also riding high with the success of David Guetta, who they release in the States. There's also Paul's show on Serious radio, which is beamed around the world. There's plans to be made for this year's Ibiza residency; Paul's going out for the whole of August. Then there's a number of film scores on the go, including the comedy *Nobel Son* and a Japanese animated film called *Vexille*, which Paul likens to an animated *Matrix*. He's recently completed music for a *Bourne Identity* video game, as well as reworking Hans Zimmer's *Pirates of the Caribbean* score for clubland; he's also about to start scoring a gangster film called *The Heavy*. 'Touch wood, I'm going to be in the new school of film composers,' says Paul. 'Electronic music is making an impact in film; a lot of the big composers are using electronic sounds – you don't hear the old sawing strings any more. I think it will get bigger and bigger. I'm looking at it as a ten-year plan. It's such a hard scene to break into – you really have to pay your dues.'

The one unfulfilled ambition Paul would really like to realise is finding that elusive world-dominating band for his label. His sights, as ever, are sky-high. 'I want to be the A&R man who signs the next Beatles,' he says. 'That's what I've always wanted to do, but I've never achieved it. It's hard to be an Alan McGee and find an Oasis, it's a one shot in a million.'

Then there's the small matter of selling Rosslyn House, the

old Victorian place in Putney which was Paul's base in the mid-nineties, which has just come on the market for an eye-watering sum. He's not selling his other London property, however. The Georgian town house in Connaught Square, Bayswater, is not for sale. Maybe Paul's waiting to have a chat to the new owner of the house next door – Tony Blair – although perhaps the former Prime Minister's influence is fading somewhat. 'I want to run as Minister of Entertainment,' says Paul. 'I think we need someone from the entertainment industry talking to the government on behalf of the industry. My idea was that I'd introduce myself as the neighbour, and then say "Listen, I've got an idea – what do you think of this?"'

There's one particular project that comes before all the others, however – Paul's new baby boy. Paul's Dutch girlfriend Else recently gave birth to Roman Hunter Oakenfold – named after the place, not the Chelsea boss as you might think – and judging by the pictures, he's a bundle of fun. Paul now splits his time between America and Europe; they haven't decided where they'll settle yet, due to Paul's commitments and Else's work as a stylist in Amsterdam. Family life is important to Paul – he's still close to his brother and sister, and to his mum Sheila and her partner Sid. 'I'm as close as I can be, given that I'm living three thousand miles away,' says Paul. 'My brother and sister are very family-orientated. They are closer to my mum, because they live near her, but I get to see them three or four times a year.'

Judging by the recent time I spent bombing round the Dutch capital with Paul on a rickety push-bike, dodging traffic as Paul sped ahead on his white two-wheeler with the 'Oakenfold' stickers on it, moving from one whisky bar to the next, I'd say

Paul is currently very happy, full of the joys of early father-hood. Roman can't beat-match yet, but I'm sure Paul's working on it.

# Notes

## 1. Southern Soul

This chapter aided by Chris Brown's Southern Soul overview *The Family Album*, and the 'Soulboys – Peace, Love & Snakebite' website – http://web.ukonline.co.uk/soulboys; with thanks.

## 2. New York, New York

For further insight into the New York disco underground, see Tim Lawrence's excellent *Love Saves the Day: A History of American Dance Music Culture 1970–1979*, which informed and inspired much in this chapter, with thanks.

## 3. From Rock the Bells to Jack Your Body

'I was fortunate enough . . . a little twist.' – Paul Oakenfold, in *Washington Post*, 24 November 2000.

'The scene was a cross . . . today in the UK.' – Gilles Peterson quoted from his biography on the www.bbc.co.uk/radio1 website.

## 4. Balearia

'When we came up on the E . . . great night out.' – Johnny Walker in conversation with Andy Crysell, in *Ibiza: Inspired Images from the Island of Dance*, edited by Ben Turner.

'At £157 a fortnight . . . body clock.' – Don MacPhearson, 'Ibiza: Holiday Babylon', *The Face*, September 1985.

'It was a completely new experience . . . so much part of it.' – Johnny Walker quoted in Sheryl Garratt's superb *Adventures in Wonderland: A Decade of Club Culture*.

'I can remember . . . loved-up experience.' – Johnny Walker, on BBC Radio 1, 1999.

## 5. Aciieed!

'In November 1987 . . . and he's ready.' – Ian 'St' Paul quoted in Jane Bussman's hilarious *Once in a Lifetime: The Crazy Days of Acid House and Afterwards*.

'The key . . . so much fun.' – Paul Oakenfold, in *NME*, 1998.

## 6. Over the Rainbow

'After Spectrum . . . going to get bigger.' – Mark Moore quoted in Sean Bidder's *Pump Up the Volume*.

'I wonder . . . has been all worth it.' – Ken Tappenden interviewed on the Channel 4 TV documentary *The Chemical Generation*, aired 27 May 2000.

## 7. Wrote for Luck

Opening Tony Wilson and Shaun Ryder quotes from ABC TV Australia's *Rage*, March 2001.

'Paul said to me . . . into the club tunes.' – Rob Davis, on BBC News Online, December 2001.

'Oakenfold didn't know . . . It wasn't very credible!' – Rob

Davis interview, *Sound on Sound*, May 2002.
'It stops him . . . frame of mind.' – Shaun Ryder interviewed by Nick Kent, *The Face*, January 1990.
'The black kids . . . the white kids woke up.' – Ian Brown, on Triple J Radio, December 2000.
Shaun Ryder and Tony Wilson quoted from Steve Lamacq's *Pills, Thrills and Bellyaches* documentary, BBC Radio 2, 2003.

## 8. Pills 'n' Thrills and Bellyaches

Shaun Ryder and Tony Wilson quoted throughout from Steve Lamacq's *Pills, Thrills and Bellyaches* documentary, BBC Radio 2, 2003.

## 9. Even Better Than the Real Thing

'After a time . . . actually quite special.' – Graeme Kelling, in *Guitarist*, 1999.
'forward-looking . . . complete about-turn' – Adam Clayton, in *U2 by U2.*
'Dance music made us jealous . . . good dance music.' 'Before Paul Oakenfold . . . that disco was the enemy.' – The Edge, in *The Muse*, January 1999.
'It was about the mid-eighties . . . *Achtung Baby*.' – Bono, in *The Muse*, January 1999.
'They were really interested . . . what was there.' – Steve Osborne in conversation with Gary Crowley, U2 Special, BBC Radio London.

## 10. A Voyage into Trance

'We created a lifestyle . . . Christmas and New Year.' – Goa Gil, in *Beam*, 1998.
'techno is the sound . . . feedback loop for long.' – Erik Davis, in *Option*, 1995.

## 11. Cream: Resident
'It is a well-established fact . . . like to control.' – Inspector Damien Walsh, Merseyside Police, in *Daily Telegraph* magazine, 1996.

## 12. Bringing It All Back Home
'I was sad . . . with that club.' – Paul Oakenfold, in *Muzik*, April 1999.
'Basically, I wanted . . . quickly enough for me.' – Darren Hughes interviewed by Ben Turner, *Cream x 10*.
'It was an event . . . gain their confidence.' – Ron McCulloch, in *Scotsman*, April 2000.
'I'm not sceptical . . . reaction against it in London.' – Dave Swindells quoted in the *Independent*, 7 September 1999.
'It's all a bit Planet Hollywood . . .' – Mark Rodol, in *Independent*, 7 September 1999.
'We're getting there . . . get on with it.' – Paul Oakenfold, in *Muzik*, January 2000.
'The decision is incredible . . . in my view.' – Ron McCulloch, in *Evening Standard*, March 2001.

## 13. Trans-America Express
'I'm on my first E . . . America' – Frankie Bones interviewed by Simon Reynolds, *Energy Flash*.
'I spent the last ten years . . . punk rock.' – Moby interviewed by Greg Kot, in *Chicago Tribune*, 22 July 2002.

## 16. Bunkka
'A poetic slice of hip hop . . .' – Pat Blashill, in *Rolling Stone*, 4 July 2002.

## 17. Thirst

'I was the warm-up DJ ... start enjoying that!' – Hernan Cattaneo interviewed for *Paul Oakenfold 24/7* DVD, HiFi Entertainment, 2007.

# Bibliography

Almond, Marc. *Tainted Life*. London: Sidgwick and Jackson, 1999

Anthony, Wayne. *Class of '88: The True Acid House Experience*. London: Virgin, 1998

Armstrong, Stephen. *The White Island: Two Thousand Years of Pleasure in Ibiza*. London: Bantam Press, 2004

Becker, Judith. *Deep Listeners: Music, Emotion and Trancing*. Bloomington: Indiana University Press, 2004

Berendt, Joachim-Ernst. *Nada Brahma, The World Is Sound*. London and the Hague: East West, 1988

Berry, Mark, and Deborah Faulkner. *Freaky Dancin': Me and The Mondays*. London: Pan, 1998

Bidder, Sean. *Pump Up the Volume*. Basingstoke and Oxford: Channel 4 Books, 2001

Bono, The Edge, Adam Clayton and Larry Mullen Jr with Neil McCormick. *U2 by U2*. London: HarperCollins, 2006

Brewster, Bill, and Frank Broughton. *Last Night a DJ Saved My Life: The History of the Disc Jockey*. London: Headline, 1999

Bussman, Jane. *Once in a Lifetime: The Crazy Days of Acid House and Afterwards*. London: Paradise/Virgin, 1998

Champion, Sarah. *And God Created Manchester*. Manchester: Wordsmith, 1990

Champion, Sarah (ed.). *Disco Biscuits*. London: Sceptre/Hodder and Stoughton, 1997

Cheren, Mel. *Keep On Dancin': My Life and the Paradise Garage*. New York: 24 Hours For Life, 2000

Collin, Matthew, with John Godfrey. *Altered State: The Story of Ecstasy Culture and Acid House*. London: Serpent's Tail, 1997

Ehrenreich, Barbara. *Dancing in the Streets: A History of Collective Joy*. New York: Metropolitan, 2006

Eisner, Bruce. *Ecstasy – The MDMA Story*. Berkeley: Ronin, 1989

Fleming, Jonathan. *What Kind of House Party Is This?* Slough: MIY, 1995

Garratt, Sheryl. *Adventures in Wonderland: A Decade of Club Culture*. London: Headline, 1998

Gilbert, Jeremy, and Ewan Pearson. *Discographies*. London and New York: Routledge, 1999

Goldman, Albert. *Disco*. New York: Hawthorn Books, 1978

Green, Jonathan. *Days in the Life: Voices from the English Underground 1961–1971*. London: Minerva, 1988

Haslam, Dave. *Manchester, England, The Story of the Pop Cult City*. London: Fourth Estate, 1999

——*Adventures on the Wheels of Steel, The Rise of the Superstar DJs*. London: Fourth Estate, 2001

Hayden Guest, Anthony. *The Last Party*. New York: William Morrow, 1997

Hewitt, Paolo. *Heaven's Promise*. London: Heavenly, 1990

Jones, Alan, and Jussi Kantonen. *Saturday Night Forever*. Edinburgh and London: Mainstream, 1999

Kempster, Chris (ed.). *History of House*. Sanctuary, 1996

Kent, Nick. *The Dark Stuff*. London: Penguin, 1994

Lawrence, Tim. *Love Saves the Day: A History of American Dance Music Culture 1970–1979*. Durham and London: Duke University Press, 2003

Leary, Timothy. *Flashbacks: An Autobiography*. Los Angeles: Tarcher, 1983

Lee, Martin A., and Bruce Shlain. *Acid Dreams*. New York: Grove Weidenfeld, 1985

Levitin, Daniel J. *This Is Your Brain on Music*. New York: Dutton, 2006

McCall, Tara. *This Is Not a Rave: In the Shadow of a Subculture*. Toronto: Insomniac Press, 2001

McCormick, Neil. *Killing Bono*. New York: Pocket, 2004

MacPhearson, Don. 'Ibiza: Hollywood Babylon'. *The Face*, September 1985

Miller, John, and Randall Koral (eds). *White Rabbit: A Psychedelic Reader*. San Francisco: Chronicle, 1995

Nuttall, Jeff. *Bomb Culture*. London: MacGibbon & Kee, 1968

O'Dowd, George, with Spencer Bright. *Take It Like a Man*. London: Sidgwick & Jackson, 1995

O'Mahoney, Bernard. *So This Is Ecstasy?* Edinburgh and London: Mainstream, 1997

Oakenfold, Paul. *24/7 DVD*. HiFi Entertainment, 2007

Pepperell, Robert, and Michael Punt. *The Postdigital Membrane: Imagination, Technology and Desire*. Bristol and Portland: Intellect, 2000

Redhead, Steve (ed.). *Rave Off: Politics and Deviance in Contemporary Youth Culture*. Aldershot, Hampshire: Avebury, 1993

Reynolds, Simon. *Energy Flash*. London: Picador, 1998

——*Blissed Out*. London: Serpent's Tail, 1990

Rose, Cynthia. *Design After Dark, The Story of Dancefloor Style*. London: Thames and Hudson, 1991

Saunders, Nicholas. *E for Ecstasy*. London: Nicholas Saunders, 1993

——*Ecstasy and the Dance Culture*. London: Nicholas Saunders, 1993

Savage, Jon (ed.). *The Faber Book of Pop*. London: Faber & Faber, 1995

Shapiro, Harry. *Waiting for the Man: The Story of Drugs and Popular Music*. New York: William Morrow, 1988

Shapiro, Peter (ed.). *Modulations: A History of Electronic Music*.

New York: Caipirinha, 2000

Silcott, Mireille. *Rave America: New School Dancescapes*. Ontario: ECW Press, 1999

Sylvan, Robin. *Trance Formation: The Spiritual and Religious Dimensions of Global Rave Culture*. New York, Abingdon: Routledge, 2005

Thornton, Sarah. *Club Cultures: Music, Media and Subcultural Capital*. Hanover, New Hampshire: University Press of New England, 1997

Toop, David. *Ocean of Sound*. London: Serpent's Tail, 1995

Turner, Ben. *Cream x 10*. London: Carlton, 2002

——Turner, Ben (ed.). *Ibiza: Inspired Images from the Island of Dance*. London: Ebury Press, 1999

Walton, Stuart. *Out of It: A Cultural History of Intoxication*. London: Hamish Hamilton, 2001

Warburton, John, with Shaun Ryder. *Hallelujah! The Extraordinary Story of Shaun Ryder and Happy Mondays*. London: Virgin, 2003

Wilson, Tony. *24 Hour Party People*. London: Channel 4 Books, 2002

# Index

Beltram, Joey 274
Benitez, John 'Jellybean' 32, 39, 43
Bentley, Jason 285–6, 332–3
Berkmann, Justin 113
Berry, Halle 281
Betts, Leah 217
Beyoncé 307, 308
Bez 128, 130, 137, 145–6
Biden, Senator Joe 263
Big Audio Dynamite 175
big beat 196, 233–4
*Big Brother* theme 266, 270–1, 294, 329
Billy's (Soho) 44
Biology 95
Bishop, Richard 269, 331
Bjork 192
*Black Echoes* 40
Blackburn, Tony 19
Blackwell, Chris 166, 167
*Blade II* 299
Blair, Tony 349
Bleasdale, Paul 212, 213, 222, 225
Blitz (Covent Garden) 44–5
Bloor, Rich 186, 188, 193–4, 194, 195
Blue Mountain 166
*Blue Peter* 41
Blue, Raymond 5
Blue Room 194
Blue, Ruza 'Cool Lady' 31
*Blues and Soul* magazine 39–40
Bodines 126
Bonds (New York) 28
Bones, Frankie 246
Bono 170, 172, 176, 177–8, 307, 308
Boor, Rich 196
*Bourne Identity, The* 284, 295
Bowery, Leigh 47
Bowie, David 103, 261
Boy George 46
Boys Don't Cry 35
Boy's Own 78, 98
Bradford, Chris 239–40
Branson, Richard 99, 100
Brazil 196
breaks 274–5
Bright, Graham 109, 263
Brit Awards (1991) 148
Brody, Michael 28, 29
Bronx River Center 23
Brown, Chris 16, 17, 51
Brown, Ian 133
Brown, James 131
Brown, Paul 228
Bruinvels, Peter 38
BT (Brian Transeau) 229, 266, 267–9, 273
Buenos Aires 325

Buller, Alfonso 147
'Bullet In The Gun' 294
*Bunkka* 282, 288–9, 292–304, 305, 308–9, 334
Burning Man festival 255–6, 265
Burton, Richard 25
Burton, Sybil 25
Burton, Tim 282
Byrd, Donald 15

Cabaret Voltaire 47
Cafe Au Go Go (New York) 25
Café del Mar (Ibiza) 62, 64
Caister Sands All-weekend event 52
Camden Palace 43
Campbell, Naomi 176
Cape Town 5, 307
Capital Radio 16, 297
Capitol Studios (Los Angeles) 139–40
Carlos (DJ) 62
Carroll, Andy 200–1, 202, 203, 204–5, 207–8, 209–14
Casey, Jane 217
Castle, Ray 183
Cattaneo, Hernan 314, 325–6
Cauty, Jimmy 101, 103, 105
CBS 37–8, 39
CDJ-1000 CD deck 337–8
Cecillon, JF 315
Certain Ratio, A 126
Champion Records 36–7, 39, 42, 54, 55, 116
Channel 4 Clapham Common party 242–3
Chapman, Mike 116
Cheatham, Oliver 116
Chelsea FC 9–10, 219, 222–3
Chemical Brothers 237, 313, 332
Cheren, Mel 28
Cherry, Neneh 273
Chicago house 53–5, 119, 201
Chile 324
*Chill Out* album 103
China 321–3
Chinn, Nicky 116
Chuck Chillout 34–5
City Sounds (Holborn) 18
Clail, Gary 162–3
Clapham Common party 242–3
Clarke, Dave 216
Clarke, Michael 85
Clarke, Vince 132, 133
Clash, The 43, 170, 202
Clayton, Adam 167, 170, 171–3, 174, 175, 178
*Club, The* 329–31
Club UK 239